PENGUIN BOOKS

A BOOK OF ONE'S OWN

Thomas Mallon is a graduate of Brown University and of Harvard University, where he received his Ph.D. He teaches English at Vassar College and is the author of a biography of the English poet Edmund Blunden.

A BOOK OF
ONE'S OWN

People and Their Diaries

Thomas Mallon

PENGUIN BOOKS

PENGUIN BOOKS

Viking Penguin Inc., 40 West 23rd Street,
New York, New York 10010, U.S.A.
Penguin Books Ltd, Harmondsworth,
Middlesex, England
Penguin Books Australia Ltd, Ringwood,
Victoria, Australia
Penguin Books Canada Limited, 2801 John Street,
Markham, Ontario, Canada L3R 1B4
Penguin Books (N.Z.) Ltd, 182–190 Wairau Road,
Auckland 10, New Zealand

First published in the United States of America by
Ticknor & Fields 1984
Published in Penguin Books 1986
Reprinted 1986

Permission credits and acknowledgments appear on
pages 303–310.

LIBRARY OF CONGRESS CATALOGING IN PUBLICATION DATA
Mallon, Thomas, 1951–
A book of one's own.
Reprint. Originally published: New York: Ticknor &
Fields, 1984.
Bibliography: p.
Includes index.
1. Diaries—History and criticism.   I. Title.
PN4390.M34   1986   809   85-21697
ISBN 0 14 00.8665 X

Printed in the United States of America by
R. R. Donnelley & Sons Company, Harrisonburg, Virginia
Set in Janson

FOR MY MOTHER

Why do we wish to be remembered, even when none remain who looked upon our face? Surely, though it must retain an element of self-consideration, it is a last acknowledgment that we need to be loved; and, having gone from all touch, we trust that memory may, as it were, keep our unseen presence within the borders of day.

—WILLIAM SOUTAR
August 13, 1943

Contents

Introduction

There are about thirty of them now — notebooks of different sizes, every page of them filled up with handwriting. They're across the room in the cabinet full of blankets and gloves and piles of papers I've meant to sort out for several years.

I hardly ever read them, but I've got one open now. December 21, 1973, was a Friday. It was a rotten day, part of a rotten time:

> Now it's Christmas, and it might have been different . . . by luck perhaps . . . I would have a notebook full of my reflections on the pretty peeling blue wallpaper in my room, the funny way C. . . smokes a cigarette, the way the Boston subway smells, the afternoon a rainbow danced on M. . .'s forehead and hair as A. . . and I watched it, smoking our cigarettes and drinking our coffee: a thousand such reflections. All of it has happened, all of it has been seen, everything is the same — except — it has not been given a second thought. I am a computer which eats the cards and spews forth no print-out. I am eating up the raw material of life like some furnace, but I don't even give out bilge. No product. No process. Just feed.

There's been a war, and Washington grinds on, and there's a great national bore called the energy crisis.

Pretty self-pitying stuff! And yet it seemed that way at the time. I remember the night I wrote it, in my room a few blocks from Harvard Yard, tired out from a semester of trying to learn Greek. Looking at the small brown exercise book, I can remember just how I felt that Friday night. (I was sitting up in bed as I wrote; I remember that, too.) I wasn't just feeling sorry for myself. I was also angry. For months I'd been feeling too rattled to keep that notebook: there's a gap between July 16 and December 21. And now I was angry over what might have been: "I would have a notebook full of my reflections . . ." If, that is, I hadn't allowed myself to become so absorbed by my own worries that I could no longer savor experience in the curious pleasure of writing it down. I resented its all being wasted; everything from the peeling wallpaper to C. . .'s cigarettes to the rainbow on M. . .'s forehead had been lost. A "thousand" things — even more than that — hadn't been put into the small book.

On Friday, December 21, 1973, I wouldn't have guessed that on Wednesday, January 16, 1974, I'd be writing this:

One of those nights when, for a moment, I think: "A thousand years won't be enough." A dusting of snow fell today, just enough to freshen the dirty pile on the ground: Nature's cosmetic. Once again each filament of bare branch is frosted . . . splendid lattices stretching under the lamps of the Yard and in front of the museum. No, a thousand years would not be enough to watch this.

That's me on both those pages, to be sure. But it's also a figure now part of the past, available to be summoned in just the way I wanted to have the wallpaper and the rainbow and the "millions of incidents" ready for retrieval. Their availability seemed important then, and his availability seems important — at least to *me* — now. I'm glad I sat down to write on December 21, and glad I sat down on January 16.

J. M. Barrie once wrote that the "life of every man is a diary in which he means to write one story, and writes another; and his humblest hour is when he compares the volume as it is with what he vowed to make it." On the whole, I think, this is a reflection appropriate to a man whose most famous creation was a boy who refused to grow up. I look back at what I've just shown you and, if I'm a little embarrassed by revealing what I thought was a private lyrical effusion, I still see someone who, while he may not have achieved every dream, got what he was so bitter about missing on December 21, 1973. No one gets a thousand years; but if you're lucky you get twenty thousand days, and the chance to put down a "million" things.

I live a pretty quiet life. I've spent a lot of what I hope is the less than half of it that's passed reading and teaching books, and one thing I've learned is that the private fingering of ordinary experience can fill up notebooks as interestingly as musings on great events; diary-writing is the poor man's art. My own diaries have outgrown the green strongbox I used to keep them in, and I've outgrown believing I'm such a shocking character that they need to be locked up. They're a permanent part of life now.

I'm always behind. I try to write each night, but I often don't get around to writing up a day until several more have gone by. But I manage to keep them all separate. It's gone on this way for seven years now without any day missing its sentences. I suppose it's a compulsion, but I hesitate to call it that, because it's gotten pretty easy. There comes a point when, like a marathon runner, you get through some sort of "wall" and start running on automatic. Of course, there are days when I hate writing the thing. If you've just lived through a perfectly miserable twenty-four hours, forcing yourself to write an account of them can be like purposely inducing a hangover. Who needs it? I'll ask myself; but I'll do it anyway. I've been grateful for uneventful days, because I've found I can be just as tired at the end of them as at the end of busy ones, but at least there's less to write. Still, it's often on days when I thought nothing happened that I'll start writing and go on for pages, a single sound or sight recalled from the afternoon suddenly loosing a chain of thoughts. I've learned, in fact, that nothing never happens.

I can recall a few times when during the day I've decided not to do something (usually something small and mean) because I realized that if I did it I'd have to mention it to the diary that night. This may be the result of a Catholic upbringing — during which confession was a deterrent to sin, not just its antidote — or it may just be an excuse I occasionally give myself to be better than I am. I know that I've often anticipated small disasters — in love, at work — in the diary, and written that if the bad thing I have in mind happens it really won't hurt so much. This attempt to lessen pain by predicting it has, I should hasten to say, never once worked. When good things have glimmered around the corner, I've sometimes hesitated to hope for them in the diary because the gods can hear and mustn't be tempted. This, too, is a practice I ought to abandon; the evidence is by now convincing that the gods don't read.

Keeping the diary is not a practice that universally endears one to one's friends. Some would prefer that their friendship be "off the record," even though they know that term rarely applies with the habitual diarist. If in a conversation they happen to remember the diary, they can become like the Indian who fears the tourist's camera will steal his spirit. I don't blame them. The little reading I've done of my own thirty books convinces me I'm a lousy judge of character in the early stages of acquaintance. Not so bad as time goes on and impressions accrue — but what a lot of paeans to jerks and brickbats to bricks those books contain!

Insofar as they turn every experience into a personal one, keeping diaries isn't such a good idea. But by hanging on to them one can manage to avoid sentimentalizing the past. If I'm ever tempted to wax nostalgic for December 1973, I've got that small brown notebook to wise me up. I also know that I have in them a thousand things to cheer me up: if I take one of them out of the cabinet I won't have to read too many paragraphs before getting to a joke or kiss I'd forgotten about.

As the volumes pile up in that cabinet I get mixed feelings. "Look at it — life! — it's all still there!" I think. But then I realize, "It's going fast; there's less and less of it to live." Even so, I've come to believe — and I think most diarists believe this — that the accumulated past makes the shrinking future more bearable. When I was nineteen someone told me that *time* was the most important word in literature. I was skeptical. What about *love*? What about *soul*? Now that some years have gone by, I'm certain she was right. Time is the strongest thing of all, and the diarist is always fleeing it. He knows he will eventually be run to earth, but his hope is that his book will let each day live beyond its midnight, let it continue somewhere outside its place in a finite row of falling dominoes. Even people who don't keep diaries proper sometimes can't bear to part with their peculiar versions of them. In *Goodbye to Berlin*, Christopher Isherwood's landlady, Fräulein Schroeder, liked to draw attention to her carpet and walls and point out which past lodger made which mark on it — whose coffee that was, whose ink. My father never kept a diary, but he never threw away a canceled check, either. When he died a few years ago I came across thousands of them in perfect order in a series of shoeboxes. Amidst stacks of others that took the family from the children's milk through his own bifocals, I found the one that paid the doctor who delivered me. My father knew they didn't audit you for 1951 in 1980; he kept those checks for another reason.

*

I would say that I've never looked at 95 percent of what's in my thirty books since the night it was written down. Every once in a while I check to see what I was doing on the same day five years ago, but mostly I just keep thinking that I'll read them "someday," years from now, when the past is indisputably longer and more exciting than the future.

Is that the only person I'm writing for — myself when older? Or is there someone else? Who is this "you" that's made its way more and more often into these pages in the last few years, this odd pronoun I sometimes find myself talking to like a person at the other end of a letter? Sometimes when I'm writing on the right-hand leaf of a notebook I catch sight of a spelling or grammatical mistake I made on the left one the night before, and I correct it. For "you"?

I can say without a trace of coyness that I have no idea who "you" is. I don't know if "you" is male or female, met or unmet, born or unborn, tied to me by blood or accident. But I do know that "you" has come to stay. What's more, I now realize that he or she has been hovering around the books from the beginning.

Whether or not they admit it, I think all the purchasers of the five million blank diaries sold each year in this country have a "you" in mind as well. Perhaps in the backs of their minds, or hidden in the subconscious strata, but there. Some people are certain who that pronoun is — the apologists in the fifth chapter of this book usually have a faithless lover or a stadium full of political posterity in mind. But most of the others in here, as well as most people who keep diaries right now, would deny that they have anybody in mind but themselves. I have to say that I can no longer believe them.

After reading hundreds of diaries in the last several years, I've come to feel sure of three things. One is that writing books is too good an idea to be left to authors; another is that almost no one has had an easy life; and the third is that no one ever kept a diary for just himself.

In fact, I don't believe one can write to oneself for many words more than get used in a note tacked to the refrigerator, saying "Buy Bread." Before another sentence is added it becomes a psychological impossibility; the words have to start going someplace. Your "you" may be even less palpable than mine, but someday, like the one you love, he'll come along. "He" may turn out to be a great-great-granddaughter, one summer afternoon a hundred years from now, going through boxes in an attic — or the man to whom she's sold the house, without remembering to clean out the garage. But an audience will turn up. In fact, you're counting on it. Someone will be reading and you'll be talking. And if you're talking, it means you're alive.

This is a book about people and the diaries they keep. It's populated by writers, dancers, madmen, statesmen, lovers, assassins, philosophers, housewives, soldiers, and children. Some are chroniclers of the everyday. Others have kept their books only in special times — over the course of a trip, or during a crisis. Some have used them to record journeys of the soul, plan the art of the future, confess the sins of the flesh, lecture the world from beyond the grave. And some of them, prisoners and invalids, have used them not so much to record lives as create them, their diaries being the only world in which they could fully live.

The books inside this one come from different centuries and continents, different motives and mentalities. But taken together I think they prove the axiom Conrad set down in *The Secret Agent*: "We can never cease to be ourselves." One can read a poem or a novel without coming to know its author, look at a painting and fail to get a sense of its painter; but one cannot read a diary and feel unacquainted with its writer. No form of expression more emphatically embodies the expresser: diaries are the flesh made word. All one really need bring to the reading of them is an interest in human beings and the things they get themselves into. As Arthur Ponsonby wrote in one of his catalogues of English diaries, "They are better than novels, more accurate than histories, and even at times more dramatic than plays." These aren't just books that were written; they're books that happened.

I've been reading them for several years now: in the library of Vassar College, where I teach; at Cambridge University, where I've had a sabbatical; under the dome of the Library of Congress reading room; at lunch; waiting in airports; in bed. This book doesn't pretend to be an all-inclusive study. There are plenty of diarists, including some of the "greats," who for one reason or another won't show up here. My own tastes and background and biases have led to what's inside and what's not. What I want to do is offer a brief tour of some of the books that have excited or annoyed or perplexed me most; to suggest the huge variety of diaries that get written; to consider why they're kept; and — most of all — to think about the people who keep them.

The next couple of hundred pages will be a bit *like* a diary at times. For better and worse they'll be the musings of a single sensibility. Occasionally they'll contradict one another. And depending on the interest or complexity of what's at hand, they'll sometimes speed up and sometimes slow down.

They'll also begin the way most diaries begin: all at once, with a rolling up of sleeves, an intake of breath — and a here goes.

I.

Chroniclers

*Oh yes, I've enjoyed reading the past
years diary, & shall keep it up. I'm
amused to find how its grown a person, with almost a face of its own.*
— VIRGINIA WOOLF
December 28, 1919

THE FIRST THING we should try to get straight is what
to call them. "What's the difference between a diary and
a journal?" is one of the questions people interested in
these books ask. The two terms are in fact hopelessly
muddled. They're both rooted in the idea of dailiness, but
perhaps because of *journal*'s links to the newspaper trade
and *diary*'s to *dear*, the latter seems more intimate than
the former. (The French blur even this discrepancy by
using no word recognizably like *diary;* they just say
journal intime, which is sexy, but a bit of a mouthful.)
One can go back as far as Dr. Johnson's *Dictionary* and
find him making the two more or less equal. To him a
diary was "an account of the transactions, accidents and
observations of every day; a journal." Well, if synonymity
was good enough for Johnson, we'll let it be good enough
for us.

The idea of the diary as carrier of the private, the
everyday, the intriguing, the sordid, the sublime, the boring — in short, a chronicle of everything — seems to have
occurred accidentally, and not much before Samuel Pepys
began what may still be the best-known diary of all. If he
cannot be said to have invented the form as we now think

of it, he very nearly did, just as he more or less perfected it within months of starting his book on January 1, 1660. The start of a decade always seems ten times as auspicious as the beginning of a mere new year, and the dawning of January 1, 1660, may have been just what Pepys needed to push him over the top of an idea that had been kicking about in his juicy mind for some time.

He can't be sure that this will be the year of the King's restoration, much less the decade of the Great Fire and the Great Plague, but he hardly needs those extra historical inducements to record once he gets rolling. He is a natural: he may not always write up each day before it is over (it feels good to know he can get twelve days behind), but during the next 3438 of them he will miss giving words to only eleven. He sets to work in Thomas Shelton's tachygraphy, which looks a little like Pitman shorthand and a little like hieroglyphics, and he keeps going for more than a million words.

Pepys passes the 1660s in the Navy Office, and is just close enough to great events to make his diary a part of history. But he is never about to leave himself on the cutting room floor of the scenes he films just for the sake of the bigger picture. When Charles II is crowned in Westminster Abbey, Pepys sees it all — except those moments when he is relieving his great "list to pisse"; his next morning's hangover, the result of the evening's festivities, isn't left out either. To Carlyle history amounted to the biography of great men; to Pepys it consists of the advancement of Pepys. He may deplore the court's sycophancy toward the King during tennis matches, and he may not record examples of his own influence with the pomposity of his contemporary diarist John Evelyn, but you don't exactly see him turning down any invitations, either. On April 17, 1665, he realizes the King knows his name, and he feels terrific.

Pepys feels terrific so often in this decade of increasing prosperity that he can't help but make a reader feel terrific, too. He is forever taking stock of himself, not in the spiritual columns of debit and credit that the Puritan diarists of his time are totaling, but in ones of earthly prosperity. And he's almost never in the red. Birthdays, New Year's Eves, the anniversaries of his successful kidney stone operation: they all make him pause and cluck about his own good luck. In 1662 Pepys delights to find himself "a very rising man," and three years later he can't believe the extent to which he's made it: "Lord, to see how I am treated, that come from so mean a beginning, is a matter of wonder to me." He realizes in 1667 that none of his old classmates at Magdalene College, Cambridge, has done any better than he, and he unabashedly puts down his joy. The diary gurgles like a full stomach and jingles like a full pocket. Never was there a man more difficult to begrudge his own vulgarity. His success has made him happy; and it's come, after all, from hard work and calculation: "Chance without merit brought me in, and . . . diligence only keeps me so, and will, living as I do among so many lazy people, that the diligent man becomes necessary . . . they cannot do anything without him."

Along with a great job, he's got a swell wife. She's prettier than Princess Henriette, so pretty that he's jealous of first her dancing master and then her painting instructor. The Pepyses argue over the accounts, and they bite and scratch and belt each other, but they always call a truce and end up "pretty good friends." He knows how to let her bad temper burn itself out by paying it no mind, and when he's been too free with the servant girls she makes sure the next one they hire has plenty of pock marks. Even their most serious row, in 1668 over the servant girl Deb, pays some connubial dividends: "I must here remember that I have laid with my moher as a husband more times since this falling-out then in I believe twelve months before — and with more pleasure to her then I think in all the time of our marriage before." This last sentence is one illustration of Pepys's knack for stumbling upon psychological truths long before psychology was invented.

Goodness knows Elizabeth Pepys has her hands full, mostly because her husband's always are — of the pliant flesh of servant girls and married ladies about the town. Pepys believes in substituting appetite for logic in these matters. He can forgive a woman for accidentally hitting him with her spittle in the theater, once he discovers how "very pretty" she is; and after he's made an assignation with Deb he can take "great hopes by her carriage that she continues modest and honest." He goes for "the main thing" with Mrs. Lane, but she says no, "for which God be praised; and yet I came so near, that I was provoked to spend." He suffers the same fate when he reads *L'Escholle des Filles*, "a lewd book, but what doth me no wrong to read for information sake." He'll even risk groping a girl in Saint Dunstan's Church — and when she threatens to stick pins in him, he goes off and gropes another one.

Being a man of some taste and standing he finds it fitting to cloak his amours in a code of broken French and Italian. Of course, one needn't be bilingual to figure out what he does with Mrs. Martin on June 3, 1666: "Did what je voudrais avec her, both devante and backward, which is also muy bon plazer." Or what happens between him and Deb on March 31, 1668: "Yo did take her, the first time in my life, sobra mi genu and did poner mi mano sub her jupes and toca su thigh." If hypocrisy is the tribute vice pays to virtue, this lunatic "secrecy" is a little bonbon virtue throws to vice. Its purpose isn't concealment; it's to give a little extra thrill to Pepys as he writes. When you're twelve and someone offers to show you a dirty postcard, you're interested. But when you're told it's a French dirty postcard, then, boy, you're really interested. In matters of the flesh, Pepys was permanently twelve.

He is blessed with a child's avidity for any new piece of entertainment, science, invention, fashion. He wants to know everything. His mind, like that of his spiritual descendant Leopold Bloom, runs away from the abstract and toward the ingeniously practical in matters scientific. He'll discuss optics just after he's discussed teeth; go see an experiment in blood transfusion performed on a dog; marvel at a bearded lady; and wonder how this Italian sport of buggery he's heard about is actually performed: "Blessed be god, I do not to this day know what is the meaning of this sin, nor which is the agent nor which the patient." He'll even listen to the antiquarian Elias Ashmole tell him how many insects and frogs "do often fall from the sky ready-formed."

He is eager to get it all into both his days and his diary: a performance of *Midsummer Night's Dream* ("the most insipid ridiculous play that ever I saw in my life"), a cockfight, the story of how his wife burned her hand or Mr. Townsend ripped his breeches. But, however vast his capacity to gather and swallow, there comes a day — June 24, 1664 — when even his senses suffer a temporary overload. The short circuit occurs in the evening, while he is being shown through the King's closet in Whitehall, "where such variety of pictures and other things of value and rarity, that I was properly confounded and enjoyed no pleasure in the sight of them — which is the only time in my life that ever I was so at a loss for pleasure in the greatest plenty of objects to give it me."

He is what the next century would call a great booby. And his willingness to be one so freely is his genius. He wakes up and gets scared by his own pillow; sets his wig on fire; bruises his finger while putting the make on Mrs. Bagwell; hurts his thumb while boxing a servant. He's embarrassed when a footboy catches him kicking a cook-maid, but not too embarrassed to tell it to the diary. He consistently confesses the same responses the rest of us pretend to have outgrown: he's less frightened to walk through a graveyard when the ground is covered with snow; the painted dew on a still life of flowers seems so real he keeps touching the canvas to make sure his eyes haven't tricked him. There may be a sucker born every minute, but an unselfconscious sucker like this comes along — well, it's difficult to think of his equal since.

The diary stops as suddenly as it begins. Fearing he is about to go blind, Pepys quits it on May 31, 1669. In fact, his eyes recover, and before his death thirty-four years later he manages to keep a few more diaries about travel and political business. But Pepys's great private enterprise is never really resumed after the decade that opened it comes to a close. It eventually goes with the rest of his books, all of them magnificently bound and cased, to his alma mater, Magdalene College, where it remains undeciphered until an undergraduate named John Smith transcribes it early in the nineteenth century.

On a visit to Eton in 1666 Pepys was taken with the self-preserving custom the boys had of carving their names in the window shutters. An entire Pepys Library now exists as his own imprimatur upon Magdalene. The six original volumes, the first one opened to January 1, 1660, are there inside a glass case. The library is open for a few hours most days of the week. Very quiet and extremely well arranged, it is the most incongruously decorous room in the world.

If you have a taste for cruel fantasy, imagine Pepys, after getting a reprieve on his eyes, being shipped from the old England to the New one, and made to live his life and write his diaries in Puritan Massachusetts. How long would it have been before he found himself in the stocks? Only if you have a very modest set of appetites, as Samuel Sewall did, could the task of writing a diary in such a time and place be congenial. Sewall is sometimes labeled an American Pepys, but this idea should be dispelled at once. First, such a thing is impossible (one might as well imagine Casanova in Kansas), and second, Sewall is not nearly so entertaining a diarist. Absorbing, yes, but in a quiet, homely way. To walk out of Pepys's diary and into Sewall's is to leave the music hall for the church recital. It's got its pleasures, but one fidgets if one stays too long.

One can do just that, because the recital runs for fifty-five years. Sewall starts his diaries in 1674, a few years after he gets out of Harvard, and keeps them going through what — as becomes appallingly apparent from the diaries themselves — was a jolly long lifetime for that continent in that century. Sewall is a pious businessman and jurist who fills his book with quiet records of one man's daily colonial round. Its readers find accounts of rainbows, squabbles among the children, changes in the weather ("a very extraordinary Storm of Hail . . . 'twas as bigg as pistoll and Musquet Bullets."), and the occasional sudden excitement, like a fire during the church service.

His career in the courts lets us glimpse the dark underbelly of our forefathers' probity. Sewall attends a multiple hanging on June 30, 1704. Upon the lowering of the scaffold, he notes, there was "such a Screech of the Women that my wife heard it sitting in our Entry next the Orchard, and was much surprised at it; yet the wind was sou-west. Our house is a full mile from the place." Sewall himself, the only judge at the Salem witch trials to admit his mistake publicly, shows as much compassion as a magistrate sitting on the hard wooden benches of Puritan New England can. In July 1701 he must try Esther Rogers for murdering her illegitimate daughter; after sentence is pronounced he has some harsh words for her, but adds that he "did not do this to insult over her, but to make her sensible."

Dead children form a grim garland around all the volumes of his diary. He fathers sons and daughters regularly, and as often as not they die in early childhood. The reader becomes accustomed to lyings-in and funerals coming within a few pages of each other. On Monday, December 7, 1685: "About One in the Night my Wife is brought to Bed of a Son, of which Mother Hull brings me the first News: Mrs. Weeden Midwife." This was

Henry, who would live for just fifteen days. Sewall describes his funeral on Christmas Eve, carefully listing the mourners and ceremonies. Then he becomes reflective: "The Lord humble me kindly in respect of all my Enmity against Him, and let his breaking my Image in my Son be a means of it." But this is not the entry's last sentence. Another one reads, "Considerable snow this night." You can hypothesize that he wanted to get his mind off the subject, or chose to see some sort of symbolism — maybe of death, maybe of burial. But, as likely as not, all that is at work here is the chronicler's habit of recording whatever dominates his recollection of the moment, regarding neither shape nor proportion, but only his own avidity for noticing and preserving.

The drama of Henry's birth and death is repeated over and over. A year later the baby is named Stephen; he survives for six months. And after that funeral, too, it is easier to list who came rather than what he felt. If there is something a little unsettling in Pepys's childlessness — all that seed without any sowing — Sewall's continual fatherings and buryings are eventually benumbing. There are too many to take in. It is only after his wife has delivered her fourteenth child, in January 1702, that Sewall ends an entry of thanksgiving with the words: "And it may be my dear wife may now leave off bearing."

The terrors of birth rival the terrors of the plague. Measles and smallpox also infect the diary. On January 12, 1690, Sewall tells his eleven-year-old son Samuel that he should be ready to die from the latter, as nine-year-old Richard Dumer just has. Sam eats an apple as he listens, seeming "not much to mind" — until he says the Lord's Prayer his father prescribes and bursts into terrified cries.

With so much mortality about, and with such a baleful view of Providence in the body politic, it isn't surprising that Sewall gives considerable attention to dreams and omens. Accidents are seen as symbols and portents. When a can of water spills it's a bad sign; and a broken glass becomes "a lively Emblem of our Fragility and Mortality." Some of Sewall's dreams, alas, are wasted on his personal modesty and limited imagination. On February 13, 1705, he dreams he is sentenced to execution, but all he says about it is that it was "a very sad Dream that held me a great while." Two years later he imagines he's been made Lord Mayor of London, "a strange absurd Dream" that leaves him "much perplex'd." One can only contemplate what Pepys would have done with these two! During the first we would have felt the sheets soaked with cold sweat, and in the course of the second we would have heard him ordering the new coach and silver plate.

How Mrs. Hannah Hull Sewall managed to live fifteen years beyond the birth of a fourteenth child is a merciful mystery. She has the reader's sympathies through all the years she spends in the diary. But from the standpoint of reader interest, it must be admitted that her passing in 1717 is something of a blessed event: "God is teaching me a new Lesson: to live a Widower's life," Sewall reasons just after his wife expires. "Lord help me to Learn." In fact, he catches on magnificently. Sewall was made for widowhood the way Pepys was made for philandering, and once (past age sixty-five) he goes respectably a-courting, standing on widows' doorsteps, bags of almonds in hand, he and the diary take unexpected, geriatric flight.

First he pursues Mrs. Denison. When he can't land her he settles for marriage to Mrs. Tilley. But after several months, on May 26, 1720, he announces: "About midnight my dear wife expired to our great astonishment, especially mine." Fortunately, widows are as plentiful as Samuel Sewall's desire to marry them is prodigious. Mrs. Winthrop is the next to be courted, and for some exhausting weeks in the fall of 1720 the diary becomes a catalogue of both Sewall's insistent proposals and her persistent rejections. By October 17 he knows it's hopeless; she's not even bothering to put on clean linen for his visits anymore. Three weeks later he is making a last pitch, but she's respectfully not buying:

> The Fire was come to one short Brand besides the Block, which Brand was set up in end; at last it fell to pieces, and no Recruit was made: She gave me a Glass of Wine. I think I repeated again that I would go home and bewail my Rashness in making more haste than good Speed. I would endeavour to contain myself, and not go on to sollicit her to do that which she could not Consent to. Took leave of her. As came down the steps she bid me have a Care. Treated me Courteously. Told her she had enter'd the 4th year of her Widow-hood. I had given her the News-Letter before: I did not bid her draw off her glove as sometime I had done.

This is his greatest disappointment, but two months later, unbowed, he's showing up with almonds for Mrs. Gibbs, and shortly thereafter they're concluding a pre-nuptial agreement that could stand up to the scrutiny of a modern Los Angeles lawyer. After the marriage enough serenity sets in for Sewall to risk a visit to Mrs. Winthrop, the result of which seems an appropriate mixture of wistfulness and sour grapes: "She thank'd me kindly, en-quired how Madam Sewall did . . . At coming I said, I kiss your hand Madame (her hand felt very dry). She desired me to pray that God would lift up upon her the Light of his Countenance."

In these last years, before his death at seventy-seven, Sewall must have marveled continually at the ripeness of the old age he was living into. He even comes to call Hannah, who had been alive when he was past sixty-five, "the Wife of my youth." Before the end of his long life and fifty-five-year chronicle finally comes, it is foretold, predictably, in his dreams. His own clock, which has run so long, is being taken from him:

Septr 10th 1728. Last night I dreamed that a little boy
had got away my watch, I found him on the Comon,
and by giving him another Watch persuaded him to
give me that round which was engraven

> Auris, mens, oculus, manus, os, pes; munere fungi
>   Dum pergunt, praestat discere velle more.

Time-lapse photography offers odd pleasures: gaudy
flowers blooming in a second, skyscrapers flinging themselves upward in half a minute. Reading someone's life in
one of these huge chronicle diaries can be a little like
watching it that way: you go through a year in maybe
an hour or two. But the effects aren't so amusing as they
are with the flower and the skyscraper. Ye gods, you ask
yourself, how many times can someone have breakfast?
In fact, the diarist doesn't eat it any more often than you
do; it's just that recording it is his tic, and by reading so
much of his book at once you've got to down a couple
of hundred eggs in a sitting. Life, from this vantage,
seems even more repetitive than it is. What's more, a
steady diet of the first person leaves anyone irritated and
malnourished, eager to assert his own ego against the one
that keeps coming up off the pages. "Up betimes and to
my office": aw, go on home, you say, having heard
Pepys tell you this a hundred times if he's told you once.
Read too quickly, even his life seems dull.

Some diaries are best read as they were written: one
day at a time. They should be set down on the night table
and consumed slowly. Certain lives, usually quiet ones,
seem meant to be slipped into for only a few minutes a
day, like a footbath. Just enough to relax you a while,
not enough to turn you pruney. *The Diary of a Country
Parson, 1758–1802*, by gentle James Woodforde, is one of
these. Parson Woodforde, who spent most of his career
in the parsonages of Ansford and Weston Longeville in
England, was a quiet, sentimental bachelor who even had

a dog named Rover. He lived the sort of life one would like to live for about five minutes each morning before getting out of bed and turning on the radio for the overnight homicide count and the outlook on the Long Island Expressway.

Woodforde was born in 1740 and studied at New College, Oxford. It is there that one catches him sowing the odd wild oat: throwing some wine around the Bachelors' Common Room, going a bit into debt with his tailor. But Parson Woodforde was not long meant for such roistering. There was nothing of the rake or slyboots permanently in him. Perhaps the raciest entry in the whole forty-four-year diary comes on May 19, 1770: "Something very agreable and with which I was greatly pleased happened this evening. It gave me much secret pleasure and satisfaction." What was it, Reverend? He's not telling.

On the job in his curacy he settles feuds, buries drunkards, sends out valentines (sixty-two on February 14, 1785), and hosts an annual winter "frolic" — a big meal and sing — for the locals who come to pay him their tithes. He distributes small sums to people, for their need and his pleasure, and makes a careful record of what he gives away. He tends to the sick and dying with duty and feeling. Sudden death is nearly as much a part of his world as of Sewall's, but Woodforde never becomes hardened to it: "I prayed for poor James Burge this morning, out of my own head, hearing he was just gone off almost in a consumption. It occasioned a great tremulation in my voice at the time." Pious without being "enthusiastic," he remains steadily aware of the proportional merits of earth and heaven. Considering the imminent death of his maid's sister, he prays that God "grant her a Speedy relief from her present Situation — to Life if it be thy good Pleasure, or happiness." Not life *and* happiness; life *or* happiness.

He is an uncomplicated, sympathetic soul, fond of fishing and not above acquiring a bit of gin from his smuggling connection. He dislikes performing forced marriages and expresses his distaste for public whippings. About as cynical as he gets is a description of Mrs. Melliar as "*fashionably* frightened into a fit by a cat after supper at the Doctor's." His dreams are like ours: in the early hours of January 9, 1785, he imagines himself being pursued by two corpses on his way to church.

The parson has some of Pepys's taste for "remarkable facts." Living in the country he has to wait longer between their appearances, but in the course of his life he, too, manages to see a bearded lady. A pineapple, a peacock's tail, a pig that can spell, a manned balloon, and a captured spider (which he tames) are among the things that catch his fancy. He may believe in inoculation but he puts faith in home remedies and wives' tales, too: rubbing one's eye with the tail of a black cat will relieve a sty, and if the same cat washes over both her ears then there'll be a change in the weather.

The ravages of love make just one brief appearance in Woodforde's quiet bachelor life. He falls for Betsy White, but, alas, she proves "a mere Jilt." That is really it. Any domestic dramas must be provided first by his wastrel brother, Jack, and then by his spinster niece, Nancy, who gets more bored with life at the parsonage as the years go by. She can be "quite bluff and rather pert," and the secrets she keeps from him hurt the poor diarist: "Nancy, Betsy Davy, and Mr. Walker are all confederate against me and am never let into any of their Schemes or Intentions &c. Nancy I think ought not to be so to me." In supporting roles there are the servants: Will gets sick "in the venereal way"; a cook who can't cook must be dismissed; Briton is tipsy; and Molly's gone and gotten herself pregnant. Woodforde must sack her, but not with any ire: "She is a very poor, weak Girl, but I believe honest."

Even this distressing duty isn't enough to keep him from noting in the very next sentence that he dined on roast breast of veal that day. Parson Woodforde is tremendously fond of his tucker; food is, in fact, one of the diary's leading topics. He dislikes "frenchified" dishes, preferring plain English ones to fill out his lists: "Pudding for dinner — Veal Cutlets, Frill'd Potatoes, cold Tongue, Ham and cold roast Beef, and eggs in their shells. Punch, Wine, Beer and Cyder for drinking." In his later years, the dinner menu is the regular climax of each daily entry. (Not, of course, that one always wants to eat with him: "sheep's heart" is the sort of thing he carries around in his pocket for a snack.) The day after Christmas, 1794, he mentions having had seven or eight glasses of port after dinner.

The small moments in the rural routine afford the most pleasure to a reader of his book. We catch his sister wearing paper curlers, or glimpse lightning creating a glow on Nancy's dinner plate. The pigs get into a beer barrel one day and are still stumbling around blotto the next morning. The chamber pots are frozen on February 28, 1785, and they're frozen again on January 25, 1795. So slow is life in Weston Longeville, and so reliable its inhabitants, that the parson bothers to pay his clock-cleaner's bill only once every five years. One can catch Woodforde slipping into a bit of grandiloquence when he reports someone's death, but a resolute plainness is more often his style. No one could accuse him of any false straining after concision and wit in his account of Mr. Custance's visit on May 26, 1796:

> Whilst we were walking to Weston House, Mr. Custance walked to our House, as we heard from Mr. Custance who soon came to us at Weston House. We went towards Morton to go to Weston House, or else we should in all probability have met Mr. Custance who came across Weston-great-Field.

Here, we think, are archaic pleasures to revel in before heading off to the drive-in teller on a Friday morning.

But was it all it was bucolically cracked up to be? In fact, no. One can't edit out all unpleasantness, even from

Parson Woodforde's life. One reads about "highway-men," and that sounds, well, romantic, until one realizes that two hundred years from now "muggers" is likely to have a quaint ring. Young Mr. Love comes to gild the parson's weathercock on May 19, 1790, and what could be more serene than that? Nothing perhaps, but it doesn't stop Mr. Love from slitting his throat fifteen months later: "He had been in a low way some time owing to his being very deaf . . . He was a great Support to a very infirm and aged Father, and afraid that he might be re-duced to want." Nancy's complaint against "the dismal Situation" in the parson's house in 1794 makes the reader shake his head in amusement. But then we remember that Nancy was making the same complaint back in 1789. That's a long time to be miserable.

Parson Woodforde wants company less and less during the years Nancy craves it. In his last decade people can get on his nerves a bit. He can be "timorous," and his entries are increasingly swollen with gout. (Is it any won-der? Friday, November 6, 1795: "Dinner to day a boiled Chicken and a Pigs Face and some beef Steaks.") But he keeps eating and writing as long as he can. The very last sentence in the diary, written about ten weeks before he died, is "Dinner to day, Rost Beef &c."

Back in 1789, when Nancy was bored, the French, of course, were anything but. Parson Woodforde, hearing of these distant convulsive events, wants them to stay just where they are. A rumor that there's to be a protest against high wheat prices at Saint Faith's Fair on Wednes-day, October 17, 1792, prompts him to observe that the real reason for such agitation is "the late long propensity of the discontented to a general Disturbance, so prevalent at present in France."

Over the next decade the ensuing war between France and Britain touches Woodforde's life but little. For the aristocratic Miss Elizabeth Wynne, however, that war is what cuts the whole pattern of life. The daughter of the

Anglo-Italian Riccardo Gulielmo Casparo Melchior Balthazaro Wynne, Esq. (a.k.a. Richard Wynne), she grows up in Italy and Switzerland with her younger sisters. We know her from the twenty-five volumes of her sixty-eight-year-long diary, which was discovered nearly a century after her death and then edited by her descendant Anne Fremantle.

The youthful volumes reveal a hugely pampered life full of tutors, masters, and lessons; marionette theaters bought by Papa; and parties thrown for the peasants ("They all ate as if they were starved"). Things are placid until the troubles in France start nibbling at the community of English expatriates in which the Wynnes figure prominently. By May 1792 there are rumors of impending risings, and a year and a half after that the news that the "unfortunate Queen of France has been *aiguillotiné.*" Elizabeth's maternal grandparents are roughed up at their country house near Lyons. It's this "abominable spirit of liberty" that dislocates everything and keeps so many people, including the Wynnes, on the run.

Elizabeth experiences, along with the fancy frustrations of exile, the usual adolescent perplexities about her diary. She'd like to write it in verse, but that's awfully difficult and time-consuming; she'd like to know how something is going to turn out even as she confides its early developments to her book; she has trouble seeing the point of writing down a conversation that afflicted her only when it was taking place; and then, of course, there is the problem of secrecy. M. Buohl, for example, is a horrible bore, and M. de Bombelles and his son are pretty awful, too, but you wouldn't want them to know that "Bets/ywa/ sver / ymiserabl / ea / tdine / ri / tbein / gcompos / do / fac / ompan/ys/odisagreable/et/oh/er." (It will take you only a minute to crack this, but compared to Pepys's continentalisms, Betsey's cipher is worthy of the KGB.)

There are numerous spectacles and scandals to be reported amidst the emigrés and exiles: a curious Jewish wedding; a man who dances on horses; another who's been struck by lightning; Miss Floyer's dalliance with a rope dancer. But Betsey's often bored, too. What she needs, of course, is a good Georgian romance, and that's where Captain (later Admiral Sir Thomas) Fremantle comes sailing in during June of 1796. At that moment the Wynnes need to hotfoot it out of Italy and away from the approaching French, and Fremantle takes them aboard the *Inconstant*, sister ship to the *Achilles*, on which they escape from Leghorn on the twenty-sixth. Betsey is delighted — though not impassioned — from the start. Fremantle is more "pleasing" than "handsome" to look at, but it is his temperament that counts: "He is good natured, kind, and amiable, gay and lively in short he seems to possess all the good and amiable qualities that are required to win everybodies heart the first moment one sees him." A couple of weeks later things are a bit more rhapsodic: "As long as we stay on board the Inconstant with this excellent man I do not care what part of the world we go to."

Unfortunately they are soon sundered, Fremantle to fight Napoleon on the seas and Betsey to sail home with another part of the British fleet. Separation, parental opposition ("Papa is worse disposed than ever"), and the unwanted attentions of old Captain Foley inject additional ardor into her affections for Fremantle before they are finally reunited. (A quick reading of her diary in this period can probably no more convey the slowness of waiting than a hundred of Parson Woodforde's breakfasts, when consumed in one gulp, can taste like a meal.) As for the reunion itself, it is possible that the volume of Betsey's diary covering it is the only one that was too hot to handle. As her descendant notes, it is the single piece of her long chronicle that's missing. Betsey says she lost it aboard the *Inconstant*; she may, in fact, have arranged to.

After a discreet report on the morning after the wedding night ("I never felt better and happier in my life than I did today"), Betsey begins her life as an officer's wife. Fremantle serves under Nelson ("I find it looks shocking to be without one arm"), and Betsey starts giving birth to children back in England. They come with sufficient rapidity that entries noting their arrival soon take on a no-big-deal sort of style: "I sent for Tookey and was safely delivered at twenty minutes after nine in the evening of a nice little girl."

For long stretches Betsey stays at home to raise her brood. On July 10, 1803, Fremantle is about to take up another commission, and she is left to worry: "He really goes to sea quite *à contre coeur* as he was now so comfortably settled here, and I feel not a little anxiety at being left alone with five such young children and so much to manage." She spends years living with her sisters and the babies, waiting for her husband's homecomings; he, meanwhile, is off gaining glory. On June 23, 1806, she records how she takes the children to see Westall's painting of "Nelson attacking a Spanish Launch off Cadiz": Fremantle is part of the canvas and the kids instantly recognize their papa. Fremantle himself, no doubt considering his wife's avidity for chronicling, sends her his own diary-letters from aboard ship, telling her of things from battles to parties, most of it exciting enough to make her future editor take more of an interest in him than in Betsey as she assembles the Wynneana. "During 1813," Anne Fremantle admits, "it is Fremantle's letters still that are news: Betsey's diary is only life."

In fact, living so long with her ancestor's diary breeds a bit of contempt in the modern Mrs. Fremantle as she gets close to the end of the third volume to be published. In her mid-thirties Betsey has "much of the waspish child in her still," and Anne Fremantle is more than a little abashed at her great-grandmother-in-law's lack of depth. It is certainly true that Betsey could be a bit brittle. She takes a good deal of pleasure in her children, but is just as often impatient with the "brats." Someone else's visiting child is "more disgusting than ever," and little Harriet

Howard is "the ugliest little ape" she's ever seen. (Ugliness is a quality Betsey has an especially hard time tolerating.) Betsey is not exactly the type to let off steam once and then forget about it. If you check out page 365 of Mrs. Fremantle's conscientious index to Volume 1, you will find such entries as:

dislikes Bombelles family, 119, 157, 164, 165, 170, 174, 175, 177–9, 183, 184, 186, 187, 190, 191, 202, 207, 208, 211, 213, 220, 224, 225, 229, 230, 231, 235, 236, 254, 260, 261, 271

But you can't really expect someone to emerge from a childhood of hot and cold running dancing masters as a model of self-sacrifice and patience. Betsey is to be credited with doing a pretty good job of living simultaneously in Fremantle's shadow and absence. By keeping a diary as she did, she was adding her book to a genre to which women have always felt especially drawn. The diary was, after all, available to them for expression in centuries when their attempts to practice other forms of literature — say, produce a play — were considered presumptuous or silly. Japanese women were confiding their emotions to "pillow books," kept in a slipcase and away from a husband's eyes, for centuries before there was anything like a tradition of diary-keeping in the West. The history of women is being written as much from their diaries as anything else. And the social history of all people is more detailed than it would otherwise be because of women's attention to the texture of the everyday in the diaries their men permitted them.

A single diary kept for many years by two men sounds unthinkable — a bit like a long race run by piggybacked contestants. But indisputably among the great chronicle diaries is the one kept by the Goncourt brothers, Edmond and Jules, between 1851 and 1870. The Goncourt *Journal* is the indispensable record of their aggressive career in the world of French writers of the mid-nineteenth century.

Gautier, Flaubert, Zola, Hugo, Saint-Beuve, George Sand, and Daudet are among those whose table talk, insults, rivalries, opening nights, and love lives fill the brothers' pages. Their journal, jointly composed but usually written down by Jules, is begun on December 2, 1851, the day their first book is put on sale and the day Louis-Napoleon masters France in a coup d'état.

The Goncourts are convinced that there has "never been an age so full of humbug" as their own, and their diary is full of what they imagine its grain to be. They overhear an era, carefully sprinkling into their journal thousands of remarks and incidents, each with the right ironic or hypocritical spin. Whereas Pepys retained a naturally wide-eyed susceptibility to life's surprises, the Goncourts do their best to appear brutal, bored, and unshockable. They confess to a "sceptical Credo" and like to top off their disgusted regard of Parisian sleaze with weary maxims of their own making: "Between the Belvedere Apollo and a legless cripple there is not half the distance there is between two minds, at one end of the ladder and the other." They pronounce themselves — and *pronounce* is the right word, for no chronicle diary was ever meant more for posterity's ears — almost totally immune to love: "One of us was once in love for eight days with a woman of fairly easy virtue, and the other for three days with a ten-franc whore. Altogether, eleven days of love between the two of us."

The brothers are forever eager for "facts," the revealing specifics of "living reality." After a visit to the home of Flaubert's brother, a surgeon, in 1863, they note that in that frugal Norman house there was "no other metal than silver-plate, which creates a rather chilly effect when you remember that you are in a surgeon's house and that the soup-tureen may represent the fee for the amputation of a leg, the serving-dish for the removal of a breast." The "facts" they collect are not the sterile statistics of Dickens's Mr. Gradgrind or the self-sufficient curiosities of Pepys, but the vivid clues to a corrupt and seductive era. For all the monstrous egotism of the *Journal* — and Edmond admits that they are "temperamental, neurotic, unhealthily impressionable creatures, and therefore occasionally unjust" — it is an outward-looking document, a cruel telescope trained on a whole city.

When Jules dies in 1870, just before Paris endures the bloody siege and the Commune, Edmond, for a while, can see no more point in going on with the *Journal*. But his appetite for the details of "living reality" soon gets the better of his mournful reluctance, and he proceeds with it for another twenty years. The events of 1870–1871 provide him with a spectacular first chance to go solo: the *Journal* becomes, for a time, less the repository of literary gossip than a lurid canvas of suffering. The besieged occupants of the most beautiful city in the world are shown eating elephants and camels from the zoo, and then killing each other with revolutionary relish. On May 23, 1871, Edmond records:

> On the other side of the boulevard there was a man stretched out on the ground of whom I could see only the soles of his boots and a bit of gold braid. There were two men standing by the corpse, a National Guard and a lieutenant. The bullets were making the leaves rain down on them from a little tree spreading its branches over their heads.

But this is not enough. After a moment the master of the meaningful particular realizes he is leaving out one of the best parts: "I was forgetting a dramatic detail: behind them, in front of the closed doors of a carriage entrance, a woman was lying flat on the ground, holding a peaked cap in one hand."

When France settles back, as she invariably does, into reaction, the *Journal* resumes its role as literary gossip and judge. By 1888 the rebellious Zola has become a Chevalier, and Goncourt predicts: "The literary revolution will one day be a Commander of the Legion of Honour and per-petual secretary to the Academy and will end up writing books so drearily virtuous that people will hesitate to give them as prizes at speech-days in young ladies' boarding-schools." Edmond continues the sort of taste-making of which Jules would have approved, and maintains their self-protecting sadism toward women, too: "I have al-ways derived indescribable pleasure from leading a decent woman to the edge of sin and leaving her there to live between the temptation and the fear of that sin."

Edmond began publishing the *Journal* in 1887, bringing down upon himself charges of scurrilousness and inaccu-racy. One reader of the seventh volume, which was serialized in 1894 in *Echo de Paris*, sent that periodical "an envelope full of soiled rags, anonymous excrement." Friends like the Daudets were upset by the appearance of extracts from what was, after all, a journal with so many potentially libelous passages that it was not pub-lished in its entirety until the late 1950s. But Edmond's increasing assurance about the value his journal had as a record of his world dovetailed, in his last years, with interior preoccupations, particularly his attempts to cheat oblivion. In 1880 he makes a record of a farewell dinner given by Turgenev, just before his departure for Russia, for Zola, Daudet, and Goncourt: "Each of us in turn spoke of the fear of death that haunted us." Flaubert and Hugo both die in the next five years, and the former's departure makes Edmond focus on their shared literary past: "The fact is, we were the two old champions of the new school, and I feel very lonely today." Edmond thinks of the human face as being like the sagging "diary of our sorrows, our excesses, our pleasures": not an encouraging simile. With no faith in an afterlife in another world, he is obsessed with the idea of "continuing" in this one, of "outliving myself, of leaving behind pictures of my house and my person. But what is the use?"

This idea of survival, along with the practice of scrawl-ing his name on all he owns, dominates his last decade.

Anxiety about preserving the journal manuscript taxes his last years, by which time he knows it will be one of the principal instruments of his continuance: "I shall die not knowing what is to become of the two great projects of my life intended to ensure my survival."

The other project was the Académie Goncourt, which still awards its annual literary prizes. But the Académie is merely a namesake; the *Journal* is the man himself — flesh, spirit, spleen, and warts. The book succeeds in keeping Edmond de Goncourt breathing and walking and sneering as no mere endowment or institution can. It is the fulfillment not only of his immortal longings, but of the *mot* he and Jules record in it on July 23, 1864: "A book is never a masterpiece: it becomes one. Genius is the talent of a dead man." The *Journal* is Edmond's only book that the common reader remembers. In it we find its bilious author still, and eternally, complaining and despairing — in some ways more alive than when he was alive.

For all George Templeton Strong cares, when he hears reports of the Franco-Prussian War far away in New York, Paris and the French can go to the devil. He'd be perfectly content with a German victory; and if the French have to endure a civil war, well, they can just go ahead and endure it. Hadn't he lived through America's own a decade before, the most anguished four years of his life? In any case, George Templeton Strong has no need to worry about Paris's supposedly incomparable beauties getting trampled, because he is a New Yorker through and through, and for all the appalling filth and violence accompanying the city's growth, it is obvious that his metropolis is on its way to becoming the world's greatest.

Strong's enormous diary of life in the city runs for forty years. We see him in 1836 as a student at downtown Columbia College, where he is dosed with the classics and mucks about with science: "Indeed my acquaintance

with chemistry is chiefly in the art of making stenches."
He may only manage to get through Horace with someone else's notes, but eventually he proceeds toward a
distinguished public career, combining Wall Street law,
service to Trinity Church, a trustee's position at Columbia, and the presidency of the New York Philharmonic
Society. Variations of this civic-minded résumé can still
be found in the city today, but no one who has ever lived
it took as much notice of its weave as Strong did.

So caught up is he in the municipal and national life
of his times that he barely makes space to tell us about
his private one. For the most part it is happy — in fact,
reasonably sustained happiness seems to be a condition
for keeping most long chronicle diaries, even if that happiness comes out of the pleasure one takes in one's own
world-weariness, as with the Goncourts. Strong's marriage to Ellen Caroline Ruggles produces three sons and
a constant flow of affection between the parties. If Ellie
is often crowded out by public triumphs and catastrophes,
Strong's diary remains one of the most pleasantly uxorious
available. We follow the couple through the building of
their house on Twenty-first Street, their financial ups
and downs, in sickness and in health. On December 28,
1857, Strong reflects on the anniversary of his first real
happiness:

Ten years ago this minute I was in Mrs. John A.
Stevens' house, in Bleecker Street, at a big party, in
the crowded supper-room . . . And I was thinking
about the young lady in blue silk (or blue something)
I'd been talking with so pleasantly and sympathetically
before supper. God bless her; she's now my dear wife
and the mother of my little boys upstairs. I remember
just where she stood, at the end of a dance, when I
plucked up a sheepish courage (doubting much whether
she'd recognize me), and accosted the young lady
and the precise topography of the sofa in the back
parlor where we discoursed somewhat at length. Just

at this hour, about one A.M., I was no doubt walking fast down Broadway with Johnny Parish and the biggest of cigars. I remember his facetious enquiry whether I had fallen in love with Miss Ellen Ruggles.

But this commemoration of love's young dream has a lot to compete with in Strong's outward-looking diary. Phrenology, hydropathy, religious revivals, Jenny Lind mania, the gold rush, temperance, women's rights: never has so much social history been so casually set down. Strong chronicles presidential campaigns from Andrew Jackson's to Ulysses Grant's, and all the extensions and shatterings and remakings of America from westward expansion to Southern Reconstruction. The Civil War, during which he serves as Treasurer of the Sanitary Commission of the War Department, is to be the climactic event of Strong's life, and he knows it from the moment he casts his ballot in 1860 for Abraham Lincoln: "One vote is insignificant, but I want to be able to remember that I voted right at this grave crisis." "GOD SAVE THE UNION, AND CONFOUND ITS ENEMIES," he writes on April 16, 1861.

The war means personal sacrifices large and small: when, for example, he goes shopping for Ellie's present at Tiffany's in 1861, he knows it's going to have to be more "economical" than usual. The destinies of his family and nation are linked now. Watching and worrying, he recognizes the need for displaying optimism, but when that is difficult, as it is on February 5, 1863, he goes off with his book and confides: "(Between me and my journal) things do in fact look darker and more dark every day." What he never loses, amidst all his ups and downs, is his sense of historical momentousness. After the latest patriotic mass meeting in Union Square, he wonders whether that place "will be held a classical locality by our great-great grandchildren."

When the war is at last over, with the news on April 3, 1865, that Richmond has fallen, he rushes up to Trinity

Church to set the bells pealing. It is one of the diary's great moments, wonderfully told, and yet a nervousness immediately sets in with its readers. They know, even if the diarist doesn't, what's going to happen on April 14; turning over each of the four pages left between Richmond and Ford's Theatre is a queasy, flinching experience. And when it happens it strikes the public-minded diarist just as one knew it would — as a "fearful personal calamity."

Throughout Strong's four million words (Pepys isn't even in the race) the temperatures, dangers, smells, and sheer energy of the city of New York are ceaselessly felt. May 9, 1839, is "positively stifling. Wall Street, always a Purgatory, has this day become a Pandemonium: clouds of dust flying, chippings of granite whizzing in volleys like grapeshot, the street encumbered with brick, blocks of stone, and huge Irishmen; the National Bank nearly inaccessible from the fact that on each side of it a big house is being pitched into the street." Always the partisan of reform and rectitude, Strong fills his diaries with news of sensational murders, divorces, bankruptcies, forgeries. The Third Avenue railroad is a "mephitic" conveyance, and where they've dug up Fourth Avenue at Fiftieth Street, through Potters Field, a pedestrian has to navigate the "debris of dead paupers. Ribs, clavicles, and vertebra . . ." Gang warfare abounds, fires are always breaking out (Strong rushes to them with an almost suspicious gusto), the Bowery is full of drunks, and crime so out of control generally that there's talk of vigilante action. (Picture such a situation!) One bright spot in the picture is the construction of Central Park, which never fails to lift Strong's civic imagination and pride: "Had myself rowed about on the lake in the twilight and among the swans. The Park gains on me at every visit. I have not found out half its points even yet." Strong is forever marveling at the city's juxtapositions of barbarity and progress — and one can't for a moment imagine him living anywhere else.

Strong is highly self-conscious about the diary. He sometimes thinks about "old Pepys, my prototype." After a year of keeping it he hopes he will "improve" as he goes on. He likes to dab the book with small mock-heroic flourishes about such human experiences as the mosquito bite: "The tormenting uncertainty with which the various performers tantalize him before finally closing in, and the series of energetic cuffs bestowed on his own countenance . . ." By the time the Civil War is in progress, Strong is certain enough of future readers to cry out "O Posterity" in one entry. But he does not keep the diary just out of civic duty to the future. He is compulsively attracted to the pleasures of writing, including its physical ones: "I'll be hanged if I am not in a humor for shedding ink tonight — feel as if I could scribble, scribble, scribble to the extent of a quart bottle full." This is no small thing to consider: unless the diarist can savor the sound of the pen point, or the feel of his palm as it slides rightward along the paper's creamy surface, his chronicle isn't likely to grow to four million words.

Strong is captivated by all the past's embodiments. When the venerable, pre-Revolutionary collection plate at Trinity Church passes through his hands on the morning of Sunday, March 22, 1868, he thrills himself by thinking "how many Brownjohns and Bartons, Templetons, Johnsons, and others had doubtless deposited their guineas, or shillings, their dollars or dimes, in that *identical depository*." Reading over some letters more than forty years old makes him feel as if he's walking down a freshly excavated street in Pompeii. Chroniclers tend to become so date-conscious that they wind up having more anniversaries than they can conveniently keep. Every time they write down the day and month they are likely to remember something they did when the same day and month rolled around once before. Strong rarely stints himself where retrospection is concerned, and he certainly isn't about to let October 5, 1865, go by without remembering how:

Thirty years ago tonight, *Egomet Ipse* George T. Strong, a Columbia College Sophomore, began this journal, kept up since that date with few considerable lapses of continuity. Would that every duty of mine had been as faithfully fulfilled. I remember nothing at all about making my first entry, but I perfectly recollect the night before — a Sunday night — when I conceived the project of a diary. It was under the stimulus of a cup or cups of strong coffee, a Sunday evening tea-table indulgence then recently introduced among the domestic institutions of 108 Greenwich Street. I perfectly remember my cogitating intensely over the project and considering what manner of book I should use. Vague aspirations were floating through my mind, I think, toward some huge folio volume like a bank ledger. While I was thus exercised, I suppose Mamma and Mary were reading by the light of an Argand lamp. My father had gone up to the library and was deep in the Septuagint or the Greek Testament.

To a man who keeps such a book for forty years and four million words, such a night is roughly comparable to the one on which he was born.

On September 21, 1849, George Templeton Strong is contentedly anticipating the deliveries that would soon fill up the "palazzo" he and Ellie are decorating on Twenty-first Street: "Furniture will soon begin to appear and the wilderness and the solitary places will blossom like the rose, with gilt gas fixtures, furnaces, and yellow brocatelle." Across the ocean, on the same day, Mr. Philip H. Gosse, zoologist, is also using his diary to take note of arrivals: " 'E. delivered of a son. Received green swallow from Jamaica.' " In his memoir *Father and Son*, Sir Edmund Gosse reproduces this entry from his father's journal, claiming not to feel slighted at having been accorded no more words than the five given the bird; nor does he believe, as it may appear, that his father necessarily reacted to each arrival with equal excitement. As he says: "What the wording exemplifies is my Father's extreme punctilio. The green swallow arrived later in the day than the son, and the earlier visitor was therefore recorded first; my Father was scrupulous in every species of arrangement." He was, as a diarist, a confirmed chronicler.

Chances are your opinion of whether the elder Gosse's respect for chronology was excessive is related to what you think of the Victorian novel as opposed to the "modern" one. In the Victorian, one thing generally happens after another. In the modern, one thing often happens not just after, but before and during another as well. Eschewing chronology for the more convulsive sweep in which our minds receive and recall events, it dispatched ordinary clock-time just as it banished the calmly consistent voice of the narrator. Distrusting what she called the "cheapness" of reality, and asserting that life "is not a series of gig lamps," one of its chief practitioners, Virginia Woolf, could devote page after gorgeous page of *To the Lighthouse* to the thoughts of Mrs. Ramsay and then kill off the same character in matter-of-fact parentheses. As a novelist she was rarely a chronicler. So when we turn to her diaries, now being published in their entirety, it is the inner life we expect to see coruscating, with all its mysterious images, backward passages, self-absorption, and self-revelation. We expect to travel the same circuitous tramway she and Joyce built for twentieth-century fiction to ride upon.

To our surprise we find something much more in the manner of Jane Austen: chronicles of the daily, the here and now caught in all their palpability by a sharp eye and ear. All the Bloomsbury companions, as familiar by now as characters in a television series, bustle about year after year: Nessa, Vita, Clive, Julian and Quentin, Lytton, the MacCarthys. The pattern of her "detached, free, harmonious" marriage to Leonard is there, strand by generous strand. Economies; the weather; the need to put a hot water range into the place at Rodmell; having to evict a mouse from Leonard's bed at Monk's House at 4:00 A.M. on April 10, 1920; the debate over whether dogs should wear leashes in Tavistock Square: all these phenomena enter her book without any fuss about proportion — as easily, in fact, as the plans she confides for creating books like *Mrs. Dalloway* and *The Waves*. Travel and parties share space with national events and family scandals: a workers' strike on the tube, Clive's woman in Leicestershire.

As the great and near great walk through her diaries, Woolf is bitchy, shrewd, and inconsistent. Harold and Vita Nicolson are "both incurably stupid" on a given day. But sometime during the next year he is "trusty & honest & vigorous," and a year after that Woolf is wondering whether she isn't falling in love with his wife. Ottoline Morrell may be "garish as a strumpet," but sometimes her "intuitions are more penetrating than many of the profoundly reasonable remarks of our intellectuals." In April 1921 Roger Fry is "entirely without meanness; always generous." Just two years later he's "become a little querulous with years. His grievances torment him; he talks of them too much." Clive Bell is found "conspicuously dumb" on May 1, 1925; but six years before, when he praised *Night and Day* as a work of genius, Woolf had to admit she did "respect Clive's judgment. It's erratic, but always springs from a direct feeling." This is, after all, a diary. And in diaries, as in life, people are much more changeable than they are in novels. Even if, like Woolf, you're in the process of reinventing the novel, you find that life resists all basic rearrangements. You can find the achievements of your competitors to be "diffuse . . . brackish . . . pretentious . . . underbred" (*Ulysses*, on September 6, 1922), and be intent on tracking the progress of your own reputation and theirs in the diary, but only literary historians have their interest wholly taken up by these things. While you're alive, you're just as much preoccupied with Nelly the housekeeper as you are with James Joyce; she occupies quite as much of your diary's attention as he does.

When Leonard Woolf published the selection of his wife's journals known as *A Writer's Diary* in 1953, he admitted that the chronicle was "too personal to be published as a whole during the lifetime of many people referred to in it," so he offered up extracts devoted principally to Virginia Woolf's craft. While it is true that she used the diary to hatch her books in ways both painstaking and explosive — we'll return to this in a later chapter — the full messy richness of her diaries couldn't really be guessed for another twenty-five years. As early as 1927, Woolf wrote, Leonard had picked up a volume of them and "said Lord save him if I died first & he had to read through these. My handwriting deteriorates. And do I say anything interesting?"

Among the most interesting observations in the thirty volumes between 1915 and 1941 are those Woolf made about diary-keeping itself. She is, in her diaries, one of the great critics of the genre. The activity is, after all, so queer, so ad hoc, and supposedly so private, that it doesn't seem amiss for the diarist to stop every so often and ask himself just what he thinks he's doing. Virginia Woolf does that as often as any diarist one can read.

Many of her reflections on diaries are prompted by her neglect of them. The journals are frequently interrupted by physical illness, madness, the press of work or social life ("This diary may die of London, if I'm not careful"), and sheer disinclination. They can stop in the middle of a thought, leaving her to ask, the next time she writes: "What is the use of finishing a sentence left unfinished a month ago?" She playfully scolds herself for the constant lapses, or makes excuses — she's lost her writing board — but she's not really worried; she knows the book always manages to get back up on its feet: "Another of these skips, but I think the book draws its breath steadily if with deliberation." The diary lives in guilty coexistence with her other writings. One Sunday morning in June

1925 she makes the "disgraceful confession" that she's writing the diary instead of a novel or criticism; but this is only two months after she'd determined to "disregard other duties" in favor of the deprived diary.

Before her relative financial success in the 1920s she could lack the money to buy a new blank volume for it — something she has to mention in the temporary notebook that gets pressed into service. (It is no good writing on loose leaves. Only "in a bound volume, the year has a chance of life. It can be stood on a shelf.") She is aware of all the difficulties and dodges the diarist must experience and practice. On October 2, 1918, she writes, in her usual fast and conversational way:

> No, I can't write to Margaret Davies. I spent on her the first flush of ideas after tea — It is fatal not to write the thing one wants to write at the moment of wanting to write it. Never thwart a natural process. I had so much to say here too. First, how the weather has changed . . .

She likes to write after tea, being herself "so inveterate an habitual" as to know the diary stands a better chance of fattening if it has a prescribed mealtime. It never loses speed and casualness, but she knows that one can learn technique for even this sort of "unpremeditated scribbling." Woolf enjoys rereading her own diaries, and thinks that's a better reason for continuing them than merely the increasing obligation one feels to keep on with something the longer it's gone on. Rather like Strong, she savors the physical and psychological pleasures of changing a pen nib, likes the idea of her diary as a "downy pillow" she can lie on when neglected by Vita, and feels it is a happily lawless enterprise compared to the deliberate shapes she gives her novels. Waiting for her tea on September 21, 1929, she thinks about how many things she has to tell the diary; yet her first sentence that afternoon, about her niece Angelica's going to school for the first time, sets her "rambling off like an old woman into the past," thinking of the end of her own childhood summer holidays.

Like most chroniclers, Woolf isn't entirely certain whom her book is for: "Whom do I tell when I tell a blank page?" But she is doubtful that she can be writing simply for her own pleasure. When on November 7, 1928, she says she is doing precisely that, she stops herself in midsentence to say "That phrase inhibits me: for if one writes only for one's own pleasure, — I dont know what it is that happens. I suppose the convention of writing is destroyed." She thinks the diaries might be useful as the raw basis for the memoirs she plans to write when she is sixty, but there are all sorts of signs that she expects an audience for the diaries themselves — in short, that she has her "you." And it's for that dimly discerned reader that she corrects her own overstatements: "This is the hottest June on record. Do not take this seriously — only it is very hot."

On August 5, 1929, Woolf wonders why Pepys wrote but never gets anywhere with an answer. She sometimes considers her own motives but never for long. In one of the last entries made, when the strains of her final madness are beginning to pull, she mentions that she is about to cook dinner, adding, "I think it is true that one gains a certain hold on sausage and haddock by writing them down." To a woman so excitable that London had to be rationed to her, the diary could be therapeutic relaxation, like knitting. But there are other motives, too. She gets closer to her own feelings, she admits, when she writes them out, and even closer by leaving them to be read later:

At the moment (I have 7½ before dinner) I can only note that the past is beautiful because one never realises an emotion at the time. It expands later, & thus we don't have complete emotions about the present, only about the past. This struck me on Reading platform, watching Nessa & Quentin kiss, he coming up shyly, yet with some emotion. This I shall remember; & make more of, when separated from all the business of crossing the platform, finding our bus &c. That is why we dwell on the past, I think.

When she gets behind in the diary, and loses the chance to recall parties and people, she realizes they've "gone down the sink to oblivion." Her fundamental motive is the same as the rest of the chroniclers' — to hold on to it all, to cheat the clock and death of all the things that she had lived. "I wonder why I do it," she writes on October 7, 1919. "Partly, I think, from my old sense of the race of time 'Time's winged chariot hurrying near' — Does it stay it?" Quoting Marvell on this matter is somewhat clichéd, but clichés get to be such only by being true. When Virginia Woolf asks, "Why did Pepys write his diary after all?" it is just one more way of saying, "I wonder why I do it."

On Monday, September 28, 1925, Evelyn Waugh makes note of two events. The first is that he "dined and drank beer at China Harry's again"; the second: "Claud lent me a novel by Virginia Woolf which I refuse to believe is good." It is this sort of open-mindedness that has propelled Waugh to a second, posthumous fame as a diarist, for there is a certain irrefutable pleasure to be had in hearing nasty things well said about other people.

As the worlds of Waugh's novels become increasingly remote, his rendition of them in the diaries becomes more strongly appealing. If you're willing to hack your way through the scores of footnotes explaining who all the hyphenated and trivial Bright Young People of the twenties are, you can find the fictional realm of *Vile Bodies* still extant, and hardly less of a cartoon, on the real-life pages of the author's journals. One can do this, that is, so long as one is willing to go on a long, vicarious bender.

Waugh is so often drunk in the twenties that one doesn't so much read his diaries as marinate in them. "More than a week has passed," he writes one summer day in 1924, "but I cannot quite remember how." Pretty much as soddenly as most of them did for him in the period before he discovered his vocation for writing with satiric disgust about the world in which he participated. On January 6, 1925, one can go out on the town with him and his friend Alistair Graham (a few of whose chromosomes were passed on to Sebastian Flyte in *Brideshead Revisited*):

We ate mushrooms and drank burgundy first at the Café Royal. At about 10.45 we went to Oddenino's where we found Audrey waiting for us under the suspicious eyes of the waiters who will not serve "unaccompanied ladies." We drank chartreuse and gradually everyone arrived. Olivia, Richard, Elizabeth Russell, Black Torry and Faith, Basil Maine, Tony Bushell and many hundreds more. A sweet man called Mr Best sat next to Olivia and smoked cigars and drank beer. At closing time we went on to dance at the 50-50. It is a bad club full of everyone one has ever heard of. I did not like it because we could not drink there, so after greeting Hugh Lygon and a few other friends Tony and I went off to 43 Gerrard Street where Miss Meyrick is carrying on in her mother's place exactly the same as ever. We drank some whisky there and wandered about and resisted the assaults of the harlots and then returned to the 50-50 — where David Greene had joined the party. It was proposed to go back to Audrey's flat so Richard and I went off in search of liquor. Miss Meyrick would not sell us a bottle but she introduced us to the most astonishing man who kept a brothel in Paris who led us to a tea shop in Frith Street called the Bohemian where a syphilitic old man sold us a bottle of gin at just over double the proper price. We gave this to Audrey and then set out to Park Crescent to look for Black Torry who had disappeared. We beat all the bells but could get no answer so we went on to Audrey where she had already arrived with two bottles of champagne. The party lasted until about 5 when we secured a taxi with infinite difficulty and saw everyone home; Alastair fell asleep. He also at some stage in the evening lost my waistcoat. Audrey made declarations of love to me, and Richard to Elizabeth and I to Olivia. I do not think Black Torry seduced anyone.

One of the especially fine features of spending such an evening merely on the page is that the reader doesn't have to do what Waugh had to — namely, arise at 8:30 the next morning.

Waugh is never actually so feckless as his reports of his partying in the twenties may indicate. He stores up material the way most novelists do, and, as his editor Michael Davie notes, he adapts his diaries to changes in his work as much as changes in his life. After his first big success in 1930, when he is in demand both as writer and as copy for the newspapers, their style becomes less extravagant and more like journalese. When he's off to Abyssinia (for Haile Selassie's coronation) shortly after that, they become a reporter's notebook full of fragmented observations and shorthand grammar. During the Second World War he keeps a diary while on active service, even though that's illegal. If captured by the enemy it can give them strategic information, but it will be useful in writing the *Sword of Honour* books. He regrets not keeping a more detailed diary of his trip to America in 1947, because he wants to gather "a store of literary material," and yet one finds him saying: "I found a deep mine of literary gold in the cemetery of Forest Lawn and the work of the morticians and intend to get to work immediately on a novelette staged there." The result, of course, was *The Loved One.*

In his early days his eye is rarely off the main chance. When he leaves his public school it isn't with nostalgia so much as calculation:

> I have left the magazine in the hands of Carew, the debating society with Lister, and the library with P. F. Machin.
>
> I am sure I have left at the right time — as early as possible and with success.

A decade later he admits that one of the reasons he makes himself part of an art subscription list is so that people will "say 'That young man is making good use of his money' and so buy more books and speak of them more tolerantly."

It is easier for Waugh to observe the life around him than to confide the one inside him to the diaries. Love is a subject resolutely avoided except in the most general terms. During his brief career as a schoolmaster ("Taught lunatics") he admits only to "the insistent sorrows of unrequited love which are ever with me in their most conventional form." There is no diary at all from the period when his first marriage was breaking up. Similarly, one finds a crippled reticence about the religion he so ostentatiously identified himself with. One might see him, at the age of eleven, bemoaning a Brighton church service as "a horrible low one" — shades of the gaudy conversion to come — but of his later instruction in the faith by Father D'Arcy there's very little, and nothing at all about his actual reception into the church.

The diary does a much better job of tracing the streak of cruelty that ran through his life from beginning to end. When a friend's midwife bothers him he frightens her with the information that the wireless causes cancer; he leaves pennies along his path home from the Hampstead tube station so that the next day he can "see how many are left. It is so cheap and charitable and amusing." He takes "great pleasure" in discharging servants, because that means he can get rid of whatever presents they've given him. The string of events he puts down during a visit home on August 22, 1930, shows a studied affectlessness that is more than a little repellent: "I returned to North End Road for the night. My father, on the eve of his birthday, has been severely bitten by his dog. My mother has just returned from visiting her relatives. Audrey seems to bear very little malice for my refusal to give her money. Kit Wood has committed suicide. The Duchess of York has had a daughter [Princess Margaret]. Birkenhead is still alive. I went to a cinema in the evening much to my father's sorrow."

Waugh knows how he swings through the parabolas of manic depression; and when he is particularly low and splenetic — especially in his later years — he uses the diary as the cup into which he can squirt a little poison and obtain release. Schoolboys, Christmas, the radio, reviewers, Americans, lapsed and liberal Catholics: they all go into the diaries' bilious stew. His own offspring join the legion of Satans provoking him: "I find the children particularly charmless." (During one magnanimous moment he goes back to read one of his own schoolboy diaries in an attempt to understand his son a little better.)

Most of us believe that ill will is all right so long as it's quotable. Randolph Churchill can be said to have justified his existence by forcing Waugh again and again to find it so thoroughly pointless. When Churchill complains that a friend has told him Waugh hasn't forgiven him for talking too much at a luncheon, Waugh assures him that " 'That is the least of the things I have against you.' " When Churchill is operated on and told the lung that's been removed was not malignant, Waugh records that "it was a typical triumph of modern science to find the only part of Randolph that was not malignant and remove it."

Actually, Waugh made that remark to a friend. That he subsequently wrote it down shows he thought it too good to let perish. It also shows that his editor's assertion — that these 340,000 words of diaries were "not written for publication" — is not to be taken as the last critical word. Waugh destroyed at least one early diary he came to find "too dangerous without being funny." The element of deliberate composition remains very strong, despite the drunkenness in which many of the diaries were apparently written. You may have enormous natural gifts of imagery and grammar, but you don't write a sentence describing a hunt near school by saying, "Pink men chased a fox about the park and excited the mad boys" without enough forethought to make it ring like crystal — and the certain afterthought that this is too good for others, however many years later, to miss attributing to you. Waugh admits at least once that an anecdote he's just put into the diary isn't fully true — it's just that he's already put it into so many of his letters that he's come to think it is.

He often found it more useful to be interesting than truthful. When he wrote an article on diaries for the *Daily Mail* in 1930 — "One Way to Immortality" — he said that his own diaries "invariably" died after a week or so because of his "deep-rooted feeling that it is a mischievous and degrading habit to write anything that will not bring in an immediate pecuniary reward." When he wrote this he was actually into a diary that lasted with reasonable consistency for several months. He was closer to fact when, chronicler that he was, he reflected in the same article: "Nobody wants to read other people's reflections on life and religion and politics, but the routine of their day, properly recorded, is always interesting." In his own case, it was a considerable achievement to turn an enormously unattractive personality into a large and compelling diary. He proves as much as anyone that there's no alchemy like grammar, and no fission like style.

*

Not all chronicles are blessed with Waugh's style, of course. Alan Dugan's poems about diaries *begins*:

> Oh I got up and went to work
> and worked and came back home
> and ate and talked and went to sleep.
> Then I got up and went to work
> and worked and came back home
> from work and ate and slept.

It's the business of Parson Woodforde's breakfasts once again. Read it or live it as slowly as you will, at a certain point the tedium can't be avoided.

There comes a time when one needs to get away from it all — to pack up the diary and go on a trip.

2

Travelers

*It would have been a very enjoyable
ride altogether, that evening's spin
along the banks of the Rhine, if I had
not been haunted at the time by the
idea that I should have to write an account of it next day in my diary. As
it was, I enjoyed it as a man enjoys
dinner when he has got to make a
speech after it, or as a critic enjoys a
play.*

— JEROME K. JEROME,
Diary of a Pilgrimage

"AN OASIS THAT I NEEDED. Edward R. Dyer USA —
12 Sept. 1982." You can find this grateful reflection in
the Visitors' Book at Saint Peter's Church on Castle Hill
in Cambridge, England. The church, in the brutal euphe-
mism the English use for the unemployed, is "redundant":
services are no longer held there. But it still attracts
visitors who enjoy signing the book. Most of us have
signed books like that — in museums, churches, at recep-
tions of one kind or another. They provide the chance
to immortalize one's movements, however tinily — to
put one's stamp on a place and leave a bit of oneself
behind. Visitors' books are the diaries travelers keep for
places, and they represent the reverse of the impulse that
causes travelers to keep diaries for themselves: namely,
to take a piece of a foreign place back with them.

Even those people not given to the desire to record the
details of the everyday will find in themselves the im-

pulse to hoard the sights and sounds of places to which they may never return. The telephone has more or less killed letter-writing, and the camera has dealt a pretty severe blow to the travel diary, but some energy for the latter survives. We all have the certainty of our own unique way of seeing places, a sense that the camera can be too objective a recorder of our trips away from home. We sometimes like the chance to say this is what *I*, not the Nikon, saw. The diary still gives that.

Whether one travels to the realms of gold or to Atlantic City matters little. If one chooses to begin a diary when one sets off, it is because one has the conviction — unlike the chroniclers, who see every day as being worthy of commemoration — that one is starting something special, that the next days or weeks are going to be more important, better, worthier of preservation than the usual run of them. And later, one will want those days to be available as an antidote to the familiar; the diary is their deep freeze. Several years ago the cartoonist Charles Saxon sketched a middle-aged couple, both of them heavy with normality. The man is slumped in an armchair, watching television, expressionless. But his wife is aglow, lost in the memory contained in a book she has just discovered in the bedroom. She has come into the living room with it and is reading aloud about charming hotels and waiters and wines on a trip to Paris in 1956. Her husband is paying no attention to her, but the look on her face shows it hardly matters. The diary is doing what she knew — perhaps just dimly, twenty years before — it would someday have to.

The earliest travel diaries were kept less for reasons of sentiment than geography. If you were exploring someplace nobody else had been to, you'd better be able to tell your sovereign how you got there. A diary would be the richest supplement to any maps drawn along the way; indeed the ship's log — like the household account and the commonplace book — is one of the forms to which the diary probably owes its murky start.

Long after the practical value of explorers' records has become obsolete, their appeal for ordinary readers remains strong. Richard Hakluyt knew this when he collected, in his *Voyages*, the stories of the discoveries made by sixteenth-century pioneers. It may be an aeronautical and diplomatic snap to get into China today, but a tale of the search for the northeast passage from Britain to Asia still has its terrific moments. When Stephen Burrough goes out to find it with the pinnace *Searchthrift* in 1556, he is well aware of the dangers involved; he was the Master of the one ship that survived Sir Hugh Willoughby's expedition in search of the same thing — the other two got stuck in the ice and everyone on them froze to death. Sebastian Cabot (head of the Company of Merchant Adventurers, which was so eager to have the route) throws a sendoff bash for Willoughby and his men on April 27, 1556, and, according to Burrough, joins in a dance with "the rest of the young and lusty company"; but Cabot isn't heading for the waters in which Willoughby and his men still lie frozen.

By June, Burrough writes, they are exploring rivers that run down into Russia from the Arctic Ocean. They have a good ship, but are so far out of their depth that the crews of the Russian coasting vessels they meet must think them a little daft. The Russians give the explorers bread and fish and advice, but this isn't a job in which you can train foreigners overnight.

In July there is horrible ice to negotiate and a whale to scare off ("At his falling down he made such a terrible noise in the water that a man would greatly have marvelled except he had known the cause of it"). And then in August, after some days along the shores of Nova Zembla, there are the Samoyeds of the Ob, a decidedly unpleasant lot, to start worrying about: "They will shoot at all men to the uttermost of their power that

cannot speak their speech." It is a lost, if exciting, cause.
By August 22 Burrough has decided not to press any
farther eastward: the winds, the ice, and the long dark
nights are simply too formidable. The men, and the log,
will have to go home. And the northeast passage will remain untraversed for another 322 years.

But at least the northeast passage actually existed. The
northwest one — which Thomas Jefferson hoped would
take Meriwether Lewis and William Clark clear across
the American continent to the Pacific — didn't. Never-
theless, that's what the President told Lewis to find in
1803: " 'The object of your mission is to explore the
Missouri river, & such principal stream of it, as by it's
course & communication with the waters of the Pacific
Ocean, may offer the most direct & practicable water
communication across the continent, for the purposes of
commerce.' " So Lewis got Clark and off they went.

There is a certain drama of failure to the journals of
their expedition. On Monday, July 22, 1805, we hear
Lewis say that the "Indian woman recognizes the country
and assures us that this is the river on which her relations
live, and that the three forks are at no great distance,"
but only two days later the mountains are still looking
awfully high, and Lewis is getting skeptical: "I can
scarcely form an idea of a river running to a great extent
through such a rough mountainous country without having it's stream intersepted by some difficult and dangerous
rappids or falls." The men on the mission are in a "continual state of violent exertion" as they press on. It isn't
meant to be; and on August 12 one of the men stands
"with a foot on each side of this little rivulet and thank[s]
his god that he lived to bestride the mighty & heretofore
deemed endless Missouri."

One can hardly blame Lewis and Clark for nature's
failure to complete the river, and aside from being a
record of disappointment, their journal, filled out from
field notes, offers up their expedition's great by-products
of success. We see them making notes of a whole con-

tinent's plants, animals, human inhabitants, and elemental
explosions. One day at the end of March 1805, Clark
notes how he

> observed extrodanary dexterity of the Indians in jump-
> ing from one cake of ice to another, for the purpose
> of Catching the buffalow as they float down. [M]any
> of the cakes of ice which they pass over are not two
> feet square. The Plains are on fire in View of the fort
> on both Sides of the River.

This combination of the precise and the huge is typical
of the observations in the journals. One entry by Lewis
mentions the Indians' methods of hunting the white bear
— rather exciting and informative stuff all by itself. But
when a whole continent is coming at you at once, it is
hardly enough to fill a single day's jotting. This entry
for April 13, 1805, also includes the account of a near
canoe wreck, the sighting of dead buffalo, and the realization that they have observed "more bald eagles on this
part of the Missouri than we have previously seen." Some
geese, sparrow hawks, and the tracks of the white bear
round out the day.

If to Lewis and Clark the Missouri River was all, to
the pioneers who actually went to settle the western
territories forty and fifty years later its tributaries were
more often a matter of hardship or nuisance:

> Everything must now be hauled out of the wagons
> head over heels (and he who knows where to find
> anything will be a smart fellow.) then the wagons
> must be all taken to pieces, and then by means of a
> strong rope stretched across the river with a tight
> wagon-bed attached to the middle of it, the rope must
> be long enough to pull from one side to the other, with
> men on each side of the river to pull it. In this way we
> have to cross everything a little at a time. Women and
> children last, and then swim the cattle and horses.

And before this laborious process could begin, a wagon had to wait its turn. When Amelia Stewart Knight wrote the above words on Sunday, May 8, 1853, there were about three hundred wagons on one side of the Elkhorn or the other.

Mrs. Knight was one of the busy traveling women (they called themselves "emigrants," not pioneers) who managed to find a few minutes to write during such waits on the trip west. The diary she kept during her journey from Iowa to Oregon between April and September 1853 is among eight hundred pioneers' journals that have survived in various archives. Most of them, according to Lillian Schlissel, the editor of *Women's Diaries of the Westward Journey*, are unemotional records of mileage, domestic details, and whether or not there was enough grass along the route for the cattle on a particular day. They were often kept not as souvenirs but as books of information to be sent home to friends and relatives thinking about making the journey.

But these diaries, unsurprisingly, cannot keep themselves free of the personalities of their keepers. Amelia Stewart Knight's steadily embodies the sort of person she is: a kind soul, humorous and sensible, almost always more thankful than sorry in the face of enormous risk and difficulty. She may be pregnant with her eighth child and eating her morning meal in the middle of a storm on the plains after already having crossed a river, but she views it all with amusement: "Got breakfast over after a fashion. Sand all around ankle deep; wind blowing; no matter, hurry it over. Them that eat the most breakfast eat the most sand." The Indians are a real threat, but even after a sleepless night spent in a spot where people are supposed to be killed each year, she gets up with a certain self-mockery: "We all found our scalps on in the morning." She feels a sense of solidarity with the other teams, but the American idea of competition extends even into these unsettled longitudes. When fifty wagons and two droves of cattle threaten to get in the way of her own party for a second time in a single day, it is time to get a move on: "While we were eating we saw them coming. All hands jumped for their teams saying they had earned the road too dearly to let them pass us again." It is such relentlessness that allows them to make twenty-five miles that day.

Amelia Stewart Knight is a good storyteller, and on ordinary days she is just as good at describing the routine regimen her family follows on its way to Oregon. Of a typical morning, just after breakfast: "It is all hurry and bustle to get things in order. It's children milk the cows, all hands help yoke these cattle the d——l's in them. Plutarch [her son] answers 'I can't. I must hold the tent up, it is blowing away.' Hurrah boys. Who tied these horses? 'Seneca, don't stand there with your hands in your pocket. Get your saddles and be ready.'" She encourages herself with gaiety, but on occasion even her humor and spirit must crumble in the face of the journey's strains. When one of the Knights' oxen drops dead in harness, on a day when they twice have had to cross Burnt River, she has to cry for "this poor ox who had helped us along thus far, and has given us his very last step." This was written after four months on the road (but there was no road), and only one month away from the end of the journey.

Like Amelia Knight, Lydia Allen Rudd, who went to Oregon with her husband, Harry, between May and October 1852, was made of strong — if not always stern — stuff. Her diary gives evidence of the decimation of so many of the wagon trains by cholera; she counts the graves along the trail. She can own up to spells of faintheartedness, but more usually shows contempt for those who turn back: "We met several that had taken the back track for the states homesick I presume let them go." Traveling down the Columbia River in an Indian canoe is a harrowing thing to have to do near the end of an already difficult journey, but you can sense the superiority she feels to the "one Lady . . . very much alarmed screaming every breath as loud as she could possibly." Hadn't she five months before seen a Dutchman walking to California with nothing but a wheelbarrow?

She can be pleasantly caustic toward her tribulations ("Started early this morning without any breakfast for the very good reason that we had nothing to eat") — and toward her husband as well. One May night he tells her to stop writing that diary and go to bed; otherwise she won't want to get up to make breakfast the next morning. Well, the next morning she's up all right, before sunrise, too, "in spite of Harry's prophecies to the contrary."

Amelia Stewart Knight and Lydia Allen Rudd were lucky. They arrived intact. People on the trail did of course go mad from grief and deprivation, and there are those journals that record as much sorrow as pluck. Jane Gould, who went from Iowa to California with her husband, two young sons, and some in-laws in 1862, was less cheerfully stoical than Amelia Knight and Lydia Rudd. "Oh dear, I do so want to get there," she hungrily confesses on August 23. She gets low; her husband, Albert, is sick; there have been bones along the trail; babies fall out of the wagons; and the Fourth of July is cause as much for sadness as celebration: "The men fired their guns. We wonder what the folks at home are doing and oh, how we wish we were there." She has no love for the Indians; they are simply "red demons" to her, and their presence looms larger as the months pass. Her entry of July 9 ("We hear many stories of Indians depredations, but I do not feel frightened yet.") is the unintended foreshadowing of what she puts down on August 15:

We were aroused this morning at one o'clock by the firing of guns and yelling of Indians, answered by our men. The Capt. calling, "come on you red devils." It did not take us long to dress, for once. I hurried for the children and had them dress and get into our wagon, put up a mattress and some beds and quilts on the exposed side of the wagon to protect us.

The attack subsides. They wait and watch until it is time to eat breakfast and move on — with bullet holes in two or three of the wagon covers.

By the end of September they are in the new civilization of California. Jane Gould marvels at what she sees in Empire City: fruit wagons, a quartz mill, new buildings. On October 1, a week before she says "Farewell to the old Journal," she records "the pleasure of sitting in a large rocking chair, the first time in five months." As she moves across the plains, the "old Journal" is a place where she can cry, a kind of domestic comfort, like an embroidered handkerchief.

The West is won, and Nova Zembla must be pretty well mapped by now. There are no uncharted worlds left into which prairie schooners can roll and ships sail — unless you count outer space; but even if you do, you have to face the fact that most astronauts cultivate a diction as gray as moondust and aren't very promising diarists. The explorer's diary seems to be defunct. Ships' captains still keep logs, but ships today tend to be cruise ships to Cancún, not clippers to Cathay. You probably go to Cancún by plane, in any case, and the chances of your suffering perils worse than misdirected luggage between check-in and arrival are very slim.

But there are such cases, and they do get recorded.

It is snowing, and Air Florida Flight 90 is sitting on one of the short runways at National Airport in Washington, D.C. It is 3:46:21 P.M. on January 13, 1982. Captain Larry Wheaton says to First Officer Alan Pettit, who is going to do the flying, "Tell you what, my windshield will be de-iced, don't know about my wing." Pettit replies: "Well, all we really need is the inside of the wings anyway, the wing tips are gonna speed up by eighty anyway . . . They'll shuck all that other stuff." They are overdue for a spraying of glycol.

A minute and a half later the two men are more relaxed. Like Stephen Burrough contentedly praising the soundness of his ship, they are marveling about the way planes and pilots have of coming through:

> *First Officer:* It's impressive that these big old planes get in here with the weather this bad, you know, it's impressive . . . It never ceases to amaze me when we break out of the clouds, there's the runway anyway, d'care how many times we do it. God, we did good! [Laughter]

Unfortunately, Flight 90 is still on the ground, and the ice is still building up on the wings. At 3:53:21 Pettit says that the de-icing is a "losing battle," and Captain Wheaton allows how it's just something that "satisfies the Feds." Still, three and a half minutes later, Pettit has to admit he hates "to blast outa here with carburetor ice all over me."

Like it or not, three minutes later he is trying, and failing, to put the plane into the air:

> 1600:50
> *Captain:* Come on, forward.
> 1600:53
> *Captain:* Forward.
> 1600:55
> *Captain:* Just barely climb.
> 1600:59
> *Crew Member:* Stalling, we're [falling].
> 1601:00
> *First Officer:* Larry, we're going down, Larry.
> 1601:01
> *Captain:* I know it.

The next thing noted by the flight recorder — the black box — is the sound of Flight 90 crashing into the Fourteenth Street Bridge. The box then goes, along with the passengers, the pilots, and their mistakes, into the freezing Potomac River. It will be recovered later.

The route from Washington to Tampa is not a matter of fresh discovery to be relayed home, like Master Burrough's route toward the Ob, or the women pioneers' reports on the Platte River Road (which is today, roughly, Interstate 80). But the black box is still a diary ready to be sent back for the instruction of those who didn't come along. More than four hundred years have passed since the *Searchthrift* did its sailing, and we can still read Stephen Burrough's reports of the "monstrous heap of ice . . . a fearful sight to see." Four hundred years from now, on a very old tape in a forgotten cabinet at a federal agency, Captain Wheaton and First Officer Pettit will still be joking about their "losing battle" with the same element.

We tend to put a great deal of faith in traveling. Bacon said it was education for the younger, experience for the elder. It is "broadening," we tell ourselves; it's what we'll do when we retire and our lives are our own. It grows us up, lets us change. Who has not had the fantasy, after clearing passport control, of dispensing with his actual identity, inventing a new one, and going forth to live it on the streets of a foreign capital? If only it worked. Alas, we don't shed skins so easily. Most of us arrive home exactly as we left. Set someone down in a different culture, come back and check on him in the morning, and you'll find just what you left the night before.

When James Boswell brought Dr. Samuel Johnson to Scotland in 1773, he was performing an action on the order of placing a hardy sixty-four-year-old growth — *Homo Londiniensis* — in a petri dish full of hostile elements. If the thirty-three-year-old acolyte wanted to show off his native land to his mentor — fair enough — he also wanted to enjoy the enormous perversity of the act. Moving Dr. Johnson at all, he wrote, was like moving Saint Paul's — but moving him to Scotland! The land he had sneered at in his mind, in his *Dictionary*, in a lifetime of conversation! What's more, moving him not just through intellectual Edinburgh, but off the mainland and around the Hebrides in small boats in bad weather! Who could watch this and believe that bear-baiting had gone out with the Elizabethans? Johnson had supposedly toyed with the idea of voyaging 'round those islands ever since he had been given an account of them to read as a child. But one doesn't have to guess long about who wheedled this fantasy into the improbable reality of their "wild Tour."

Once they're there, Boswell can scarcely believe he's done it. There's Dr. Johnson eating Scottish spelding, and hating it! Dr. Johnson waxing sensible and obnoxious on such topics as Scottish emigration, the phoniness of the Ossian poems, the pathetic state of Scotland before her union with England — in front of Scots! In Scotland! His guide admits that in point of fact neither one of them "had much taste for rural beauties," but that hardly matters on a trip whose purpose was less delectation for the eye than provocation of the spleen. Boswell says he regretted how Johnson "did not practice the art of accommodating himself to different sorts of people," but any reader of the *Life* knows this for the disingenuous piffle it is. Getting a rise out of Samuel Johnson, LL.D., is the whole point of the thing. Boswell is certain that Johnson won't get on with the Scottish judge Lord Monboddo; so he makes sure they pay a call. When the two actually hit it off, he is clearly disappointed. But on a journey three months long there are plenty of opportunities for upsetting a sage: trick him into admitting a fondness for oatmeal — after what he said about Scots and oats in his *Dictionary*! Or get Lady Lochbuie to offer him a cold sheepshead for breakfast!

Somehow, Boswell assures us, Johnson came to look back on the trip as "the pleasantest part of his life." And Johnsonians have ever after marveled at the idea and results of the Great Lexicographer in such peculiar circumstances. Legends began as soon as they made it back from the Hebrides to the mainland. Johnson, perhaps recalling Stephen Burrough, says, " 'I am really ashamed of the congratulations which we receive. We are addressed as if we had made a voyage to Nova Zembla, and suffered five persecutions in Japan.' " He has a point. Even though one can't help but admire the fat old boy, bouncing down hills on horseback and sailing uncomplainingly through squalls in an open boat, one also can't lose the sense that what we have here is mostly just Johnson being Johnson and Bozzy being Bozzy. It is the same doctor as ever: melancholic, grumpy, playful, as definite as a periodic sentence, his moods carefully monitored and managed by the Scottish lawyer who is sometimes more like Pepys than Pepys: a trifle more self-conscious perhaps, but unafraid to appear a little ridiculous if that will get him his momentary heart's desire. On September 25, 1773, he's drinking too much, and on September 26 he's confessing the result: "I awaked at noon, with a severe head-ach. I was much vexed that I should have been guilty of such a riot, and afraid of a reproof from Dr. Johnson. I thought it very inconsistent with that conduct which I ought to maintain, while the companion of the Rambler."

Such chagrin aside, Boswell is absolutely delighted with what he's achieved in dragging his guest all the way up here and not having to share him with the other wits back at the club in London: "I compared myself to a dog who has got hold of a large piece of meat, and runs away with it to a corner, where he may devour it in peace, without any fear of others taking it from him." He knows that if he is to keep Johnson talking he has to keep the ball rolling pleasantly — don't let him get bored, and make sure he joins in the Highlanders' amusements. After a month he knows he's managed it. "I must take some merit from my assiduous attention to him," he writes in self-congratulation, "and from my contriving that he shall be easy wherever he goes, that he shall not be asked twice to eat or drink any thing (which always disgusts him), that he shall be provided with water at his meals, and many such little things, which, if not attended to would fret him." Boswell was a veritable American Express card; Johnson could never have left home without him. In turn, Johnson wasn't so much a traveling partner as he was the land Boswell traveled *to*.

Boswell published his *Journal of a Tour to the Hebrides* twelve years after he made the trip. In the printed version he freely inserted passages written long after the events that took place. A reader of the *Journal's* third edition will find paragraphs beginning "At breakfast this morning" lying not far from remarks Dr. Johnson made years later. One of the latter comes in a passage where Boswell apologizes for his extreme fidelity to detail: "Dr. Johnson said it was a very exact picture of a portion of his life." Johnson was allowed to read the *Journal* throughout the trip, and was, Boswell swears, very pleased with it, going so far as to suggest, on September 19, 1773, that " 'it might be printed, were the subject fit for printing.' " What both he and Boswell were approaching, however obliquely, was the great biography for which the *Journal* would prove, with its peculiar combination of immediacy and retrospection, a kind of dry run. Indeed, it is in it, on October 14, that Boswell records his historic intention: "I shall collect authentick materials for *The Life of Samuel Johnson, LL.D.*; and, if I survive him, I shall be one who will most faithfully do honour to his memory." Johnson read this passage and consented to its contents. And so we see Boswell, like a pregnant woman eating for two, keeping not just his own diary, but Johnson's as well.

As Queen or Empress of every pink place on the world's map — and that used to be a very large portion of it — Victoria could make an awful lot of royal "progress" without ever leaving what was, legally speaking, home. She was a lifelong diarist, but we know her best in that role from her Highlands journals, the ones she made on her own trips to Scotland over many decades, first with Prince Albert, whose observations were reverently quoted, and then with her loyal attendant John Brown. Extracts from them were published in 1868 and 1883 and became Victorian (naturally) best sellers.

In them one can find the odd bit of royal business, such as her declaration of intent, on August 12, 1849, "to create Bertie 'Earl of Dublin,' as a compliment to the town and country." (One suspects Her Royal Highness didn't ask the average Dubliner's opinion.) But mostly they record things seen and done on holiday, and in a way quite similar to the ordinary traveler's. Many of her observations are less than startling: "We got back to Balmoral, much pleased with our expedition, at seven o'clock. We had gone forty-two miles to-day, and forty yesterday, in all eighty-two." Things tend to be "pretty" or "lovely" or "fine." The Queen is a plain writer and takes royal care not to lose dignity of language any more than dignity of person. Recording a carriage accident she and Princess Alice suffer on October 7, 1863, she puts it this way: "There was an awful pause, during which Alice said: 'We are upsetting.' In another moment — during which I had time to reflect whether we should be killed or not, and thought there were still things I had not settled and wanted to do — the carriage turned over on its side, and we were all precipitated to the ground!" Victorian monarchs do not take pratfalls; they precipitate.

Still, it would be a mistake to assume that the Queen is never emotional about what she sees on her Scottish travels. Attempting to convey the sight of Ben-y-Ghlo and the river Tilt, she exclaims: "No description can at all do it justice, or give an idea of what this drive was . . . Oh! what can equal the beauties of nature!" She is capable of being substantially amused, as well as horrified. The sight of a man who appears to be drowning one day in September 1850 causes her considerable agitation: "There was a cry for help, and a general rush, including Albert, towards the spot, which frightened me so much, that I grasped Lord Carlisle's arm in great agony. However, Dr. Robertson swam in and pulled the man out, and all was safely over; but it was a horrid moment."

Some English readers were annoyed by the attention and affection lavished on the Scots in the Queen's journals (just as a lot of Scottish readers were put off by what they perceived as Johnson's contempt). But you can't please everyone, and when you're ruler of what must often have seemed like nearly everyone, life must be especially difficult. Victoria could not, of course, be freely critical in the portions of the journals she chose to publish. Leveling charges against the weather on September 16, 1848, as being "most provoking!" and against Leith as being "not a pretty town," is about as censorious as she can get.

Certain phenomena engendered along the route by the Queen's royal status, like crowds, are noted matter-of-factly: "There was a great crowd at Cupar Angus, and at Dundee a still larger one, and on the pier the crush was very great." Her way of recording this event is rather like that in which a present-day tourist on a Super Apex ticket might remark on the Tokyo subway or a bottle-neck at La Scala. In fact, to read Victoria's journals is to be impressed first and foremost by the continuing ordinariness of a woman in unique circumstances. Her regal diary contains all the telltale marks of those kept by commoners. Its sense of immediacy: "After dinner I tried to write part of this account (but the talking round me confused me), while Albert played at 'patience.'" The doubling of experience by living it and then writing it, such as in her account of hearing of the death of Louis Napoleon, the Prince Imperial, in the Zulu war during 1879: "Beatrice . . . came in with the telegram in her hand, said, 'Oh! the Prince Imperial is killed!' I feel a sort of thrill of horror now while I write the words." And the tendency of the diarist to annotate his entries in the light of later experience: on October 16, 1861, Victoria wonders whether the "delightful expedition" she and Albert have been on from Balmoral to Ca-Ness will be their last. On December 14, the Prince dies. Rereading the journals in 1867, in order to prepare them for publication, the Queen appends the note: ("IT WAS OUR LAST ONE!")

If the Grand Tour of the eighteenth century seems to have been an elevating way for aristocratic English families to get rid of their sons for a while, a hundred years later it presented itself to rich American industrialists as a way to dispose of their wives and daughters. Miss Julia Newberry came from the prosperous and civic-minded family that would give Chicago the Newberry Library, and at fifteen is happy to pronounce her home "worth all London Paris & New York put together." This declaration of June 6, 1869, is prompted by her relief to be returning from a trip to Europe made with her mother and sister. Now she can catch up with friends, eat corn bread, and celebrate the Fourth of July at home. Unfortunately, her American contentment is not to last. She will be back traipsing through Europe in a little more than a year. After all, her mother, newly widowed, has just inherited over a million dollars, and in those days when a million was a million, what else could a mother with a marriageable daughter do?

Julia Newberry will have none of this travel-is-broadening business: "How much trash is talked, & enthusiasm wasted on traveling, when it is the greatest bore under the sun." Show her the Rhine and she says: "Deprive it of its castles & I dont think much would be said about it." Just contemplating this repetitious trip to Europe gives her the "HORRORS"; she'll once again have to be pursued by oily and effeminate flatterers like Mr. Francia: "I just despise him, with his red shirts, & green neck-ties, for he does dress like a perfect fiend. — The lazy lives these foreigners lead, are enough to disgust any one." Of course, show her somebody like nice sensitive Mr. Burroughs, and she has to think a little harder: "I never liked him as much as when I knew he was going off, but then that is always the way, — when they run after me I don't care for them, but if they stay away I want to see them. I hope I am not a flirt & yet sometimes I believe I am."

Her father used to tell her to " 'be somebody,' " and she envies the immortality of a Shakespeare or Napoleon compared to the fate of "we poor ordinary mortals." What, she wonders, on her seventeenth birthday, has her life amounted to so far? Pointlessly stranded in a hotel in the south of France, she tabulates her experience against her innocence:

> I have been twice to Florida, & three times to Europe. I have been to two boarding-schools, & gained a great many friends in diffirent ways. Have been run-away with twice, & had my portrait painted. I have learned how to faint, & have inheireted a fortune. Have been through a long illness & had a terrible sorrow! And I might have been married if I had choosen.
>
> On the other hand I have never had on a long dress, or been into society as a young-lady; Nor in the conventual form, have I been to my first ball. — I have never given my photograph to a young man, or any other souvenir either, nor have I made my hair uneven by distributing locks, among my friends. I have never waved my handkerchief, to a male biped on the other side of the street, or appointed a rendevous on my way to school. — I have never sworn eternal friendship to any one, nor written poetry since I was eleven years old.

Julia applies this wonderfully total self-centeredness to whatever she encounters on her travels, and that includes events of international significance. On September 22, 1870, Edmond de Goncourt is writing about the impending siege of Paris: "The horizon is just mist and dust, with a few puffs of white smoke which one assumes to come from the guns." A day later, from the Grand Hotel

Vevey in Geneva, Julia is declaring: "If Paris surrenders, I shall be utterly crestfallen!"

A year later she is back in a once more peaceful Paris, ordering gowns and wondering if Mr. Little wants to marry her. Then the familiar tedium of travel is suddenly interrupted by news of a calamity at home, one that shakes her bored touring diary into frightened life. On October 13, 1871, she writes: "Half of Chicago is in ashes, it is too awful to believe, to dreadful to think about. And the suspense is so fearful, the reports so vague & no one can get direct information . . . I cant & wont imagine our house is burnt." Four days later she knows that the Newberry home has indeed perished — and along with it her early journals. "I have no home anywhere," she writes on the nineteenth.

For more than fifty years Julia's travel diary rested with other family papers. No one broke the lock (the key had long been lost) on the morocco-bound six-and-a-quarter-by-nine-inch volume until 1930. But three years later it was published, its editors assuring readers that there was "in her work a possible indication that with Julia Newberry a mute, inglorious Jane Austen died."

No, that's not right, you think. Miss Barnes and Miss Fairbank have got it wrong. For one thing, Jane Austen could spell; and for another, she could size up the world from her parlor without having to be dragged through its older districts. A Jane Austen *character* perhaps: Julia is often ogling and dancing with members of the regiment, after all. But even this isn't the right parallel. Surely it is Miss Daisy Miller of Schenectady, New York, she most reminds you of in circumstances and spirit — even if Miss Miller was willing to admit that Europe could be "perfectly sweet." The flirtations with foreigners, the un-Continental exuberance, the purposeless movement from hotel to hotel. Yes, it is Daisy Miller Julia Newberry reminds you of, you're certain — even before you get to the black-bordered notice reproduced at the end of her diary: "DIED At Rome, Italy, on the 4th April, 1876, of sudden inflammation of the throat, JULIA ROSA NEWBERRY, only surviving daughter of Julia Butler and the late Walter L. Newberry."

Not only was Julia Newberry not an incipient Jane Austen; she had no desire to be. Nor to be any other kind of artist, either. She had none of the young artist's usual eagerness to travel in search of the mores he believes necessary to the doing of his visionary work. After those seeking political freedom, expatriates (if only temporary ones) are more likely to be artists in search of breathing space for their corseted sensibilities than anyone else. When Gauguin wrote *Noa Noa*, an account of his journey from France to Tahiti, he explained what his purpose had been with a capital letter: "I had a sort of vague presentiment that, by living wholly in the bush with natives of Tahiti, I would manage with patience to overcome these people's mistrust, and that I would Know." Gauguin's urges have been readily comprehensible to generations of English and American painters and writers; what they've had a harder time trying to understand is how it could be so necessary to leave France — since that has so often been the Tahiti of their own fantasies. The *Paris Journal* that the young English poet David Gascoyne kept between 1937 and 1939 is a lovely overwrought example of the diaries kept by those who actually got there. It is full of sad self-absorption, a young poet's suicidal questions and complaints, as well as quivering responses (both self-induced and real) to the spectacle of Paris. How he can go on about him*self*:

After all, — the expression: *myself* indicates that my "self" — the tiring body that one pushes around, the brain-box full of seething grey matter, the bundle of nerves continually being plucked and played upon by one's solitude or by one's contact with the outside world, and all the wearisome superstructure of conflicts and contradictions.

Oh, enough already! It's September 23, 1938, and you're in Paris, for God's sake. One can write stuff like this *anywhere*. How can you waste a moment of Paris, and a page of your book, on this? — especially when you know better, when your own diary shows you capable of fleeing these sterile and obligatory abstractions for the glorious gluttings of the real and sensory. How can you have forgotten? You were sitting with the person you loved. Just look back to May 13:

> Last night we sat alone in the Place Dauphine, under chestnut trees. It was so warm, the sky so blue and clear. A perfect May night. (Even the *pissoir* nearby sounded like a fountain playing in an Italian piazza!) The white steps of the Palais de Justice glimmered like a more romantic balustrade in the background. — We were silent most of the time. Some people went by with their dog. We were there for perhaps an hour. I shall never forget it.

You certainly seem to have forgotten it by September. It's a good thing you'll have this book to bring it back to you. Anyone who's sat in that little square can tell you it's still just like that — the benches, the chestnut trees, the white steps. But someone else's reminders won't do. Someone else's chestnut trees aren't your chestnut trees; and his white steps aren't yours, either. You want the ones *you* had on May 13, 1938. Above all you want the detail of that dog going by, and the jokey way you were struck by the *pissoir* — chance particulars that will really let it come back to you, that will let you open the diary forty, fifty years later and hear it playing your song. Elsewhere you say that "in the end, perhaps, the real reason for keeping a journal is vanity or narcissism." Yes, but what are "vanity" and "narcissism"? More abstractions. The fact is you wrote down those things about May 13 because otherwise *you would have lost them.*

You ended the journal on November 1, 1939. Despite the war you were feeling flushed with artistic purpose, ready, in fact, to write about a vision of a new world. You closed your book, feeling it had helped get you to that point, that it had "served its purpose." But you really knew that paragraphs like the one you wrote on May 13, 1938, only serve their purposes years later.

Before she was barely open for business, America was receiving visitors from the Old World eager to experience her and send back their judgments — often via diaries — to those left behind. Years before de Toqueville made his survey, his future sovereign, Louis Philippe (1773–1850), was taking the new continent's measure. He seems to have enjoyed himself, even if it was not strictly a pleasure trip. Like Charles II's, Louis Philippe's travels were sponsored by a revolutionary government. The French Directory agreed to let his two brothers out of jail on the condition that all three of them go to America. So Louis Philippe traveled with them — the Duc de Monpensier and the Comte Beaujolais — and kept a diary of what they saw in 1797.

The twenty-four-year-old future King carefully notes landscape, architecture, and manners among the Americans in the first year of John Adams's presidency. He is a game and gracious traveler, willing to experience and grateful for hospitality, but not beyond taking offense when he has a right to. For all the industriousness he finds, he also sees plenty of shabbiness and boorishness, and he records it all. He has a sense of humor and a sense of justice. He duly notes how the whites cheat on the Indians in the continual effort to push them farther west, and with a certain prescience he comments on the inevitability of the slaves' emancipation: after a visit to George Washington and Mount Vernon he remarks that three quarters of the 770,000 inhabitants of Virginia are black. He sees Washington, D.C., as it is being built, and visits the newly settled areas of Tennessee and Kentucky. When he makes the acquaintance of some Cherokee Indians he exhibits genuine feelings for them, as well as

predispositions gained from reading the eighteenth century's "noble savage" literature.

It is the Americans' rough-and-readiness, their improvi-
sational approach to their new lives, that most perplexes
and amuses the three traveling aristocrats. During a visit
to Captain Chapman, a strident opponent of taxation who
lives north of Nashville, Louis Philippe comments at
length on the sleeping arrangements, in a passage that
should find its way into all books regulating etiquette and
sexuality, and which must certainly be reproduced at
length:

There were only two beds in the one room that was
the house's entire living area, and we were granted
only what they call here *house-room*, that is, permission to spread our blankets on the rough planks of the
floor, with our bedding arranged so that all four of us
lay abreast with our feet to the fire, between the two
beds. Captain Chapman got into one bed with his wife,
which seemed perfectly straightforward to us. A rather
pretty girl who we knew was unmarried got into the
other, and that too seemed perfectly straightforward.
A strapping young man of about 20 or 22 arrived
shortly afterward, while we were settling into our bedding; not standing on ceremony, he undressed and
plunked himself into the girl's bed; and while that was
indubitably natural, it occasioned a certain surprise on
our part. It had no such effect on the captain, who, to
relax from the day's fatigues, was enjoying a prose
with his wife of which we (though present) were the
topic, and in the course of which he found us *odd
fellows*, to leave our *home* and undergo all the travail
of a painful journey to see deserts, savages, and a
thousand other things that a man might reasonably
think not worth all the trouble. Nor was he distressed
by the young man's intimate manner with his daughter. His other daughter blew out the candle and
slipped into the young people's bed, so that the young

man was in the middle. That seemed to us even more extraordinary; but the flow of matrimonial conversation abated not a whit. We four paid close attention to these goings-on, and saw to our left, by the gleam of the fire, the young man and the first daughter get up and settle again at the foot of the bed; in a word, we saw all that one can see, while the paternal word-mill continued to grind away as before.

This must be what the English actress Fanny Kemble meant by the Americans' horror of privacy, something she noted in a Philadelphia hotel in 1832 when she was ushered into a single room containing two bathtubs. Kemble was on a tour with her father that year, keeping a journal that would later be published. Americans had to get used to regular bashings by British travelers in the nineteenth century — Frances Trollope's *Domestic Manners of the Americans* and Charles Dickens's *American Notes* could scarcely be considered rave notices — and Fanny Kemble's observations would later be met with a certain resentment by the audiences that fought for tickets to her onstage performances. But her journal actually reveals a traveler more than willing to be carried away — just unwilling to be taken in.

She's quite ready to be rhapsodic over both the Hudson and Niagara, but for the same New York of the young George Templeton Strong she can only come up with scrupulously mixed reviews. It is a badly lit and badly paved place, and her hotel is nothing to write home about. But she admires the ease and civility of the evening strollers on Canal Street (the men even take their cigars out of their mouths when women pass); in fact, they compare very favorably with Londoners. If only the Americans would stop spitting everywhere! The Catholic priests she sees in Washington, D.C., do it even during Mass; "Every place is made a perfect piggery of." She admires what the Americans have built upon the land ("No one, beholding the prosperous and promising state of this fine country could wish it again untenanted of its enterprising possessors"), but, like Louis Philippe (by now regnant in France), she is troubled by the enforced retreat of the Indians. Sometimes the actress seems so intent on taking the mixed view that it is difficult to tell whether a single sentence is meant as tribute or sneer. Consider her reflection on Utica, on Thursday, July 11, 1833: "The gentlemen went out to view the town, which twenty years ago *was not* and is now a flourishing place, with fine-looking shops, two or three hotels, good broad streets and a body of lawyers who had a supper at the house where we were staying and kept the night awake with champagne, shouting, toasts and clapping of hands: so much for the strides of civilisation through the savage lands of this new world."

If her own views are complicated, she thinks the Americans themselves, with their misguided equation of "ill-breeding" and "independence," are very nearly schizoid. In the shops she meets with insolence or familiarity, depending on which the proprietor thinks a better demonstration of his personal and national autonomy. Even in church the Americans refuse to kneel or respond on cue: "I suppose their love of freedom will not suffer them to be amenable to forms, or wear the exterior of humbleness and homage even in the house of the Most High God." All this from a people who still keep slaves, a horror Fanny finds insupportable, and which eventually makes her bad marriage to Pierce Butler, himself a slave-owner, even worse than it was in its boring early days: "I do not keep a diary any more," she writes after she's settled down with him in Pennsylvania. "I do not find chronicling my days helps me to live them. Perhaps I may resume it when we set out for our plantation in the South." She did in fact take it up again, and her *Journal of a Residence on a Georgian Plantation*, published in 1863 (long after her divorce from Pierce Butler), was once thought by some to have helped prevent England's recognition of the Confederacy.

There is a formidable combination of percipience and arrogance in Fanny Kemble. (Queen Victoria, still a princess, read her first American journal and concluded that even though there were "some very fine feelings in it," its "authoress must be very pert and ill-bred.") But one is always inclined to give her a hearing. Her temper may get the better of her judgment, but she does not operate from arid presupposition when she takes impressions in a country not her own. She is not, that is, like Simone de Beauvoir who, in her journal of travels through the United States in 1947, *America Day by Day*, said she hoped to show "how America revealed itself to a single conscience day by day: my conscience." Not consciousness, but conscience — in her case an unimaginative little moral machine, inelastic, obtuse, and willfully intent on disapproving of all that won't slide uncomplainingly through her ethical mill.

De Beauvoir's New York is unlike anyone else's has ever been. The subway is too fast for her; the crosstown bus is "agreeable though slow." (One gets the feeling it is the French who possess the golden mean in these things.) She goes stompin' at the Savoy with Mr. and Mrs. Richard Wright and oozes guilt (although, she says, Wright's presence finally "seemed to absolve" her). The blacks' style of dancing shows their superior freedom and gaiety and sexuality — so "different from the stiff cold formality of Americans." It does not seem to occur to her that the blacks are also Americans. She is determined to have her political sentimentalities confirmed and in order to do so she meets the folks. In San Antonio, she points out, her waiters are "real Mexicans." (Had she met imposters somewhere else?) On a bus to Houston, catching sight of the "huge fields and black earth where in a few months' time the fleecy cotton would blossom," she instantly reminds herself that this is the same cotton "so hard on the hands of the pickers." Mlle de Beauvoir's existential ethics are *very* sensitive: watching ice skaters in Central Park she recoils at the way "many young people sealed up their ears with wads of plush fixed to a semi-circular celluloid band, braiding their hair like ribbon: it was quite awful." One may have to run this passage by one's eyes a second time before realizing that Mlle de Beauvoir is making an impassioned plea against earmuffs. Her first rule as a traveler seems to have been: see everything as you expect it will be. Her second apparently was: believe anything you are told: for example, "A woman employee, a secretary, must devote about twenty-five percent of her salary to hair-dressing expenses and beauty products."

Only one year earlier her countryman André Maurois was also in America — as a visiting professor in Kansas City. To read his book *From My Journal* is to wonder how two visitors to the same shores can arrive on such different planets. Maurois does not expect too much of people ("Whoever would exact of men an abstract perfection . . . ends by hating them"), and so he sometimes is pleasantly surprised. There is a terrible piano player who practices in the building where Maurois lives. The fellow spends months trying to get the hang of just a few notes of the birds' song from *Siegfried*, combining "infinite patience with incredible incompetence." Maurois marvels at him; Simone de Beauvoir would find him to be evidence of some national characteristic of which she was already certain. Maurois spends his months in the Midwest as America experiences its first year of unquestioned pre-eminence in the world. He neither scrapes nor scolds; he weighs things. He compliments the general good will he finds, even as he criticizes the national susceptibility to emotional hogwash in making up its political mind.

Even before Simone de Beauvoir has her visa stamped for the States, Maurois manages to locate her difficulty:

There are travelers who insist that America "has no spiritual life." Oh, how I dislike these peremptory judgments! And how curt that particular one seems!

What can it mean? That no one on this continent is concerned about human destiny, about moral problems? On the contrary, here concern and scruple are present in most men's minds. But the traveler does not know the living, thinking populace. He judges a people by its organized amusements, which are inferior in almost any country, more through the producer's fault than through the spectator's.

Perhaps Maurois and Simone de Beauvoir should have traveled together. Maybe his empiricism would have unclouded her ideology. But then again, maybe not. Joint expeditions to foreign parts don't necessarily produce unanimous diaries. In the summer of 1867 Mr. C. L. Dodgson — better known as Lewis Carroll — took a trip to Russia with his longtime friend the Reverend Henry Parry Liddon, who wanted to have a look at the Russian Orthodox Church. The two of them kept separate journals of their travels, and the results show how people with different hopes from a journey set rather different store by the same sights and experiences. While good-humored enough, Liddon lacks Dodgson's lively whimsy; the religious motive for the journey is far more serious to him than it is to his companion, and his journal is considerably more reflective.

Of course, people can differ on anything; it doesn't take religious principle. On July 15, after they've gone from Brussels to Cologne, Liddon recalls "Dodgson's delay about the tickets" and notes that 2.50 francs are missing from their joint fund. Dodgson seems to find the first matter excusable and the second inconsequential: he mentions neither of them. The main event of the day was, after all, their viewing of Cologne Cathedral, which Dodgson allows is "the most beautiful of all churches" he has seen or can imagine. A rave, certainly, but hardly the reaction his traveling companion claims to have witnessed in him: "Dodgson was overcome by the beauty of Cologne Cathedral. I found him leaning against the

rails of the Choir and sobbing like a child. When the
verger came to show us over the chapels behind the
Choir, he got out of the way: he said that he could not
bear the harsh voice of the man in the presence of so
much beauty."

On July 20 Liddon records that Dodgson argued with
him about the "obligation of the daily Service." Liddon
says his friend argued "fiercely" that there was no such
obligation; but if he did, Dodgson never mentions it.
Three days later Liddon is miserable with a tourist's
stomach; Dodgson never mentions this, either.

When they at last reach Saint Petersburg and tour
Kazan Cathedral, Dodgson is more interested in the
peculiarities of the people around them than the spiritual
dimensions of the visit. "They were doing all the bowing
& crossing before the Eikons . . . I was waiting outside
for Liddon (I went out when the sermon began)." Still
inside, Liddon is having a more profound experience:
"Today I feel that for the first time in my life, I stand
face to face with the Eastern Church."

He finds her "imposing." But the Mohammedans they
meet farther east are another matter. Liddon cannot get
comfortable with the followers of the false prophet, and
concludes on August 8 that he is "delighted to *have been*
at Nijni Novgorod." But Dodgson is enchanted — he
might be walking through one of his own books: "It
was a wonderful place. Besides there being distinct
quarters for Persians, the Chinese, & others, we were
constantly meeting strange beings, with unwholesome
complexions and unheard-of costumes."

A month later they are home, landing at Dover. All
Liddon writes is: "Walked along the pier by moonlight
until 11 p.m. Most enjoyable." But Dodgson can't resist
rounding off his journal like a well-told tale. The lights
at Dover, he tells us, gradually became more definite,
"till that which had long been merely a glimmering line
on the dark water, like a reflection of the Milky Way,
took form & substance as the lights of the shoreward

houses" and welcomed home the boatload of travelers —
whom Lewis Carroll compares, naturally enough, to
"homeward bound children."

In the last century, without new worlds to explore, travel
diaries have often had to depend on dramatic circumstance, and not just exotic geography, in order to engage
readers. We look for events taking sinister turns, and
strain to see not one culture unfolding, but two cultures
clashing. When, for example, both the American and
British publishers of W. H. Auden and Christopher Isherwood asked them, in 1937, to do a travel book about the
Orient, they spent some time deciding just where they
would go. They finally settled on China because of the
Japanese invasion that August. The resulting *Journey to
a War* is one of those books that show how travel diaries,
if they are to find an audience, must now be about not
just a place, but a time as well.

To be shipped abroad with an army during wartime is
to be offered the ultimate package tour. Everything, as
in the modern travel agent's version, is prescribed and
guaranteed — except, of course, a return ticket. The
diary the English poet Siegfried Sassoon kept during the
First World War starts out not so differently from diaries
kept by those who have toured France in peacetime.
Early in 1916 he is still waiting to see action, and is walking through Amiens Cathedral with a lot of other foreigners: "The Army Service Corps and Red Cross men
are everywhere, walking up and down with the foolish
looks of sightseers, who come neither to watch nor to
pray." Returning from a stand-to he even writes, like a
uniformed Pepys: "And so home to bed." But the useless bloodletting soon begins in earnest, and the diary
fills up with the sounds of bugles, 5.9 shells, and the 110
paces men can march in a minute. On July 1, 1916 — the
day the British lose twenty thousand men in the opening
of the Battle of the Somme — Sassoon makes an almost
hour-by-hour record of what he sees and does, perhaps

because he senses the day's historic nature, and probably just to help get him through it: "Since 6.30 there has been hell let loose . . . I could see one man moving his left arm up and down as he lay on his side: his head was a crimson patch."

It wasn't only this present diary that steadied him. After his first leave home, he returned to the front with one he had kept during his peaceful, fox-hunting days before August 1914: "Discomfort — and the chance that I might never hear the horn again — endowed the diary with heart-easing capabilities," he wrote years later in his autobiography. "There was something between those pages which anyhow couldn't be taken away from me." And yet in time the soldiers on the western front, Sassoon included, would come to feel more rooted to its bloody muck than they had ever felt tied to home. As the playwright Enid Bagnold wrote in the diary she kept of her experiences as a VAD nurse to soldiers invalided back to England: "Isn't it curious to wish so passionately for the day which may place them near to death again?"

Those who stay home during wartime may still manage to have the sense of abruptly quickened circumstance that one gets at the start of a journey. They record sudden thrills and disruptions of ordinary life in something like the manner of the traveler. And if a family member or a lover has gone off to the war itself, the home-front diarist attempts an imaginative journey to be with him. Several years ago the World War II diaries of Clara Milburn, a middle-aged, middle-class Englishwoman of the Midlands, were published. She called her book "Burleigh in Wartime," naming it for the house she occupied with her husband, their servant Kate, and their dog Twink.

For nearly the entire war her son Alan is a POW in Germany, and keeping the diary is her way of keeping faith in his return. She hopes each of the diary's fifteen volumes will be the last, but in the meantime she busily fills her book with news of the household and news of the war: whatever comes over the wireless, good or bad, is recorded avidly and optimistically. She stuffs her journal with newspaper clippings, maps, and telegrams. The book serves to keep up her spirits, as well as those of her diminished family circle: they sometimes read from previous volumes before the evening news comes over the wireless. She even sends bits of it round to a friend.

It is all there: Dunkirk, the destruction of nearby Coventry, the Blitz, D-Day, the progress of the Allies across the islands of the Pacific. Alongside the war's enormities are the stories of her gardening struggles, price increases, and shortages — by 1944 even the exercise books in which she keeps the diary have become scarce. And there is the continuing story of the coughing man who ruins each Sunday's church service. When he's absent, it's a treat: "The Sunday service without that man's cough was very pleasant indeed. Nor was he at the next Service of Remembrance, thanks be, for we had 'Onward Christian Soldiers' and 'Fight the Good Fight,' both of which he ruins."

Mrs. Milburn, as her enthusiasm for martial hymns may indicate, can make Mrs. Miniver look like a positive quisling. "Is there anything more heartening than the Union Jack!" she writes on May 13, 1943, after the British victory in North Africa. She cheers Monty and the boys on against "the beastly Hun" with the same vigor she uses to scorn any squeaks of Labour opposition to Churchill ("He is a lad!"), and any striking or shirking by the miners. Her patriotic credulity is such that she occasionally lapses into officialese: "The British advance in Libya is being pressed with the utmost vigour."

She amply exhibits the insularity and understatement that so endear the British to some Americans. Early in the war she writes: "I can do with the Italians as a nation, but now they are Mussolinied they have lost their courtesy and charm." While writing during an air raid on November 14, 1940, she notes: "Heavens! What a bang!

The house shook then. I think we could do without any more of this."

Goodness knows it is this sort of national self-possession that has allowed the British to resist aggression from the days of Philip of Spain to General Galtieri of Argentina. One must admire Mrs. Milburn's grit, the stuff that allowed a nation "to stick it and *stick it*, and STICK IT till the war is ended." But there are moments when her upper lip is a bit too stiff, almost frightful in its determination first to bear and then avenge. One sympathizes with her when she describes fantasies of Alan's return ("And then off one goes into dreamings and imaginings till one finds oneself doing the same thing twice, or going upstairs when one meant to go in the garden — even picking up the kettle to go and feed the hens!"), but at other times one is chilled by her sang-froid. When in 1942 the Germans begin to manacle prisoners of war, she writes, with Alan in mind: "We certainly hope he won't have his hands tied but, if this indignity is forced upon him, that he will bear it as becomes a British officer — and get a bit of amusement out of it, too." One would almost prefer to see Mrs. Milburn give in for a moment to that most mortal of sins, despair.

But despair, or even mild discouragement, was not part of her make-up during war. In fact, one can hardly come away from her diary without feeling that, despite her genuine revulsion and anxiety over the sufferings caused by it, there was a fundamental part of her that loved the war. It vitalized her more, one suspects, than anything else ever did. The war threw everyone into the same bomb shelter; there were no outsiders, only participants: "Everyone's life is so full these days," she writes. She cries out, "Oh this cursed war, separating families and destroying home life!" — and she means it. But she gives the war news from the Continent and says, "Things are so intense that one's mind goes to it again and again." The seductiveness of that intensity is something that doesn't bear looking into too deeply; but it's what makes Mrs. Milburn's diaries so eminently salable.

Alan comes home — on May 10, 1945. The telegrams and phone calls preceding his arrival are mentioned in the diary and can be read with the same satisfying thrills to be found in the last reel of a good war movie. "Burleigh in Wartime" offers us a dénouement of two days, during which we see Mrs. Milburn and her son resume their normal lives. On Friday, May 11, she writes:

> Everything is *very* good. All the old familiar noises about the house, the same cough, the same bangs here and there. The doctor came after lunch and stayed a long time, and just as we were finishing tea out of doors the Clay family came. As they didn't go till after seven, it was a bit late when we had supper, and then Alan walked Twink to fetch medicine from the doctor's. And so ends another good day.

A bit curious, the first and last sentences of that paragraph — they make it seem as if she had to convince herself that May 11, 1945, really was a good day, as if she was aware, perhaps guiltily, that something was missing — a certain intensity perhaps.

Clara Milburn may not have fully understood the ambivalence toward the war that is so apparent to a reader of her diaries. But she did understand two important truths about time — matters of retrospect and prospect — that need to be known, if only instinctively, by any good diarist. She knew the value of accumulating the past: "As one gets older and there is so much background, one can't be dull, but can just open the heart's store, look round the shelves, take down the memory and live it over again. Grand!" And she knew the terrors of the future: "It is as well we cannot see ahead — our hearts would break."

Certainly we would be afraid to travel.

3

Pilgrims

*Huddled in front of my fire with a
teapot as dawn breaks, I go over the
last scenes [before Nancy's suicide
attempt], the last letters in my mind,
a substitute for the coldnesses, the un-
kindnesses, the lukewarmnesses, the
words and phrases I wish now I had
used. In course of time, I daresay, I
should have come to think I really did
use them — if this diary did not con-
front me with the truth.*

—J. R. ACKERLEY,
My Sister and Myself

A BREED APART from the diarists who write simply to
collect the days or preserve impressions of foreign places
are those who set out in their books to discover who they
really are. These are generally very serious people, more
in the way of pilgrims, with inward destinations, than
mere travelers. Some of them are after the sight of God;
others are out to realize their full "potential," spiritual
and otherwise; and some of them are carrying burdens of
suffering they are unsure they can shoulder — they want
to use their diaries to test, and add to, their strength.
Some of them succeed in getting where they want; others
talk themselves into believing they've done that; and
some clearly, if honestly, fail.

I am living this 27th of June, 1840, a dull, cloudy day
and no sun shining. The clink of the smith's hammer

sounds feebly over the roofs, and the wind is sighing gently, as if dreaming of cheerfuler days. The farmer is plowing in yonder field, craftsmen are busy in the shops, the trader stands behind the counter, and all works go steadily forward. But I will have nothing to do; I will tell fortune that I play no game with her, and she may reach me in my Asia of serenity and indolence if she can.

This self-satisfied declaration of contentment in the here and now, made, just as he says, on June 27, 1840, by one Henry David Thoreau, Harvard graduate, pencil maker, transcendentalist, walker, recluse, and gadfly, is belied by the other two million words in the thirty-nine notebooks he wrote between 1837 and 1861. Not only were these the greenhouse for thoughts that would flower fully in his published work; they were also the place where, with neither serenity nor indolence, he discovered and manufactured a "self" as precious to him as Whitman's was to Whitman: "May I love and revere myself above all the gods that men have ever invented. May I never let the vestal fire go out in my recesses." These are not words from "Song of Myself"; they are from Thoreau's journal of August 15, 1851. Whitman's "sensuality" might be something Thoreau felt most men and women weren't pure enough to handle, but on the preciousness of themselves the two men were in agreement.

Thoreau sees his diary as, literally, a container for the effervescings of a soul moving ever further toward enlightenment. "My Journal," he writes on February 8, 1841, "is that of me which would else spill over and run to waste, gleanings from the field which in action I reap. I must not live for it, but in it for the gods. They are my correspondent, to whom daily I send off this sheet postpaid." These small *g* gods come and go, but the "me" remains, and the journal goes on and on perfecting it. "He enjoys true leisure who has time to improve his soul's estate," Thoreau writes in the proverbial manner

that is one of his journal's stylistic workhorses; he is
determined "to meet [himself] face to face sooner or
later." It is nature, he knows, that will give him the
symbols he can read his own life by, and the seasons that
will give "tone and hue" to his thoughts; but without the
journal he will not be able to make it all clear to himself.
A friend criticizes his unabashed dependence on it: "He
finds fault with me that I walk alone, when I pine for
want of a companion; that I commit my thoughts to a
diary even on my walks, instead of seeking to share
them generously with a friend; curses my practice even."
Thoreau says he will accept the curse on his book and
habit if he really is such a "cold intellectual skeptic," but
the diary stays. More than one friend's loss is confided to
its pages; but those pages keep increasing until just months
before their author's death in 1862.

Thoreau was one of those men who are their outlooks.
The liberating insights and mean little prejudices recorded and repeated in his books are not so much a man's
expression as the man himself. It is in the journals that
we find Thoreau telling himself (and us, for these books
are not shy about using the second person) to stay at
home and find beauty there, to learn one place deeply
instead of smearing footprints over half the globe, to
"migrate interiorly without intermission" toward that
supremely consequential being, oneself. He tells us that we
live too quickly and coarsely, that moonlight and mountains are better than men, that we should cultivate poverty and live, as he did, deliberately.

It is a heroic and wearying solipsism that he cultivates:
"I do not judge men by anything they can do," he writes
on February 18, 1841, when he is twenty-three. "Their
greatest deed is the impression they make on me." Almost
a year later he is reading Chaucer, and finding that poet
more or less worthy of his own company: "I can at length
stretch me when I come to Chaucer's breadth; and I
think, 'Well, I could be *that* man's acquaintance,' for he
walked in that low and retired way that I do, and was not

too good to live. I am grieved when they hint of any
unmanly submissions he may have made, for that sub-
tracts from his breadth and humanity." If Thoreau was
to be without a patron, so must everyone else. There is
something magnificent in the way he fails to see how
snobbish his own humility can be. He admits it is impossible for him "to be interested in what interests men
generally," but when those interests occasionally do rub
up against one another in conversation it is usually
Thoreau who is right and "men generally" who are
wrong. Men tell him to bring a spyglass with him when
he goes up the mountains, but he knows better. "The
facts of science, in comparison with poetry, are wont to
be as vulgar as looking from the mountain with a telescope. It is a counting of meeting-houses." It is almost
ever thus in these journals.

But it is difficult to write two million words without
putting down some that have a charity redeeming pride-
fulness. Nearing forty, Thoreau reflects on how long his
neighbors have put up with his transcendentally pro-
prietary tramplings across their fields without ever pull-
ing a gun on him: "For nearly twoscore years I have
known, at a distance, these long-suffering men, whom I
never spoke to, who never spoke to me, and now feel a
certain tenderness for them, as if this long probation
were but the prelude to an eternal friendship." The self-
aware crank finds it in him to pay tribute to the un-
enlightened, and the journals suddenly gesture more
warmly, more includingly, toward the reader who is
tired of being hectored for his failure to meet spiritual
tests he has, when he thinks about it, little desire to pass
in the first place.

The journals are speckled with lovely, lyrical moments, ones when Thoreau's homespun prose suddenly
silkens, when all the plain and overpraised vegetables of
simplicity get cleared away for a platter of sweets. "The
stars are the apexes of what triangles!" he writes: they
connect one man to any other looking up at them at the

same instant. The new "telegraph harp" is celebrated in spite of its suspicious modernity; and the snowflakes falling on January 5, 1856, are "glorious spangles, the sweeping of heaven's floor." Such outbursts make up for a lot of the belligerence that goes with striving to be a saint in Massachusetts.

As he sought in the journals to comprehend the world, and to simplify and perfect his place in it, Thoreau frequently meditated on the proper balance of the concrete and the abstract. He wants the "daily tide" to "leave some deposit on these pages, as it leaves sand and shells on the shore," but he worries that he sees too many details at the expense of wholeness. And yet — his friend William Ellery Channing's notebooks seem too idealized and ethereal to him, all forest and no trees. The solution, at last, is not to banish facts, but to get the right ones down: "Facts should only be as the frame to my pictures; they should be material to the mythology which I am writing." Thoreau tells us on February 18, 1852, that he keeps one notebook for facts and another for poetry, but that he finally has trouble keeping them separate, "for the most interesting and beautiful facts are so much the more poetry and that is their success." (In their last years the balance does shift in such a way that for long stretches the journals read like a naturalist's data bank.)

He knows, finally, that the journal provides the perfect form for his writings. Since thought begets thought so quickly in him, and since to defer recording an insight can be to let it expire like a dream we forget the next morning, the journal's immediate and constant availability is its greatest attribute. On August 18, 1858, he forgets to bring his notebook on his walk: no matter — he strips off some birch bark and uses it for paper instead. "The writer who postpones the recording of his thoughts uses an iron which has cooled to burn a hole with."

The journal's freedom from formulas and convention and public exposure makes him sometimes prefer it to books that get published and sold — publication being, as another part-time transcendentalist put it, "the auction of the mind." When on October 28, 1853, 706 unsold copies of *A Week on the Concord and Merrimack Rivers* are sent back to Thoreau by his publisher, he seems to return to his journal with a kind of relief. (And, to be sure, rationalization: "Indeed, I believe that this result is more inspiring and better for me than if a thousand had bought my wares. It affects my privacy less and leaves me freer.")

The journals are Thoreau's essential work, the books wherein he came to know himself and by which we will always know him best. In them we see thoughts not just as they soar full-grown, but as they hatch in the nests of circumstance:

> I do not know but thoughts written down thus in a journal might be printed in the same form with greater advantage than if the related ones were brought to-gether into separate essays. They are now allied to life, and are seen by the reader not to be far-fetched. It is more simple, less artful. I feel that in the other case I should have no proper frame for my sketches. Mere facts and names and dates communicate more than we suspect. Whether the flower looks better in the nosegay than in the meadow where it grew and we had to wet our feet to get it!

The journals show him wetting his feet during the whole twenty-year trek toward himself. He was sufficiently pleased with the discovery to believe others would will-ingly wet theirs for the chance to see it also.

About 125 years after Thoreau went to live at Walden Pond, the poet and novelist May Sarton, during a spell of nervousness, anger, and uncertain love, decided she, too, needed a period of living deliberately. She determined to spend time by herself in her New Hampshire home to see what she could sort out. From this year (1970–1971, shortly before she turned sixty), and from this house she once compares to a nunnery, comes her *Journal of a Soli-tude*. She is convinced that her existence truly begins when she is apart from others. "I am here alone," she writes on September 15, 1970, "for the first time in weeks, to take up my 'real' life again at last." She sees the journal as the place where she can "break through into the rough rocky depths, to the matrix itself," the place where she can find herself being herself. She is one of those people who "can think something out only by writing it"; and so, for the job she has in mind, the journal is more a matter of need than indulgence.

It is not easy work. She confesses to being depressed by it after just two pages, but she has an orderly as well as stubborn temperament, and she gets herself back to her book most mornings. She has the sort of mettle one needs if one decides exercise or therapy is in order — she likes her cupboards neatly arranged, and when there is a gap in the journal she tends to explain it — partly to work off guilt, and partly to keep the record complete. *Journal of a Solitude* reminds us of the remarkable immediacy the diary has for both keeper and reader ("The sun has suddenly come out and there is a bright blue sky — all this happened while I wrote a few words!") even as it allows us to see things unfold over time: her relations with flowers, a parrot, cats. When near the end of the book the wild cat — who has padded around the house and the journal like a motif — is pregnant once more, forcing Sarton to call the Humane Society rather than face a plague of kittens, the reader realizes again the diary's trick of turning into narrative almost without meaning to. Suddenly we are at the climax of a story we hadn't even realized *was* a story.

But mostly what one finds in May Sarton's journal is what the author wants to find, namely, herself. She recognizes a woman who is constitutionally "ornery" and too frequently subject to depression and fury. In exploring that anger she uses the journal to confess and then gain absolution. After one bout of bad feeling she rebukes herself and then attempts to find a few mitigating circumstances and unanticipated compensations. She moves toward an equilibrium. But a week after such productive meditation, she is once more taken hold of by an ugly mood: "I woke in tears this morning. I wonder whether it is possible at nearly sixty to change oneself radically. Can I learn to control resentment and hostility, the ambivalence, born somewhere far below the conscious level? If I cannot, I shall lose the person I love." One of the things she must face in the course of her year alone is the decline of her lesbian love for "X." She manages that — not without some anger and regret, but with a moving stoicism:

> Maybe patience is the last thing we learn. I remember Jean Dominique, old and blind, saying to me, "*On attend toujours*." I was under thirty then and she was over sixty and I was amazed to think that someone so old could still wait for someone so intensely. But now I know that one does so all one's life.

She admits that her moods take her to heaven and hell a dozen times every day, and she keeps recording her failures — even though she's far too shrewd to believe in her own, or anyone's, perfectability. It is her frustrating habit to chastise herself for her flaws and then berate herself for excessive guilt over them. This honest inability to get out of a vicious human circle — a holding pattern very different from the little rings of self-satisfaction Thoreau is inclined to float through — makes her journal a bleakly appealing thing. It has integrity.

Sarton's honest ambivalence extends to the solitude she has decided to put her faith in. If she offers it praise, she stays aware of its price: "Mine is not, I feel sure, the best human solution. Nor have I ever thought it was. In my case it has perhaps made possible the creation of some works of art, but certainly it has done so at a high price in emotional maturity and in happiness." She can be reduced, at the end of the day, to feelings of relief when the faces on the television news beam their way into the house, and she sympathetically reads an essay that criticizes the contemporary taste for Thoreau as unrealistic in a time when social relations are more inescapable and crucial than ever. The reader of her journal likewise questions the solitude that gives it birth when he notices the perceptible — and temporary — increase in its energy when someone comes to call. Carolyn Heilbrun, the first scholar Sarton sees paying serious attention to her, comes for a visit. The journal suddenly prospers with complication, the sound of one good mind involved with another, instead of the hum of a solitary poet contemplating herself or the locals before her moods once more beleaguer her.

And yet, on balance — and balance is the state the journal searches for — Sarton's solitariness, after a year, carries her through to some hard-won and genuine enlightenment. Being apart has probably aided her in breaking away from "X," a process of apparently great pain and ultimate relief that is not much elaborated upon. An honest peace, which is to say a compromising, nonecstatic one, has descended by September 30, 1971:

> I begin to have intimations, now, of a return to some deep self that has been too absorbed and too battered to function for a long time. That self tells me that I was meant to live alone, meant to write the poems for others — poems that seldom in my life have reached the one person for whom they were intended.

It is, however, an equilibrium that will not last. Several years later a bad review in the *New York Times* sends May Sarton into a psychological quicksand from which she emerges only by again resorting to solitude and a journal — one she calls *Recovering*. But the absence of final triumph does not diminish what she accomplishes in *Journal of a Solitude*; it, in fact, authenticates it. When human beings are playing for stakes of happiness and self-knowledge, the only believable victories are probably the temporary and partial ones.

It was perhaps Anaïs Nin's preference for total fulfillment to partial victories that made her in the 1970s a more likely cult figure than May Sarton. If Sarton was subject to gloomy solitudes — however therapeutic — Miss Nin could assure thousands of diarists eager to reach her extremes of creativity and awareness that her life had always been "very full and very rich." A friend of Henry Miller, a patient of Otto Rank, a fledgling artist living in a houseboat on the Seine in the 1930s, the author of lyric and surreal fiction once appreciated by only the truly sensitive and cognizant, and finally a sort of delicate California guru, Miss Nin lived a life that allowed her to fill her endless diaries with an artistic glamour that only added to their appeal for readers eager to follow her into the realms of realization.

She begins them as a young girl, originally intending them to be a kind of letter designed to entice home her Spanish father, who had abandoned his family to America. As Anaïs Nin matures the diary takes on many different functions; but above all it becomes the place for "organic cellular growth," the crusader's highway on "this quest for the self, the emotional evolution, the overcoming of obstacles, the fears that we shared, the timidities, the confusions, the conflicts, and then the step-by-step struggle finally to come out of them into a state of freedom and harmony." The books grow huge in number. She was photographed one day with stacks of them in the Brooklyn bank vault that kept them safe for the rest of the world. Miss Nin was an extremely beautiful woman, and this was not the only photograph to be included in the diaries as they were published (in radical condensations) in the 1960s and 1970s. Another shows her at a masquerade party with a birdcage on her head: "Coming out of the bird cage," she later explains, "was a sort of ticker tape of the unconscious, long strips of paper on which I had copied a great deal of writing. This was, of course, a very clear symbol of how I hoped to escape from my cage." So dependent on the diary does she become that when she abandons it temporarily, at the suggestion of Dr. Rank, she suffers withdrawal symptoms she subsequently compares to an opium eater's.

Let us catch Anaïs Nin in midflight, in Volume 4 of the published diaries (culled from Volumes 68–74 of the original ones). This puts us between 1944 and 1947, a cataclysmic time for the globe, but, as always, a fruitful one for Miss Nin. Here, as in the other volumes, we will find, according to Gunther Stuhlmann (editor and keeper of the flame of self-fulfillment), the same things we find in other volumes: Number 4 is an "intensely personal document" in which the author attempts "to gain a totality of experience"; "exploration, unfolding, growth" are the essence of this volume, too, and in it we once again find Miss Nin seeking "meaningful personal relationships."

Public events are not entirely absent from Volume 4. Atomic bombs and the liberation of continents do sometimes intrude upon its pages. But it is hardly a chronicle of the times, for Miss Nin feels one can become too absorbed in an event like D-Day. Her friend Gonzolo, "who lives glued to the radio," certainly is, and it is doing him no good at all: "Because he only has *one* life, the one he shares with the present, in history, because he is not creating an antidote to the poisons of history, Gonzolo has no hope. He is crushed by events. He has no inner life to sustain and alchemize events." To those among us who find the idea of living outside history at best uncivil and quite possibly unhealthful, Miss Nin says not to worry. It is all right to isolate yourself for a time until you have, as she has, "solved the personal world" and are ready to go beyond it.

One solves this personal world more by feeling than analyzing. Dr. Rank teaches her that "too much lucidity creates a desert" and her habit of diary-writing teaches her "enthusiasm, naturalness. The emotional reality of the present. A respect for the present mood." She pities the defenses erected by others who cannot flourish as she does in her book. "The real Anaïs is in the diary," she writes in November 1945, "even the destructive Anaïs who refuses to destroy in life." She is convinced that her books contain not only the keys to herself but to the mysteries of her sex. Male friends clamor for revelation. Harry, speaking like a "predatory invader," demands entry: " 'I want to read all the diaries. I want to know the secret of woman, to incorporate this knowledge into my writing. I feel I must know it. No other woman can give me the truth.' " Next year it's Leonard who is begging to know what they contain, especially about himself: " 'I will hypnotize you, make you open the safe, and read them all.' " In her published interviews, and on film, Miss Nin can be extraordinarily charming, but the diaries themselves are full of an off-putting Delphic pride, and what seems a biological inability to refrain from recording expressions of praise that have been directed to her by others — in letters, conversation, reviews. As for words of censure, she records them and then proceeds to explain their inaccuracy.

She admits that her diary is "an effort against loss," a way of saving things that would otherwise disappear. She denies, however, that she is a hoarder: "I keep nothing to remind me of the passage of time, deterioration, loss, shriveling." In this last statement we see the aggressive denial of neurosis appropriate to a disciple of Dr. Rank. But the real story lies more nearly in that picture of her in the Brooklyn bank vault. She wasn't paying the bank management to preserve only scrolls for others' enlightenment; she was paying it to preserve herself. She admits in her late years that she can "remember every time I used to hear a fire engine, I used to think: 'The diaries are burning.' "

In a letter to Leo Lerman, inserted into the diary in December 1946, she wrote: "I am more interested in human beings than in writing, more interested in love-making than in writing, more interested in living than in writing. More interested in becoming a work of art than in creating one. I am more interesting than what I write."

Without putting too fine a point on it, one must express the wistful hope that she was. Because if life is short and art is long, she managed to make her diaries even longer.

Miss Nin insisted she was not a narcissist; more than once she said that by encountering the deeply personal, one inevitably hits upon the universal. Toward the end of her life, as she received the accolades of her fulfillment-hungry admirers — and answered their letters — she came to think that the message her diary finally imparted to others might have been its chief reason for being all along. First we solve "a problem of the soul" and then "we become truly collective or communal, giving and outgoing." Mr. Stuhlmann, writing in 1971, declared that this wonderful simplicity united Miss Nin with the young revolutionaries seeking to bring " 'new consciousness' " to America. Two years later Miss Nin herself observed, happily, that Americans were finally coming around, however late, to the habit of diary-keeping: "We're taking it up as an instrument for knowing ourselves, for creating ourselves."

Are we ever!

We're really writing in Boston; in Pittsburgh, Pennsylvania; deep in the heart of Texas; and 'round the Frisco bay. And in Huntsville, Rabun Gap, Des Plaines, Porchatoula, Cohasset, Ossining, and Saskatoon, too. We're writing journals according to the method developed by Dr. Ira Progoff and taught in his Intensive Journal® workshops and seminars. One has been in your area and another will be there soon. Almost four hundred of them were held in 1980. The Life Context workshop costs $75 ($65 if you've been registered previously) and the Process Meditation workshop is $65. Register for both and you pay just $120.* If Dr. Progoff's operations seem to be on the order of Smokenders, or Evelyn Wood Reading Dynamics, it must be remembered that he offers nothing so paltry as the chance to kick cigarettes or increase one's

---

* Summer 1983 prices.

reading speed. He is offering, to all who register, a new life.

At a Journal Workshop ("The basic text and guide for using the *Intensive Journal*® process") explains that if you follow his methods, "allowing them to stretch over as long a period as they require, an exciting awareness like the breaking of dawn will come to you." Keep it up and you will be embarked upon "an ongoing, open-ended program of personal growth." It took Dr. Progoff many years to develop it. The premise for what he hath wrought is described in an appropriately interplanetary simile, for certainly Dr. Progoff's reality is like no other to be found on this sphere: "The concept that underlies the *Intensive Journal* approach is that the potential for growth in a human being is as infinite as the universe."

Participants in groups led by the doctor himself or his approved Journal Consultants are issued workbooks with multicolored separators marking off the "mini-processes" they will investigate within their own lives. The workshops involve lots of quiet and deep breathing, but mostly they involve writing. A participant keeps a Period Log (concerning whatever phase his life now seems to be going through); a record of the Twilight Imagery that flows to him ("In the twilight atmosphere of our imagery we feel the wholeness of life, and the fullness of time in its ongoingness"); and a Daily Log (after asking himself two pages of cue questions that Dr. Progoff recommends for beginning the assessment of each day, the participant will find that he is still not out of bed). In other sections of the Intensive Journal he will record his existence's Steppingstones and make his Life History Log (aided by the rather safe assumption that "since our entries in the Life History Log involve a calling back of memories from the past, we will not necessarily remember everything at once"). The participant will also dialogue (a word Dr. Progoff likes to use as a verb) with persons, works, his own body, events, situations, circumstances, society, and a figure representing Inner Wisdom to him (it could be

Gandhi; it could be Susan B. Anthony). The "dialogue script" that will result from each of these exercises comes, Dr. Progoff assures us, rather automatically. A little work with dreams is also included. The color-coded sections seem very sharply differentiated at first, but eventually the participant will go back and forth from one to the other, filling up his Intensive Journal as if it were an accordion file. As Dr. Progoff explains: "Those who work actively and continuously with the *Intensive Journal* workbook have found that the use of different colors to distinguish the major divisions of the Journal helps them move more fluidly through the many interrelated aspects of their lives and expedites the self-integrating process within them." It is all meant to help them get to "a new Now . . . the Open Moment of our life."

Although he is an admirer of Anaïs Nin (as she, not too surprisingly, was of him), Dr. Progoff has registered his suspicions of "literary" diaries, and those ordinary ones that tend to go " 'around in circles' " without, presumably, pushing a person toward his Open Moment. In fact, Dr. Progoff really cannot be said to believe much in writing. He says, "We should pay no attention at all to [its] style." As for himself, he is more inclined to purée words than connect them: "the gradual and cumulative work by which an individual recognizes the nonconscious guidance that has been directing his personal life involvements . . ."; "the energy that carries the life toward its meaningful unfoldment . . ." He likes his metaphors mixed ("The seed of the person is reaching out to a new avenue of experience"), his reasoning circular ("That can become a very important piece of information, as it may be very meaningful to you at a later time"), and his flights into meaninglessness sublime ("Basic to the Dialogue Dimension is the realization that the main aspects of our existence unfold as persons in the universe").

Dr. Progoff says you can pick up the Intensive Journal® method from *At a Journal Workshop*. But there is no substitute for the mutual support to be gained through

the "*active privacy*" available at the workshops themselves, where participants can, should they wish, read
their jottings aloud. If they decide to, they will meet with
no est-like abuse; in fact, they will not meet with much
reaction at all. Dr. Progoff reminds them that those listening will still be busy writing: they may pick up only the
speaker's "psychic vibrations" and not his words. If people
plumb such depths that they break into sobs, the proper
response from their colleagues in the group is supportive
quiet. In the cathedral of the workshop (Dr. Progoff's
comparison), maintaining the proper atmosphere is most
important.

He is vigilant toward any bad contingency his journal-
ists may meet on the road to the Open Moment, among
them "the misuse of journal-keeping when it is done
without the guidance of dynamic principles and without
a protective discipline" — which is to say without the
guidance of an approved Journal Consultant. The *Intensive Journal* workbook each participant receives at a
workshop has a number that is registered with Dialogue
House in New York City. The participant's name is not
on it, but Dr. Progoff assures him that if the journal is
lost, and then returned to Dialogue House, he will get it
back. So names and numbers would seem to be not entirely unconnected. Whether or not the participant ever
loses his journal, he can be sure that he will remain on
Dr. Progoff's mailing list until the last day of the last
diary kept on earth.

The world as we know it does not seem terribly near
those realms to which Dr. Progoff promises passage. All
his diaries have happy endings; that is chiefly what distin-
guishes them from those that go " 'around in circles.' "
It never occurs to him that the earth goes around in
circles, too; that it is a place where things may not come
out all right; where some of us may end up unhappy;
that this planet, for all the intermittent joys of living on
it, is less a spaceship to bliss than a hospital from which
no one, finally, gets out alive. Dr. Progoff urges his

participants to keep up their journals, according to the methods they have learned, after they complete the workshop. Their books are meant to be a continuing (he would no doubt say "ongoing") part of their lives, lives that they ultimately will *control*. Thousands of people believe in Dr. Progoff; but thousands of people still believe in the Reverend Moon and laetrile. The success of the Intensive Journal® seminars testifies not only to the deep appeal of books we can write by and about ourselves, but also to the great American hunger for awareness and transcendence. It has been Dr. Progoff's genius to franchise his tasty diaries of the spirit, his I-in-the-sky. He has become the Burger King® of self-realization. Follow him and you can have it your way.

On December 18, 1860, one of the Goncourts, back from a tour of a women's hospital ward undertaken on the recommendation of Flaubert, recalled reading "somewhere that people who look after the sick are more given to making love than others." Tending to the chronically ill, or the intermittently mad, or the slowly dying, is exhausting work, and if the balm of sex or love isn't always available or adequate, the journal may be the other presence called on for comfort. To bear witness to another's suffering and to attempt to soothe it can be ennobling; carrying such a cross can transform and elevate, and people who keep diaries about their days among the sick and dying are often conscious of going through a phase that will take them to higher spiritual ground. But getting there is chancy.

For example, it isn't easy bringing up "a damned retard." That's the way Josh Greenfeld, the journalist and screenwriter, characterizes his brain-damaged son on June 4, 1972. *A Place for Noah* is the second of his diaries about how he and his Japanese wife, Foumi, try to raise both their handicapped child and his gifted older brother, Karl.

Noah may be autistic, but Greenfeld won't call him that, because there's a grotesque chic to the word. He's had to put up for too long with sentimental notions that kids like Noah are really " 'angel children' ": "An actor friend was at the house yesterday, with his American Indian girl friend. 'The Indians believe children like Noah are inspired,' she said. 'Ugh!' I replied." Whatever tantalizing mystery there may be in things like Noah's annual utterance of the word *strawberries* is there to be pondered by clinicians, interested outsiders. At home the Greenfelds must deal with "all the shit-cleaning work [their] tired flesh has become heir to." Those who sigh over books about "angel children" don't have to cope with the vagaries of Noah's bowels and bladder, and don't have to ask a salesman in the linen department whether a particular bedspread they find attractive is also edible.

Throughout his diary Greenfeld worries the question of what must eventually be done about Noah. Where is the place for him? On September 19, 1974, he writes: "It took two of us, Foumi and me, to cut Noah's toenails. What happens in six months?" To glimpse the prefigurings of adulthood in Noah's face, when he is six, or to see him emerge from the bathtub with an erection when he is ten, is to be forced into admitting that he will someday be too big and uncontrollable to remain at home. And to admit that is to picture, a moment later, Noah "no longer a kitten, prowling through a life of endless hospital corridors." On one day Greenfeld is able to assert: "Noah must go. And we both know it." On another he asks himself why they can't keep him after all:

> Who is to say that what is best for Noah may not be best for us as a family? Why should our family be dedicated to my writing or Foumi's painting or Karl's maturing? Why can't our family be dedicated to the care of Noah? What finer principle? After all, everything we do — in spite of how we try to squirm out of it — is because of Noah anyway.

Aside from being the place where Greenfeld ponders alternatives (actually the lack of them), the diary is the place in which he collects ironies and releases anger. On November 1, 1973, announcements come from both Noah's and Karl's schools: "A meeting of the parents of the autistic children. A meeting of the parents of the gifted children." The family has Chinese food one night and Noah's fortune cookie tells him: " 'A little conversation can remove great hindrances. Try it.' " "Outside these pages," Greenfeld writes, "rarely do I bemoan Noah's condition or let his fate get to me." But in them he can admit he sometimes hates the son he loves, and can write out some bad black jokes: he goes out at night and notices that "other people were walking their dogs; I walked my son"; "fifty percent of the time he chooses the right shoe." He writes such sentences as a sort of shock tactic against himself. If he drains the anger as quickly and brutally as he can, he'll be left with more stamina for his real business in life, which is taking care of Noah.

Greenfeld admits that he "can never kill the dream that is my son," and one Valentine's Day he goes so far as to say "Our love must do for Noah what we cannot do." But most of the time he knows better than this. Love can have power only if it remains united with practicality, and Greenfeld's diary shows that where Noah is concerned one's energy is invested in simple hygienic maintenance more than anything else. The hospital will eventually become Noah's place and thereby solve the problem, dreadfully. In the meantime Greenfeld has to deal with Noah "on a transient — or existential — basis." Which is to say day by day. The diary's greatest usefulness to him is that its daily call forces him to note all his changes of mood, all the tired oscillations between hope and realism. In its lifelike resistance to consistency and neatness, it helps him realize there is no satisfactory way to master certain miseries; it helps him simply to endure.

Hours on — and around — a deathbed can provoke the surrender of pride as well as flesh. The diary that the screenwriter Aram Saroyan kept during the last illness of his estranged father, William, shows the huge value the smallest concessions of the dying can have on the living. The younger Saroyan's book, *Last Rites*, reads like the faltering EKG wave of a fatally sick father-son relationship. The son keeps pounding on the father's heart, determined to keep the wave from going flat before some kind of peace can be made between the two of them.

Between mid-April and mid-May 1981 William Saroyan is dying of cancer. Aram Saroyan begins his journal on April 14, when he gets the news that things are hopeless. The book that emerges during the next month is less a vigil than an exorcism. Aram Saroyan informs his reader (and he certainly intended, from the start, that there would be readers) that far from being the genial, wise, and endearing figure the public imagined him to be, the author of *The Time of Your Life* was a lonely, bitter man, swollen with a sense of his own greatness and septic with resentment against the woman with whom he went through two marriages and two divorces. Aram Saroyan is convinced of his father's own bad will toward him: "He wanted me to die, he wanted me to be a disgrace and a failure, to be a blot on his good name — the hopeless fuck-up son of a great man." And Aram disappoints him by emerging from a smart-assed hippieish phase (he named his two daughters Strawberry and Cream) and becoming a responsible man who can certainly write ("a suggestion that sank like a stone within the already deeper fluencies in the room"). William Saroyan's ego was such, his son says, that he refused the Pulitzer Prize rather than have to feel grateful for it, and that "probably the last genuinely intimate telephone conversation of his life had been with the Associated Press." Still, this is no easy death for Aram Saroyan to anticipate; he is sensibly frightened of the change about to take place in his "own interior architecture: as if a huge wall were to be suddenly removed and sunlight to flood in where for years what has grown has been an issue of darkness."

He has long been estranged from his father, but is

determined to use the journal to stay in touch with his dying. "Each day I pick up my pen to write, as if to stave off what amounts to a deepening dissociation between myself and what is, in fact, happening to my father." He is determined to survive by soberly comprehending ("The only way I can hold my own now is by writing it down day by day until the terrible game is over at last"); and he refuses to give way completely to a "desire to cry out at the grim, smug, humorless, and finally horrifying inhumanity of every claim he made against my mother." He wants to communicate with both himself and the audience that for decades thought of William Saroyan as a benevolent mustachioed sage.

So Aram Saroyan goes over the past as he waits for his father's time to stop. He meditates not only on his own childhood, but on his father's as well. He seeks Freudian comfort in the explanation that his father's orphaning and overnight success made his later cruelties inevitable.

Saroyan's book is an odd combination of spontaneity and contrivance. There is clear address to an audience ("I will get to the substance of these attacks in a moment") and just as clear evidence of later revision. But there is also great urgency (on April 18 he begins writing at 6:00 A.M. and is still going six and a half hours later) as well as some of the tremendous drama a diary conveys when it is kept not just after, but *during*, events: "I just called the hospital." *Last Rites* builds, of course, to a climactic meeting between father and son. We wait for it, and get decidedly nervous. But if Aram Saroyan teases us into suspense, he forcefully depicts his own nervousness. He writes about the moments before he goes into his father's room:

In the snack bar, Cream got Hawaiian Punch and I got a piece of pumpkin pie. We sat down in the brightly lit white Formica eating area, in a no-smoking alcove where only one other person was seated (smoking), and we were finished with our food almost immediately. I took our tray and dishes to a service wagon, and then returned to our table and took Cream's hand and we walked through the eating area, lingering for a moment at the food and drink machines, as if, perhaps, we might want to buy something more. But neither of us were actually hungry, and we went back up in the elevator now . . . We ended up sitting in the fourth-floor lobby for five minutes.

The only way to replicate the feeling of waiting is to allow chronology and detail to tyrannize over the entry.

A tentative peace is made between father and son. The little girl, Cream, helps mediate it, and this satisfies our sense of fitness. The father kisses his son, and the son holds his dying, gaunt father. "As I was closing his door, now outside in the corridor, I heard him saying loudly, 'It's unbelievable! . . . It's unbelievable!'" The emotional pleasures are diluted — and kept honest — when Aram Saroyan tells the reader that in some ways this peace was really more in the nature of an exhausted truce; when he tries to turn this healing encounter into regular visits during his father's last days, the elder Saroyan's rebuffs are felt once more. But Aram Saroyan has been sufficiently strengthened by several weeks' writing so as not to despair: "I have lived half of a full lifetime with these sad and maddening emotional impasses." He settles for the little he got in the hospital room during the afternoon of April 29, 1981.

Among the things we learn about William Saroyan from his son's book is that he kept diaries from 1938 until his death, and that he was an obsessive saver of rocks, nickels, magazines, carbon copies of his own letters, envelopes, jars, boxes. His diaries record "minutely . . . physical processes such as getting up (exact time), showering, shaving, writing a story, eating breakfast, walking, picking up groceries and laundry, eating lunch, stopping at a bookie joint, etc., until getting to bed that night (exact time)." The son, in one of the most believable psychological explanations the book offers, speculates that with all these diaries and all these collections his father was "writing his name over and over and over again," that they amounted to "a kind of *willed* immortality" on the part of the orphan who made good. Saroyan left absolutely all of these things to the William Saroyan Foundation, which his own estate would finance: "In effect, he left his estate to himself. He took it with him." In fact, the time of Saroyan's life was not a peak moment to be lived, but the whole huge mass of hours to be hoarded, kept, forever unrelinquished. One of his father's books, Aram reminds us, was called *Not Dying*.

The different attitudes that both Saroyans had toward keeping diaries were one more thing that kept them apart. The elder had, it seems, an almost hysterical case of the chronicler's reluctance to let the sun go down on any day. But his son used the diary to let go.

During a deathwatch the observer may experience a flow of emotional adrenaline that makes a diary unnecessary to the survival of the ordeal. It may be only later, when the mourners are gone and the house is empty, that the trial of loneliness, with none of the practical tasks hospitals and funerals provide, really begins. At that point there may be only a diary to talk to. By 1960 the English writer C. S. Lewis has grown used to talking happily both with his wife, the former Joy Davidman Gresham, and with God. But with Joy's death that year, Lewis finds himself cut off not only from her, but from Him as well. Anger and skepticism invade their conversations. Deprived of the unexpected happiness of his marriage (meant to be a matter of convenience between friends, it had turned happily sexual), he must now entertain the notion of God as a "Cosmic Sadist," an "Eternal Vivisector," before experiencing guilt over what his remaining faith tells him is "filth and nonsense." *A Grief Observed* tries to map the caves of loss and doubt that Lewis stumbles through in the months after Joy's death.

He quickly learns to spot how grief resembles fear and to be appalled by the lazy self-pity it forces on him; he wonders whether the "terrible little notebook" to which he is confiding all this isn't doing him more harm than good. Does reflecting on pain only double it? "I not only live each endless day in grief, but live each day thinking about living each day in grief . . . But what am I to do? I must have some drug, and reading isn't a strong enough drug now. By writing it all down (all? — no: one thought in a hundred) I believe I get a little outside it. That's how I'd defend it to H. [his pseudonym for Joy]. But ten to one she'd see a hole in the defense." A reader of the diary does, too. In it Lewis constantly refers to previous entries. So, not only does he recollect pain; he recollects recollecting it. This may be an exorcism, but it is a painful and obsessive one.

Lewis is troubled by the realization that he is building an imaginary Joy in his mind, that his memory no longer matches life; he is even losing a sense of what she looked like. It's easier for him to remember the face of a casual acquaintance; when a man thinks on the face of his beloved he realizes he has seen it from too many angles, and in too many moods, to have it flash, like a single slide, when he summons it. He experiences all of grief's nasty ironies, including worry over what will happen when grief finally goes away: "Does [it] finally subside into boredom tinged by faint nausea?" Like a survivor of combat who has seen his comrades fall, he feels guilty about any lessening of pain — is it a sign of insufficient devotion to the departed?

At one point in *In Memoriam* Tennyson despairs that he has "no language but a cry." Lewis, disgusted by some of his own denunciations of God, characterizes one of his entries ("Time after time, when He seemed most gracious He was really preparing the next torture") as "a yell rather than a thought" the day after he writes it. But so exquisite is grief's cleverness that it makes sure Lewis cannot win for losing where God is concerned. When he

tries to effect a reconcilation with Him, he must trouble
himself about ulterior motives: "Am I . . . just sidling
back to God because I know that if there's any road to
H., it runs through Him?"

Lewis's diary does not carry dates, so a reader cannot
know exactly how long the different stages of his be-
reavement took to pass. But his book makes clear how
interrupted and disorderly one's progress against grief can
be. At points in his journal calm and time seem to be
doing their work, but then: "Tonight all the hells of
young grief have opened again . . . The same leg is cut
off time after time." Mourners backslide more often than
drunks.

Lewis's book ends with a kind of victory, the sort one's
reason knows from the start is the only one possible, but
which one's heart must be exhausted into accepting. He
lets God have Joy: "How wicked it would be, if we
could, to call the dead back! She said not to me but to
the chaplain, 'I am at peace with God.' She smiled, but
not at me. *Poi si tornò all' eterna fontana.*" It is a victory
that comes more through time and grace than will. And
it is a victory in which the diary has only a doubtful part.
When Lewis begins his fourth notebook about his loss, he
wisely decides it must be the last, because he has come to
realize how the diary-keeping is feeding his grief as much
as purging it. The fourth notebook is the last empty one
he can find in the house, and he decides to take this as an
opportunity to consider — and then stop — what he has
been doing:

> I resolve to let this limit my jottings. I *will not* start
> buying books for the purpose. In so far as this record
> was a defense against total collapse, a safety valve, it
> has done some good. The other end I had in view
> turns out to have been based on a misunderstanding. I
> thought I could describe a *state*; make a map of sorrow.
> Sorrow, however, turns out to be not a state but a
> process. It needs not a map but a history, and if I don't

stop writing that history at some quite arbitrary point, there's no reason why I should ever stop.

For this relief, in other words, much thanks. But beyond that Lewis is right: it would be foolish to claim too much for the diary against grief. The only true relief is brought by time, and in its marriage to chronology the diary reminds its keeper how slow that relief is in coming over the hill. It can be a medicine with gruesome side effects.

The benefits and dangers of actual medicine provide the Hobson's choice that Laurel Lee, a thirty-year-old Oregon mother with Hodgkin's disease, has to make. Her hospital journal, *Walking Through the Fire*, published in 1977, shows her enduring not only the pain and vomiting and balding that are the normal consequences of radiation therapy, but also the possibility that the child with whom she is pregnant will be born retarded as a result of the treatment the mother undergoes to save her own life. Her religious faith guides her to make the decisions both to submit to the therapy and to resist an abortion. Caught in "a very firing squad of circumstances" (including a lack of money and her husband's desertion a few days after she comes home from the hospital), Laurel Lee remains as faithful and humorous as Lewis is doubtful and depressed. Her cheer is never gooey or mindless; she seems endowed by an authentic optimism and fortitude as she puts up with the unthinking cruelties of doctors. (During a lymphangiogram she asks how long certain chemicals will remain in her body; " 'Oh, for years,' " a technician replies.) Rather than waste time in resentment, Laurel Lee spends her depleted energies on the approachable. She tells Dr. Cris Maranze how she can "live on fifteen dollars a week for groceries. It was a life-style that made my mind as sharp as a stockbroker over the price trends of inseason produce . . . She wanted to know the stories of a lady at home, and I wanted to know the stories of a lady as a doctor."

One emerges from this journal certain that its author's inner life survived because she remained so avid an observer of the one outside her. Not only are there her children to be attended to ("Matthew found in a plastic bag of fruit one more mottled than the rest. 'Look Mom, it's got Hodgkin's disease'"), but also doctors to observe and classify and unexpected empathies to chart: "I suffered from many of the common geriatric problems."

One of the few times one observes her angry comes when she contrives to read some nurses' reports she is not supposed to see:

> I found if a nurse was conscious that the notes were available to the patient, it produced one kind of recording of physical movements. The notations tucked within a chart held at the desk were another style, often dealing with their perception of the patient's emotional realm.
>
> I found what seemed like tender concern from a nurse would elicit my tender confidence, only to find it distorted and recorded for the hospital world. I felt betrayed and limited their probes to the external.

Laurel Lee probably felt this sting with particular force because her own diary-keeping was so guileless. She wrote her journal for four student doctors whom she was proselytizing — in exchange for embarrassed and indulgent nods, one suspects — about Jesus Christ. She was looking for nothing else from the book, but a summertime colleague of one of the student doctors sent it to a New York publisher, and Laurel Lee, a lily of the field, suddenly found herself regarded and provided for in ways she had never expected. Her diary was acclaimed by people like Joan Didion and May Sarton, and in places like the *New York Times*. It is the sort of book that jolts a reader out of his condescending patience, the sort whose author turns from being pleasant to impressive as the 150 pages go by. That such a shift in attitude can occur is less surprising when one considers just one of Laurel Lee's nonchalant revelations, which comes on October 4, 1975: "Even the meditation of death progresses."

There are diarists who use their books to come to terms with death's more usual forerunner, old age. Alan H. Olmstead was a newspaper columnist and editor of the *Manchester Evening Herald* from 1941 until 1972. Faced that year with his sudden retirement, he decides to ease his way into the next phase of his life by transforming himself from one kind of journalist into another. The public commentator becomes a private diarist. "What would I be doing with my time now if something other than the typewriter had been the tool of my trade?" he writes in the preface to *Threshold* (1975), the published volume of his retirement diary, which turned his commentaries temporarily public once again.

In his first entry, made on Monday, September 4, 1972, he says bluntly: "I have no job to go to tomorrow morning, and I am frightened." Retirement strikes Olmstead as an imprisonment instead of the promised ticket to leisure and fulfillment. Faced with the realization that there is no longer anything "out there, in the world, which really depends on me," he panics a bit — enough to conceive of the diary as a strict daily discipline, something that will impose regular obligation, keep him from going to seed. In addition to being exercise, a sort of thinking man's golf game, it becomes the place where he can meditate on the difficulties of his new life. Some of them are small, humorous: no longer having an excuse to put things off until Sunday; having to listen to his wife run the vacuum. Others aren't so easy to dismiss in a line or two: Will he have the imagination and resignation to practice the economies forced upon him by having a Social Security check instead of a salary? Will he be able to call up enough self-esteem to fight off the cold, sweaty suspicion that he never accomplished anything in his life's work? "When I quit working in the idea factory I at first had the idea that nobody could replace me. That subsided, rather swiftly, in favor of the still comforting conclusion that nobody could fill the place as well as I had. That in turn is now yielding to a new and much less comforting realization. I am beginning to think it would never have made any difference if my particular factory had not been operating at all."

Olmstead keeps the diary for 192 straight days, from that afternoon of September 4, 1972, until March 14, 1973. Each of the entries has the relaxing shape of a "sketch" and concludes with a pleasant little exit — you can tell they were written by a man who spent years composing editorials and the occasional "Talk of the Town" *New Yorker* piece. But all those days in a row: that is not a sign of relaxation. Self-pity comes and goes, and when it comes he gives in to it. Two days after being encouraged by the recovery of a birch tree from an ice storm, he finds himself "demoralized by a feeling that this is getting to be a losing battle, after all — that the lows are going to get lower and longer, and the capacity to snap back weaker, until I am ready to sink down and bow my once foolishly proud crest in the admission that life defeats me." When he thinks about death, on Friday, February 23, he reports, almost shamefacedly, that he began "to choke up and feel passionately sorry" for himself. If this reflex fails some test of heroism, it can still be said to have sprung from a healthy love of the life that was receding, a life he could honestly recommend to the young so long as they not "expect too much happiness from any source."

In the preface to *Threshold*, written between the last entry and the time, two years later, that the book was published, Olmstead tells us he is doing well, that "pleasures and satisfactions have deepened," and that he looks forward to the returns of spring. He says that the diary-keeping not only encouraged his spirits, but has now turned out to be of practical value as well: he anticipates making some money off his new book. So we leave him with things looking up — and we wonder what happened to him beyond 1975, closing his book with that familiar disappointing feeling that every diary is a novel with its last chapters ripped out.

When Florida Scott-Maxwell — suffragist, playwright, novelist, and psychologist — reaches her eighties, she discovers that that decade of presumed senescence and decrepitude is actually a time of turbulence: "My seventies were interesting, and fairly serene, but my eighties are passionate. I grow more intense as I age. To my own surprise I burst out with hot conviction." She marvels at her "now wild heart that never used to be wild." Instead of slowly dying she is left with more life "than seems likely, convenient, or even bearable." And she suspects that what is true for her is true for others her age.

It is only when she reaches eighty-two, in 1965, that she begins a notebook, where she can follow the experience. It is to be her companion (she regrets that it cannot laugh), the place she can both speculate and moan. In it she experiences the pleasures of generalizing, being definite, assertive. Being alone comes to seem a way of being more alive, a state where it is impossible to flee the questions that keep coming to her so ungently. Who, really, is our neighbor? *Should* we have an egalitarian society? Is there a value to shyness? How many kinds of love are there? The relations between men and women; the similarities of hate and love; the afterlife — all these things are on her mind.

She was trained by Jung — but apparently not the same Jung that Nin and Progoff are so redolent of. She might agree with them that our "whole duty may be . . . to make our consciousness a finer quality," and she may describe her own experience of the unconscious as the central one of her life, but she remains aware of the intractability of evil and unhappiness in ways some of the other self-discoverers we have encountered rather frantically avoid.

She wonders whether the loss of a sense of sin has, in our time, meant a corresponding loss of emotional inten-

sity, and whether goodness can have any meaning without
the acknowledgment of its opposite. "I never found it
possible to ignore man's plight even when I was busy
living it," she explains, "and now in my idleness it has
me by the scruff of the neck." So it is man's plight that
goes into the notebook as much as her own. Florida
Scott-Maxwell shows that traveling outward and inward
at the same time is less a matter of physical impossibility
than a condition of mental health and moral well-being.
Her notebook becomes a more supple and scrupulous
document the more she fills it, and it is only when she
gets the rare chance to do some literal traveling that she
would prefer to drop it. "I am off," she writes, after the
surgeon tells her she is sufficiently recovered from a gall-
bladder operation to visit her grandchildren, "and I leave
my note book behind. What need of a note book when
one is out in the world?"

The genesis of diaries kept for spiritual purposes isn't
completely clear, but there is substantial evidence to suggest that the practice began among Reformed clergymen
in East Anglia late in the sixteenth century as a means of
magnifying their godliness. As the historian of diaries
David Shields has written, the diary became the place
where these divines examined their consciences and prepared themselves for encounters with God in prayer and
communion. There is even some evidence that these East
Anglians (meeting secretly, much against Queen Elizabeth's liking) exchanged their diaries, like Puritan Pro-
goffians, for each others' additional edification. A great
Protestant art form had been created, and during the
middle of the seventeenth century the habit of charting
one's spiritual progress in a diary was extremely common
among Nonconformists, who were writing wagonloads
of diaries that were as self-punishing as Pepys's was self-
indulgent. By 1656 John Beadle's instruction manual on
how to keep *The Journal or Diary of a Thankful Christian* had appeared.

The practice spread to America, where for a long time it was the habit only of the clergy. Despite its relative confinement, though, its products remain of great importance to American history and literature: as long as there have been Americans there have been American diaries. They were, in fact, being written as the first boats approached the shores. Richard Mather, father of Increase and grandfather of Cotton, came to America in 1635, when he was thirty-nine, and soon became a minister in Dorchester. His journal of the Atlantic crossing — in a ship with twenty-three seamen, a hundred passengers, twenty-three cows and heifers, eight mares, and three sucking calves — includes an account of a terrible storm off Cape Ann on April 15, 1635, a calamity in which one Richard Becon lost his right hand while trying to help some of the seamen with a cable. The subsequent meditating the Reverend Mather performs in his diary allows him to accept God's will: "But in all yᵉ grievous storme, my feare was yᵉ lesse, when I considered yᵉ clearenesse of my calling from God this way, and in some measure (yᵉ Lords holy name be blessed for it) he gave us hearts contented."

A century later, Jonathan Edwards would be keeping strict accounts of his spiritual life in a journal he begins (at least in the manuscript that survived for a time) when he is nineteen. The diary seems to have grown out of a series of resolutions Edwards made, and against which he would sometimes dovetail the record of his actual conduct. For example, on Saturday morning, July 13, 1723, he writes: "Transferred the conclusion of June 9, to the Resolution, No. 57; and the conclusion of May 27, to No. 58; and May 12, and July 11, to No. 59; and of July 4, *at night*, to No. 60." And so on. He can berate himself for feeling "dull, dry and dead" on a given day, and although he is aware of the dangers to one's health from excessive self-mortification, he has enough resoluteness to commit himself to an occasional cold shower of mathematics: "When I am violently beset with temptation, or cannot rid myself of evil thoughts," he resolves, on July 27, 1723, "to do some sum of Arithmetic, or Geometry, or some other study, which necessarily engages all my thoughts, and unavoidably keeps them from wandering." When he is a tutor at Yale, in 1725, he chides himself for a lack of gentleness. A few years later, serving with his grandfather as a minister in Northampton, Massachusetts, he combines his spiritual self-exhortation with some of the Franklinesque industry that was soon to be such a hallmark of the American character: "I think Christ has recommended rising early in the morning, by his rising from the grave very early." He keeps some of the diary in cipher, and for this measure in aid of privacy he also has a biblical justification: "Remember to act according to Prov. xii, 23, *A prudent man concealeth knowledge.*"

If Edwards's Protestantism chills us with its rigor, it is nothing less than soothing compared to the prescriptions for Christianity bitterly spat into the last journals kept by Søren Kierkegaard before his death in 1855. In these books he doesn't search for certainties; he proclaims them, and decries all those who pervert or shrink from their manifestness. These last journals are marked by a sustained hysteria, perhaps even madness. But it hardly needs saying that madness is a relative term. Kierkegaard's earth may be the bleakest vale of tears a theologian ever imagined, but looked at another way his consistent doomsaying can still be a bracing antidote to the Pippan gladness of Progoff and Nin. He is not concerned with finding himself; he is intent on seeing men lose themselves in absolute obedience to God's majesty. The Christianity of the New Testament, he tells us, is a fire, a wound; Luther made a mistake when he saw it as a source of calm. Kierkegaard again and again cries anathemas against world history (a thing of no importance); priests and professors ("parasites" who have made good livings by softening Christianity and making it available to all on a come-and-get-it basis); and the state Church (most powerfully personified in the worldliness of the late Bishop Mynster). In order to love God, one must hate the world and one must suffer.

These writings are for the most part impersonal in a manner appropriate to someone who loathed the inconsequentiality of being human. But occasionally Kierkegaard does use his journal to comment on the loneliness of being the *vox clamans* in the bourgeois Danish wilderness. Refusing to shrink from his task — "to put a halt to a lying diffusion of Christianity, and to help it shake off a mass of nominal Christians" — he suffers from the "immense strain" imposed by his "heterogeneity," and considers the public humiliations inflicted on him by the newspapers to be part of a new kind of martyrdom. Even after he passes through the extremely strait gate toward his reward, he still expects to suffer the ironic punishment of having his writings (including the journals) pillaged by those for whom he always had the greatest contempt: "When I am dead all that I have said will be grist to the mill of the professor."

When the young Thomas Merton keeps a journal, between 1939 and 1941, before his entrance into the monastery, he has occasion to consider Kierkegaard's idea (which he paraphrases) of "the essential incommunicability of the highest form of religious experience." Most of Merton's journal is written while he is a graduate student at Columbia and an instructor at Saint Bonaventure University. It also covers a trip to Cuba (Havana is "an analogy of the kingdom of heaven") and a retreat — a kind of trial run — to the Abbey of Our Lady of Gethsemani in Ohio. During all this time he ponders what form his service to Christ will take. Kierkegaard's rather brutal distinction between kinds of religious experience and sacrifice probably stays in his mind as he attempts to choose between a monastic life and a more socially involved one at Friendship House, a Catholic mission in Harlem founded by Baroness Catherine de Hueck.

During the two years before he enters the monastery

Merton shows himself receptive to revelation. He realizes
that we sometimes grasp whole truths more suddenly than
we later come to understand their aspects and details. On
April 29, 1940, after listening to children singing a hymn
in the church of San Francisco in Havana, he writes:

> To say that this was the experience of some kind of
> certainty is to place it as it were in the order of knowl-
> edge, but it was not just the apprehension of a reality,
> or a truth, but at the same time and equally a strong
> movement of delight, great delight, like a great shout
> of joy, and in other words it was as much an experi-
> ence of loving as of knowing something, and in it love
> and knowledge were completely inseparable. All this
> was caused directly by the great mercy and kindness of
> God when I heard the voices of the children cry out
> "I believe" in front of the altar of St. Francis.

Were Kierkegaard able to read this account he would no
doubt probe it for evidence of slackness and sentimentality; but there are certainly parallels to the "indescribable joy" he himself experiences at 10:30 A.M. on May
19, 1838.

Merton relishes the idea of new beginnings. He mentions, on December 4, 1940, the pleasure of tearing out
the pages of old journals, and four months afterward,
when he first goes to the abbey for his retreat, he writes:
"I should tear out all the other pages of this book, and
all the other pages of anything else I have ever written,
and begin here." A few days later, Holy Thursday, he
witnesses the ceremony during which the monks wash
the feet of poor men, and in relieved astonishment at the
genuineness of it, he writes: "What all the spring I had
looked forward to finding, when I started from St. Bonaventure, is here." In fact, this discovery would still be
followed by some indecision. Months pass before he
actually enters the order, and on the last page of *A Secular
Journal*, Merton is still wondering: "Would I not be
obliged to admit, now, that if there is a choice for me

between Harlem and the Trappists, I would not hesitate to take the Trappists? Is that why I hesitate to find out if the choice exists? Is that my roundabout way of evading my vocation?" Only at the bottom of that page does he admit the "awe" and (somewhat paradoxically) "desire" he feels at the idea of giving up *everything*. "I shall speak to one of the Friars," he at last decides.

To read Merton is to witness a sort of measured ecstasy. He brings one neither to the stone floors of Kierkegaard nor the slaphappy apogees of the self-actualizers. He admits that, finally, our identities can be known only to God, and that insofar as we can approach such knowledge at all, we are approaching the pleasures of humility rather than any pride in our potential. Thinking about Dante, he considers that it may be "easier to write well of a difficult progress, like the arduous climbing through purgatory, than of the swift, breathtaking movement through the nine spheres of heaven," a suspicion the reader of some of the diaries in this chapter may well share.

Merton's *Secular Journal* shows the spiritual movement that would take him from the *vita activa* to the *vita contemplativa*. But its publication, in 1959, offered an ironic boon from the latter life to the former: royalties from it went to Catherine de Hueck Doherty's Madonna House, whose works involve "the broad Social Apostolate of the Church."

If Kierkegaard's journal shows faith's fierce certainty, and Merton's its gradual movement to vocation, other journals record its crises and crumblings. The American poet Annie Dillard's book *Holy the Firm* covers but three days in her life, but manages to preserve both the sudden undermining and reaffirmation of her belief in God. She lives alone — and deliberately — on Puget Sound, seeing herself, in her one-room house, as "a backdrop to all the landscape's occasions," and finding calm but transcendent meaning in the movements of the ordinary. November 18 is a Wednesday, a clear day with no wind:

Terry Wean — who fishes, and takes my poetry course
— could see Mount Rainier. He hauls his reef net gear
from the bay; we talk on its deck while he hammers at
shrunken knots. The Moores for dinner. In bed, I call
to me my sad cat, I read. Like a rug or wrap rolling
unformed up a loom, the day discovers itself, like the
poem.

But the next day something happens: "Into this world
falls a plane." Its wing gets snarled in a treetop; it crashes
and explodes, and a seven-year-old girl named Julie Norwich has her face burned off. Dillard had seen the girl
just once, two weeks before, and been struck by a certain resemblance between the two of them. Now God has
done this: He is "a brute and traitor," a malevolence that
"despises everything, apparently." *Is* this God's work?
Or is He without any hand in it, merely indifferent, "a
holy fire burning self-contained for power's sake alone"?
Dillard sits at the window and chews on her wrist and
tries to pray for Julie and her parents. But she believes —
today — that God is a "glacier."

By Friday she is ready, desperate, to worship Him "by
any means ready to hand," telling herself that we do
need, perhaps, these reminders that God is free to let
time move as it will, and to refrain, if He wishes, from
sticking "a nickel's worth of sense into our days." We
control nothing. She meditates on Holy the Firm, "matter at its dullest," a substance thought to be found lower
than salt and therefore touching the base of the Absolute:
"Does something that touched something that touched
Holy the Firm in touch with the Absolute at base seep
into ground water, into grain; are islands rooted in it, and
trees? Of course." She decides in the end that Holy the
Firm is the philosopher's stone — and it seems to lead her
to an acceptance of Julie Norwich's fate. She imagines
a future for her as a nun, a kind of ecstatic, saved from
earthly love by her horrible facelessness. The burning
comes to seem like a baptism.

But at the last minute Dillard changes her mind. She decides that plastic surgeons will make Julie Norwich's face all right, that the crash will be just a story to tell her husband someday; that she'll be happy, have children: "So live. I'll be the nun for you. I am now." What does one make of these sudden swings? Can one take them seriously, believe in them as resolution? If they are that, does the final portion of the meditation imply that God burned Julie Norwich's face for *her*, for Annie Dillard? On the day of the crash, Dillard writes: "Give the mind two seconds alone and it thinks it's Pythagoras." Is her conclusion about Julie just a two-second theorem, a fake palliative that could never withstand the real geometry of the universe? Has anything really been concluded? Perhaps we have had a demonstration of journal-keeping's autosuggestiveness, its ability to soothe, like driving or plate-breaking, if it is done quickly and assiduously enough during a crisis. Between November 19 and 20 Annie Dillard appears to have written enough to fill fifty pages. She in fact worked on the book for more than a year, but if its original, raw form contained as much as the final version, one still wonders: Is there something about writing so much so fast that inevitably leads to a kind of drained resolution, the pen having been turned into a runner that knows, perhaps not consciously, that it will break the tape and collapse in exhausted victory? If that is so, when one wakes from the rest that follows, is the victory still real, still there?

The journal of Angelo Roncalli — Pope John XXIII — was kept for more than sixty-five years, and if its reader looks for a crisis of doubt on the order of Annie Dillard's, he will look in vain. It is not a diary in which one finds the hard lecturing of Kierkegaard, or the tentative gropings toward a mission that one sees in Merton. One finds only the long record of a soul certain of its task and doubtful of its worthiness. The long diary was kept haphazardly, sometimes in notebooks, sometimes on loose sheets, sometimes in handwriting, and sometimes

on a typewriter. During his papacy, John went over the
material and made a few revisions, mostly to style. When
he went over the pages from 1895–1899, his editor tells
us, he said, "with his mild eyes suffused with tears . . .
'I was a good boy, innocent, somewhat timid. I wanted
to love God at all costs and my one idea was to become
a priest, in the service of simple souls who needed patient
and attentive care. Meanwhile I had to fight an enemy
within me, self-love, and in the end I was able to get the
better of it.' "

The journals written when he was a seminarian reveal
a very different person from the twinkling John of old
age. They show a serious young man always at war with
pride and the flickers of ambition. To those not called
to the religious life they will seem self-tormenting. There
is little record of the outer life in them. They are used
to sharpen his conscience and commitment. They are
never relaxed or humorous. In the seminary he frequently
rates the day as bad or not so bad on the basis of how
well he has maintained his devotion. It is perhaps a reflection of our secular selves that we see such appraisals
as more abstract than intimate. (And yet John is reported
to have said, " 'My soul is in these pages.' ") Even so there
remains the intimacy produced by sheer immediacy. The
bell rings for the end of the retreat, and so an entry must
be broken off; or, one April Sunday decades later, the
day's notes end with the sound of Easter bells nearby.

The entries are a steady stream of resolves. In 1897, as
a seminarian in Bergamo, Angelo vows to fight any lustful sensations by putting a rosary around his neck and
sleeping with his arms folded across his chest. More than
sixty years later, as pope, he can review his life during a
retreat at Castel Gandolfo and make the entry: "*Sins*:
Concerning *chastity* in my relations with myself, in im-
modest intimacies: nothing serious, *ever*." Going on a
retreat in 1950 he brings with him the journals kept over
the past twenty-five years, hoping they will serve as an
aid to self-examination. Their usefulness lies in their the-

matic constancy: pride continues to be the sin they fight down, year after year. In 1904, the year of his ordination, Roncalli is criticizing the ego that fueled his intense studying, "which was really [done] with a view to cutting a dash in the examinations." On a retreat in Istanbul thirty-five years later, when he is making his way up the ranks of the church, he feels compelled to note: "There is no lack of rumour around me, murmurs that 'greater things are in store.' I am not so foolish as to listen to this flattery, which is, yes, I admit it, for me too a temptation."

His rise is not spectacular. In 1945 he is sixty-three years old and trying to cope with the approach of old age; his election to the papacy is still thirteen years away. In 1961, three years into his unexpectedly innovative reign, he reflects:

> When on 28 October, 1958, the Cardinals of the Holy Roman Church chose me to assume the supreme responsibility of ruling the universal flock of Jesus Christ, at seventy-seven years of age, everyone was convinced that I would be a provisional and transitional Pope. Yet here I am, already on the eve of the fourth year of my pontificate, with an immense programme of work in front of me to be carried out before the eyes of the whole world, which is watching and waiting. As for myself, I feel like St. Martin, who "neither feared to die, nor refused to live."

He knows he is surprising people, and he is enjoying it. He cannot resist giving in ever so slightly to the pride he has always used the journals to quell. It is not easy to fight the ego in a diary. Whenever one attempts it, one is fighting on the opponent's home ground.

John XXIII reigned in Rome during that period a quarter century ago when the world was directed by more remarkable personalities than it is today — Kennedy, Khrushchev, and De Gaulle among them. If at that time the whole world had at least a nominal leader, it was

the Secretary-General of the United Nations, Dag Hammarskjöld, whose book, *Markings*, reveals intensities of
reflection and anguish one hardly associates with a diplomat, who is after all supposed to be the calming conduit
between overwrought adversaries.

Beginning in the 1920s, and with more urgency through
the 1950s, Hammarskjöld keeps a private book filled with
short poems, quotations, questions, orders, and rebukes,
a book in which he tries to bring his lonely personal life,
cluttered public life, and tentative spiritual life into some
kind of balance acceptable to God. *Markings* is an extremely abstract work: there is no reference in it to particular public events; individuals are never more than
pronouns; entries may or may not appear with dates.
Like Thoreau's journals it is full of pronouncements on
universals; but unlike those books kept a century before,
it rarely shows us the concrete incident provoking the
axiom.

Still, a picture of a man emerges, in however bleak a
fashion. Reading *Markings* is not unlike watching a
movie by Hammarskjöld's countryman Ingmar Bergman.
(It even contains scenes of surreal symbolism, such as one
of men waiting at a counter that appears to be a "polished
black marble tombstone.") Hammarskjöld is proud but
guilty, self-absorbed but self-loathing, trying constantly
to convert despair into duty, forever fueling himself with
"that pain in the soul which drives us beyond ourselves."
The first entry, made around 1925, asks, "Shall I ever
get there?"; thirty years later he confronts his continuing
failure to arrive: "*Never* at your destination. — The
greater task is only a higher class in this school, as you
draw closer to your final exam, which nobody else will
know about, because then you will be *completely alone.*"

Dag Hammarskjöld seems to have been alone nearly all
his life. The sense of solitary misery given off by *Markings* is at times overwhelming. He tries to tell himself that
"loneliness can be a communion," but on the same page
he must admit: "We reach out towards the other. In

vain — because we have never dared to give ourselves."
There is an enforced and embittered sexlessness throughout the years of jottings. He worries about the dangers of
lust, and makes attempts to find any compensation he can
for his unrequited passions:

> Perhaps a great love is never returned. Had it been
> given warmth and shelter by its counterpart in the
> Other, perhaps it would have been hindered from ever
> growing to maturity.
>
> It "gives" us nothing. But in its world of loneliness
> it leads us up to summits with wide vistas — of insight.

He tries to reason himself into the belief that when the
Lover ceases to expect anything from the Beloved all will
be well for both of them. But finally he must return to
his own sense of guilty estrangement: "How undisguised
your thick-skinned self-satisfied loneliness appeared before his naked agony as he struggled to make a living
contact. How difficult you found it to help, when con-
fronted in another by your own problem — uncor-
rupted." He knows his "personal" feelings must be sub-
ordinated to something larger; but he also entertains the
possibility that "it is better for the health of the soul to
make one man good than 'to sacrifice oneself for mankind.'"

Hammarskjöld comes to preside over the organization
identified more than any other in the world with idle
words and cocktails, even though he knows how exhausting being "sociable" is: "In miniature, one of the
many ways in which mankind successfully acts as its own
scourge — in the hell of spiritual death." His chief hope
is that his loneliness will somehow mutate into usefulness, that it will propel him toward "finding something
to live for, great enough to die for." More than once he
expresses hope that he can pursue a vision, a course of
action, single-mindedly. He subscribes to the Kantian
maxim, "Treat others as ends, never as means," but realizes that self-interest is tolerable if it can be made to

serve a larger goal. By the time he has his UN post he knows that "the road to holiness necessarily passes through the world of action."

On occasion Hammarskjöld confesses to a sacrificial death wish, and in reading these entries one of course recalls his actual end in a plane crash over Africa during September 1961, when he was on his way to mediate the Congolese war. But the editor of *Markings*, W. H. Auden (whose own notebook we will encounter shortly), properly steers us away from seeing that end as an appropriate, if horrifying, fulfillment of Hammarskjöld's need to give himself up to the doing of God's work: "It could happen to any of us, regardless of any 'commitment.' " More than any picture of successful sacrifice, it is in fact Dag Hammarskjöld's laceration of himself that makes an impression on the reader. He attacks his own vanity, his spiritual pride, his tendency to take on responsibility out of "laziness, ignorance, consciousness of an audience (were it only your own reflection in the mirror)"; he propounds the need for self-effacement, an active humiliation. It is, however noble, a bleak world of unworthiness that he continues to inhabit.

His fearful awareness of pride is very much connected to keeping the diary itself. He may at one point view it as an automatic enterprise ("the book my days are writing"), but he knows in fact that it is his ego scratching out the entries, just as it is his ego he catches preening for posterity in all its daily actions. On November 29, 1956, he credits Faulkner with the reflection that "our final wish is to have scribbled on the wall our 'Kilroy was here.' " He worries about taking pride of authorship in what began as personal aids to reflection; by 1956 it is implausible to assume they will not be seen by others as well: "These notes? — They were signposts you began to set up after you had reached a point where you needed them, a fixed point that was on no account to be lost sight of. And so they have remained. But your life has changed, and now you reckon with possible readers, even, perhaps, hope for them. Still, perhaps it may be of interest to some-body to learn about a path about which the traveler who was committed to it did not wish to speak while he was alive. Perhaps — but only if what you write has an honesty with no trace of vanity or self-regard."

The idea of other readers grows slowly in him. A number of times before this entry he considers their possibility and remains uncertain. But by the mid-fifties, when he is known throughout the world, it is inevitable that the public will be invited into what he finally calls, in a letter to the Swedish Permanent Under-Secretary for Foreign Affairs instructing that it be published, "a sort of *white book* concerning my negotiations with myself — and with God." He knows the markings will constitute the only reliable biography that could be written of him, since he has come to recognize this lifelong act of "anamnesis" — remembering, calling to mind — as the "Ariadne's thread" that strings the elements of his existence together. And, finally, the book would also be his belated cry to the Other he apparently could never reach. Stark and "white," *Markings* is a journey into something like light, but it is the light given off by a midnight sun.

4

Creators

*26 April . . . Welcome, O life! I go
to encounter for the millionth time
the reality of experience and to forge
in the smithy of my soul the uncreated
conscience of my race.*
— *A Portrait of the Artist
as a Young Man*

STEPHEN DEDALUS WROTE the words above just before leaving to seek creative glory on the Continent. He
would, alas, come back to Ireland a failure, and have to
content himself with becoming only the chief supporting
player in the most important novel of the century. But
unless an artist's creative reach is allowed to exceed his
grasp, then what's a diary for? The makers of earthly
objects of beauty have needed books in which to sketch
and brainstorm, private pages on which invention's au-
dacity can fly or fail, where the words and shapes and
rhythms and systems that educate humankind's sense and
imagination can first come to life. In this chapter, as in
the others, I will suggest the waterfront more than cover
it, as we look at the private books of some poets and
novelists, as well as scattered representatives of painting,
photography, architecture, dance, science, and philosophy. This particular shoreline is especially slippery, not
just vast, because the books in question so often hesitate
and shift between the personal and the professional. In
some of them notes for projects are crowded by reports
on romance and the weather; in others, more sober ones,

the subject matter is more strictly, if never quite hermetically, the creative business at hand. Just as the distinction between *journal* and *diary* eludes clarification, the point at which a diary becomes a notebook, and vice versa, is difficult to locate.

One forerunner of the diary has historically been used more to regard art than create it. It was the practice of making a record of one's reading, or of whatever information came one's way, that gave rise to those diaries still known as commonplace books. The special interest of those kept by artists is obvious: What piece of reading or news may have triggered a particular line of verse, or perhaps a whole painting? For writers, especially, commonplace books are the records of influence, but they have for centuries been kept by blocked writers and nonwriters as well. We do not have Shakespeare's commonplace book, but we do have evidence that one of his creations, perhaps the most blocked person of all time, kept a sort of commonplace book: "My tables, — meet it is I set it down," Hamlet says in Act I, Scene v, making a note of what he has just learned from his father's ghost — namely, "That one may smile, and smile, and be a villain." He hopes the notation will be a spur toward revenge.

Someone still unknown in a Sussex manor house during the fifteenth century was filling one of these books with sayings, prayers, bits from the poet Lydgate, puzzles, a saint's life, a religious play, and other pieces of practical and literary knowledge that came his or her way. In the same book also went writings about manorial law; and when Robert Melton, who may have been the Cornwallis family's steward, got hold of the book and found there was yet some blank space in it he used it to keep his accounts. Somebody else stuck in a prescription for yellow jaundice: "Fresh rosmary, tyme, betany, nepe, izope, selendyn. safurun, long pepur, clowes, grennys, hony, tarmaraks. Nutmygges, and greynys, and long peper, senamun and clowes, masys." This five-hundred-year-old volume (published as *A Common-place Book of the Fifteenth Century* in 1886 by Lucy Toulmin Smith) shows that such books could be not merely elastic in function but promiscuous in ownership as well.

Inside most commonplace books there is a personal diary trying to get out. One can rarely read without reacting, and once one begins to comment as well as list, the engines of personality and narrative have started running. John Manningham, a law student at the Middle Temple in the final days of Elizabeth I's reign, seems to have done more listening than reading in whatever spare time he had for self-improvement. He was a great sermongoer, and he left behind a kind of auricular commonplace book full of detailed accounts of what he heard the great preachers of London and Cambridge saying at the beginning of what would turn into the most religiously contentious century in England's history. So detailed are some of his reports that his posthumous editors suspect he had his four-by-six-inch notebook right on his lap at church, or at least some paper there on which to make shorthand notes for later transcription. Manningham does not content himself with recording the preacher's reflections on the day's text; he also judges the performance. There is, in fact, a bit of the opening-night critic in him. One minister speaks his piece with "a hanging looke, a gloting eye, and a tossing learing jeasture."

Manningham's notes about and quotations from books — bits from Themistocles and *Albion's England* — are generally less interesting to modern readers than his eye-witness clerical dispatches. But a few of Manningham's reports on writers have proved memorable. There is in town along with him a young man named Donne, also working at the law, and Manningham transcribes a list of his colleague's paradoxes that have begun to circulate. Marston and Greene and Spenser are all on the scene, and Manningham puts down a few of the things they've been saying, too. He is not much of a playgoer, it seems, but there is the following report: "FEBR. 1601. 2. At our feast we had a play called 'Twelve night, or what you will' . . . A good practise in it to make the steward beleeve his Lady widdowe was in Love with him, by counterfayting a letter, as from his Lady, in generall termes, telling him what shee liked best in him, and prescribing his gesture in smiling, his apparraile, &c., and then when he came to practise, making him beleeve they tooke him to be mad." This is not perhaps very penetrating criticism, but we see he got the jokes. As for Shakespeare himself, the story that he kept Burbage (who had just played Richard III) from a woman's bed by reminding him that William the Conqueror came before Richard was kept alive by Manningham's book.

Manningham has enough appetite for the life of his times that his sermon summaries keep getting jostled by other matters: news of "connycatching" schemes current in London; military news from the Continent; the latest in Italian manners, the rage for shuttlecock; and who's up and down at court are among the items that creep into his pages. Early in 1603 the rumors of Elizabeth's illness, the news of her death, the anxieties over the succession (and rumors of rebellion), and the relief at the apparently smooth accession of James I, come into the book. So does news of an Elizabethan medical breakthrough: "They make incision and then grope for the stone with an other toole which they call a duckes bill. Yf the stone be greater then may be drawne forth at the hole made by the seame, the partie dyes for it." This is the operation Pepys would pull through in 1658. Had he not, Manningham's fellow alumnus of Magdalene College would never have begun the diary that each year marked March 26 as the happy anniversary of his surgery.

Although he shows little of their cynicism, Manningham has something of the Goncourts' knack for overhearing things: "A whore is noe worse then a Catt, for she plays with her tayle, and a whore does noe more.

(One in the tillbuow as I came from Lond.).) "The better remarks of his legal friends Edward Curle and Charles Danvers also get into his book. Manningham was no genius. He was not, like Charles Dickens, a whiz at short-hand about to go on to great feats of the imagination. But he was clearly clever, and he was no less a wit-monger than the average university graduate trying to make it in Elizabeth's London. He probably used his book to store up snappy comebacks he hoped he'd get the chance to use at a later date. As his editor, Robert Parker Sorlien, shrewdly notes: "He used the Diary partly as a training ground to exercise his wit." And so he was something of an artist. What was it he hoped to create? Well, an impression. He does not want to quote as obsessively as Dr. John Reynolds ("He does as yf a begger should come and pouer all his scraps out of his wallet at a riche mans table"), but he does want to remember a reasonable number of good ones to fire off. He sees his commonplace book as the magazine from which he can reload.

He also seems aware, like any other diarist, of what his book may do for him with audiences he will no longer be alive to address personally. On folio sheet 64b is a couplet apparently of his own making:

> Goe little booke, I envy not thy lott,
> Though thou shalt goe where I my selfe cannot.

If Manningham was a young man in a hurry, John Milton, who would be a contestant in the religious wars dimly discernible in the former's commonplace book, was about as deliberate as a man could get. By his own admission "long choosing, and beginning late" when it came to his epic subject, Milton prepared himself with more lengthy and intentional learning than any poet before or since. His commonplace book is not thick, but it does suggest the university of philosophy, history, and poetry that he made his own before presuming to justify the ways of God to man. Scholars have made more use of it than of any document of its kind. The custom of keeping such books has managed to survive in a more relaxed manner among poets as recently departed and famously sloppy as W. H. Auden. A few years before he died Auden published *A Certain World*, an arrangement of his commonplace book under alphabetized subject headings. It seems very much the work of the "later" Auden — mature, convivial, and cagey — especially when it comes to the lip-smacking biographers he knew were waiting to pick bare his imaginative remains. He didn't like the notion of writers' lives being written (he called upon his correspondents to destroy his letters), and he offered up his commonplace book as a sort of substitute autobiography. It was "a map of [his] planet," he conceded, and as much as a reader was going to get out of him in any case. Alas, the snippets and annotations of *A Certain World* are pretty whimsical and evasive. If it's a map, it's on the order of the road map one laughs over after having given up trying to fold it. One thing, however, that does emerge from it is that Auden liked to read and think about diaries, among them the clergyman Francis Kilvert's, Virginia Woolf's, and Goethe's — including the latter's remarks on limestone, the subject of Auden's most famous poem of praise. But his anti-biographical suspicions were alert here as well. Think of the harm a diary can do to a person who makes only a single appearance in it, he warns. After he quotes from Benjamin John Armstrong's diary of January 3, 1854 (" 'In the evening went to a party at Mr. Anfrere's. Very slow — small rooms, piano out of tune, bad wine, and stupid people' "), Auden sighs: "Poor Mr. Anfrere! No doubt he had many virtues, but to posterity he is simply an incompetent host." It is only in his poem "The Horatians" that Auden seems to look with real kindness upon diaries, as he considers those written by ordinarily sane mortals, those even-tempered and unexciting people who keep the world going:

Some of you have written poems, usually
short ones, and some kept diaries, seldom published
    till after your deaths, but most
    make no memorable impact

except on your friends and dogs. Enthusiastic
Youth writes you off as cold, who cannot be found on
    barricades, and never shoot
    either yourselves or your lovers.

Dorothy Wordsworth was certainly one of these who
served and waited — upon her famous brother William.
In fact, she could even be said to have kept his commonplace book for him; for while her Grasmere journal
(1800–1803) is of great interest as an account of how life
in the English Lake District affected her own receptive
sensibility, it is also the most complete record we have
of her brother's reading and movements in his most creative years. She decides to keep it because she can "give
Wm. pleasure by it," and it is indeed brimful of sisterly
solicitude and anxiety. Dorothy copies his poems, reads
to him, keeps quiet for him, pets his headaches, and frets
over the toll his creativity takes. On Thursday, October
23, 1800, William is "not successful in composition in the
evening"; the following Monday he has "fatigued himself with altering"; a month later he is "very well, and
highly poetical." Living among geniuses in the process
of redirecting poetry from classic to romantic could be
trying, and Dorothy's sympathy is not always appreciated:

November 10th, Thursday. Poor C. [oleridge] left us
. . . Every sight and every sound reminded me of him
— dear, dear fellow, of his many walks to us by day
and by night, of all dear things. I was melancholy, and
could not talk, but at last I eased my heart by weeping
— nervous blubbering, says William. It is not so. O!
how many, many reasons have I to be anxious for him.

If there seems to be here more than a hint of the imperious Poet Laureate who was to live on in ever-increasing self-esteem for another fifty years, the reader should not jump to the conclusion that the charter Romantic thought all tears mere "blubbering." On February 2, 1801, for instance, he can himself be found crying, over Book XI of *Paradise Lost*, which Dorothy is reading aloud after tea.

Dorothy thrills before the products of genius ("Read L.B. [*Lyrical Ballads*]. Blessings on that Brother of mine!"), but without her Grasmere journal we would have less of an idea about how casually certain such products come into being. "To a Butterfly," for example, first came to Wordsworth one Sunday morning when he had gotten up, not for the last time, on the wrong side of the bed:

> William had slept badly — he got up at nine o'clock, but before he rose he had finished *The Beggar Boys*, and while we were at breakfast that is (for I had breakfasted) he, with his basin of broth before him untouched, and a little plate of bread and butter he wrote the Poem to a Butterfly! He ate not a morsel, nor put on his stockings, but sate with his shirt neck unbuttoned, and his waist coat open while he did it. The thought first came upon him as we were talking about the pleasure we both always feel at the sight of a butterfly. I told him that I used to chase them a little, but that I was afraid of brushing the dust off their wings, and did not catch them. He told me how they used to kill the white ones when he went to school because they were Frenchmen. Mr Simpson came in just as he was finishing the Poem.

That evening he is making alterations to the poem in which Dorothy, recognizable despite her alias, appears:

> Oh! pleasant, pleasant were the days,
> The time, when, in our childish plays,

My sister Emmeline and I
Together chased the butterfly!
A very hunter did I rush
Upon the prey: — with leaps and springs
I followed on from brake to bush;
But she, God love her, feared to brush
The dust from off its wings.

The most casual report of literary history in Dorothy's journal occurs about two weeks later: "A divine morning. At breakfast William wrote part of an ode." It was "Intimations of Immortality."

Dorothy Wordsworth's sisterly aid to scholars of Wordsworth has a counterpart in Mary Shelley's wifely assistance to pursuers of Shelley. The journal she keeps during her marriage to the poet is a very full record of Shelley's and her reading; of his current work and her assistance to him in copying it out; and of the progress of her own drawing and study. Many of the entries are lean and tabular, but they are invaluable evidence of what Shelley's mind and hers are up to on a given day: May 14, 1817 — "Read Pliny and Clarke. Shelley reads 'History of the French Revolution,' and corrects 'Frankenstein.' Write Preface. Finis."

This being the late Romantic era, other sons of light inevitably show up in the journal's pages. On February 5, 1817, a day Mary walks on the heath and reads "Tales of My Landlord," "Messrs. Keats and Reynolds sup at Hampstead." This is the first appearance Keats makes in the journal; his last comes on July 12, 1821: "Write. Read Homer. Dine at Pugnano. Read Shelley's 'Adonais.' " We know that the elegy first went to press the very next day in Pisa.

In that poem Shelley speaks of joining Keats on the unknown waters of the afterlife. When a year later the seas have quite literally claimed him, his widow puts the journal in which she has made a record of their creative work to new use. It changes from being an elaborate commonplace book and calendar to being the chamber in which Mary Shelley can discharge her grief. Nearly three months after Shelley's death she once more takes up the book she had last written in the day Shelley's boat sank off Via Reggio:

> And I begin again? Oh, never! But several motives induce me, when the day has gone down, and all is silent around me, steeped in sleep, to pen as occasion wills, my reflections and feelings . . . I have no friend. For eight years I communicated, with unlimited freedom, with one whose genius, far transcending mine, awakened and guided my thoughts. I conversed with him . . . and my mind was satisfied. Now I am alone — oh, how alone! The stars may behold my tears, and the winds drink my sighs; but my thoughts are a sealed treasure, which I can confide to none. But can I express all I feel?

Even as she doubts her ability to find words adequate to her sorrow, she is finding them, writing them — in short, using the journal to the very end she doubts its pages can reach. She even uses it as a medium through which she can speak with Shelley himself: "Well, then, now I am reduced to these white pages, which I am to blot with dark imagery. As I write, let me think what he would have said if, speaking thus to him, he could have answered me. Yes, my own heart, I would fain know what to think of my desolate state; what you think I ought to do, what to think."

In the preface she wrote to the first collected edition of Shelley's verses (1839), Mary explained how she used her still-fresh impressions of her life with Shelley in fashioning notes about the different poems' origins. The journals helped keep those impressions clear and useful. Mary Shelley in fact clearly preferred the first spare ledgerlike life of her journals to their later expansive and emotional one. A dozen years after Shelley's death, she wrote: "It has struck me what a very imperfect picture (only *no one* will ever see it) these querulous pages afford of *me*. This arises from their being the record of my feelings, and not of my imagination." She wished, it would seem, for posterity to see what her life was with Shelley, but not what it became afterward. But her parenthetical note is not much more than the diarist's usual way of protesting too much. Late in 1822, after all, Mary Shelley wrote: "But people must know little of me who think that, abstractedly, I am content with my present mode of life." The journal was, as she no doubt knew it would be, one more means of setting them straight.

One imagines much in the writings of Mary Shelley that would displease Helen Bevington, scholar of neo-classical literature and maker of light verse with neo-classical regularity. But there are some parallels to be found between her journal and the one kept by Shelley's wife and widow. *Along Came the Witch* is a sampling of Mrs. Bevington's diaries from the 1960s, and it demonstrates that the commonplace book habit is still alive. Mrs. Bevington, a professor of English at Duke, shows herself to be dauntingly well read and invariably equipped with the apposite quotation, or a half dozen of them, for whatever situation life puts her into. Her journals are full of snippets that chain-react into lists:

Name-calling:
   Sydney Smith called Macaulay "a book in
      britches."
   Macaulay called Horace Walpole "a heartless
      fribble."
   Horace Walpole called Lady Mary Montagu
      "an old, foul, tawdry, painted, plastered
      personage."

There are nine more before she concludes with a verse of her own:

Fools, sots, buffoons,
Dolts, noodles, loons —
Mere names to call
But true withal.

She seems to be one of those excessively sane people who react to everything in life with exasperating (and sometimes a trifle smug) good sense. Still, if her reading and quotation verge on the compulsive, it is useful to remember that there are worse compulsions: Mrs. Bevington knows this herself: "How does [Anaïs Nin] sound? As longwinded as the *Decline and Fall*, the *Ring* cycle, or the wooing of Penelope." She prefers books on the order of the old French *"choses vues . . .* things seen, noted because there they are to look at."

She is right. The outer life is in the long run a healthier thing with which to glut ourselves than the inner one. And one would rather lose patience with Mrs. Bevington's endless barrage of other writers' pellets than dwell too long in the fluid depths of Anaïs Nin's consciousness. Yet Mrs. Bevington, like Mary Shelley, comes to bend her journal to new purposes when circumstances press her. Although she takes what seems to be admiring note of those diarists who disdain recording the unpleasant in their books, this reflection is prompted by the doubt she is feeling about her own ability to hold to their tradition of pleasantness; she has on the day she makes it (June 24, 1963) just gotten some bad news: "B. [her husband] was operated on today at Duke Hospital. A brain tumor. A malignancy." He died not long after, and while Helen Bevington's journal remains mostly a book of *choses vues* and things read, it also becomes a place where she can confide loneliness, lay down grief, indulge and relieve bitterness. By October 1968 she can record: "Montaigne wrote, 'I have gone to bed a thousand times in my own home, imagining that someone would betray me and slaughter me that very night.' My record is better than Montaigne's. In more than four years alone, already it adds up to nearly 1500 nights. We have lived in bad times, Montaigne and I. Yet he sought and found a 'scandalous serenity.' " Refusing to claim any such serenity herself, Mrs. Bevington still acknowledges the homely companionship of her commonplace book as something not to be scorned.

If Mary Shelley sought to inform readers of the "origin and history" of Shelley's poems, the poet's own notebooks — great messes of English, Italian, Greek, Spanish, and Latin written right side up, upside down, and diagonally — show the poems themselves, growing and shrinking and mutating before one's eyes. If you look at his work on "To Night," you will see him doing both the routine business of craftsmanship (smoothing line 19 from "When the Day turned him to his rest" into "And the weary Day turned to his rest"), as well as the more purely poetical work of loading every rift with ore:

> Kiss her asleep [no, not right]
> Kiss her to sleep [no, still not right]
> Kiss her till she be wearied out.

Trelawny is supposed to have snatched Shelley's heart from the funeral pyre, and one needn't have Auden's exaggerated disdain for the archivist's mentality to find this a bit much. But who could consign these notebooks, which give such hints about how it is done, to oblivion?

Gerard Manley Hopkins was on his way to being a poet before he became a priest, and the diaries he kept when he was about twenty show his sense that poetry was more a matter of the spirit's rushings than the assemblage of shopworn bits of received poetic diction. In the spring of 1864, he writes: "It is a happy thing that there is no royal road to poetry. The world should know by this time that one cannot reach Parnassus except by flying thither." His own trip there is postponed many years by his novitiate in the Society of Jesus, and this same early diary shows the tension between literary and religious exhortation. In August 1864 one finds the reminder: "Mem. To read Gray's Poems, *Vanity Fair*, *Henry V, VI*, and *VIII* and *Richard III*, Coleridge's *Greek Classic Poets*."; but on January 22, 1866, the resolutions are rather different in nature: "For Lent. No pudding on Sundays. No tea except if to keep me awake and then without sugar. Meat only once a day. No verses in Passion Week or on Fridays. Not to sit in armchair except can work in no other way. Ash Wednesday and Good Friday bread and water." In fact, for his first several years as a Jesuit, until in 1875 he is asked to write "The Wreck of the Deutschland," there are to be "no verses" at all.

But he keeps another diary as well, one full of notes on arcane words, plants, Irish expressions, pictures at exhibitions, fairy stories, and, above all, nature — astonishing combinations of accuracy and afflatus. There are obvious premonitions of the poems several years off: the journal has, among other things, pied skies and pied pigeons in it. But Hopkins's journal from the late 1860s and early 1870s is also something different from a poet's usual storehouse and scratchpad. If there are meticulous nature-observations in language that has yet to be leavened into poetry, his chosen and enforced silence in verse often makes him use his prose book as an available substitute for poetic expression. Just as there are no other poems in English that sound like "The Windhover," there are also no prose descriptions of nature that sound like some of the ones in Hopkins's journal; they are too replete with poetry's rhythms: "In returning the sky in the west was in a great wide winged or shelved rack of rice-white fine pelleted fretting." After this, the verse "I caught this morning morning's minion, king- / dom of daylight's dauphin, dapple-dawn-drawn Falcon, in his / riding / Of the rolling level underneath him steady air" is not such a shock to a reader. There is the same combination of precision and ecstasy. It makes a certain sense

that Hopkins did not bother to continue with the journal after he was free to write actual poems.

In our own time, Allen Ginsberg, whose ecstasies have
been somewhat more randomly directed than Hopkins's,
has often transfused his verses with his journals. The
title page of *Reality Sandwiches* promises " 'Scribbled
secret notebooks, and wild typewritten pages, for yr own
joy,' " and in one of the long poems in that book, "Siesta
in Xbalba," Ginsberg speaks of

> my own crude night imaginings,
> my own crude soul notes taken down
> in moments of isolation, dreams,
> piercings, sequences of nocturnal thought
> and primitive illuminations

In that poem, based on a trip to Mexico in the early 1950s,
Ginsberg sometimes simply chops up journal prose into
verse: "As I leaned against a tree inside the forest expir-
ing of selfbegotten love I looked up at stars absently"
becomes, in *Reality Sandwiches*,

> As I leaned against a tree
>   inside the forest
> expiring of self-begotten love,
> I looked up at the stars absently.

But before one smirks at this confirmation of the Beats'
arbitrary or nonexistent sense of metrics, one does well
to look for some of the more complicated transpositions
from journals to poem. In the former is this account of
a bus ride:

On the bus Coatzcoalcos to Vera Cruz, sleeping on
codinetta, in the night gloom toward dawn passing
Lago Catemaca with the great sense of an inland sea,
hills and lunar mounts proceeding up out of lunar
darkness — I had in my eyes also an image, of Giotto,
the likeness of a heavenly file of female saints ascend-

ing in the starry sky on miniature stepped golden rainbow stairway snaking upward curved, the thousands
of little saintesses in blue hoods, with round sweet smiling faces looking out directly at me (thru the picture
wall to the beholder), their hands beckoning as they
go up — salvation it's true, as simple as that in the
strange picture.

In "Siesta in Xbalba" the passage is transformed into this:

> another image descending
>   in white mist
> down the lunar highway
>   at dawn, above
> Lake Catemaco on the bus
>   — it woke me up —
> the far away likeness
>   of a heavenly file
> of female saints
>   stepping upward
> on miniature arches
>   of a golden stairway
> into the starry sky,
>   the thousands of little
> saintesses in blue hoods
>   looking out at me
> and beckoning:
>   SALVATION!

This is considerably more arresting than the prose in
the journal. It is, in fact, poetry, and for a sense of what
Ginsberg had in mind when he was sculpting the one
into the other one can return once more to the journal,
to an entry he seems to have made a couple of months
later while meditating on the poem-in-progress:

> Break up the line?
> into emotive or meaningful or musical
> complete images or
> abstractions or sensations — whole, each, however.

The editor of Ginsberg's journals says that the poet started keeping them in 1947, and that the eighteen books he examined and edited included big ones for the bedside and small ones for the subway and bus. The notebooks contain not only early versions of Ginsberg's poems, but also lists of his reading, descriptions of the men he follows on the street — and dreams, dreams, dreams, recorded in exceptional detail and with plenty of tedium. He sometimes wishes himself that he could concentrate more often on "the real world" around him, but he gives in, again and again, to the inner flow. He writes: "I must put down every recurrent thought," and it is this tendency that does him in as a diarist as often as it does him in as a poet. Still, Ginsberg's incontinence is only an exaggeration of modern poetry's sense that the minutiae of daily life can be transmitted to poetry with less filtering and selection than earlier centuries supposed. Robert Lowell's *Notebook* and Louis MacNeice's *Autumn Journal*, to cite just two examples, show the possibility of raising the diary up from being imagination's sketchpad and cupboard to being the poem itself.

It would be difficult to think of a more incendiary example of an artist's will to succeed than that provided by the late poet Sylvia Plath. Her deep and narrow talent found spectacular expression just before her suicide in London at the age of thirty; her recently published *Journals* make for exhausting reading, not only because of the strain one feels while waiting for the catastrophe one knows is going to take place, but also because the journals show, through all her late adolescent and adult life, a self-absorption far beyond anything like the necessary self-consciousness of a poet. There are glimpses in the diary of "outer" life and community (some intriguing sketches of faculty colleagues at Smith College around 1957 and, later, of her neighbors in Devon, England), but the journals are more than anything else a relentless record of punishing self-exhortation — to write and to succeed.

Readers of her poems and fiction can find her using in the journals the images of Lazarus and the bell jar as well as favorite words like *stasis*. They can find her writing about her relationship with her mother in a slightly less emphatic form of the fairy-tale language she would use in her most famous poem of all, "Daddy." The premise of her poem about being hospitalized for an appendectomy, "Tulips" —

> The tulips are too red in the first place, they hurt me.
> Even through the gift paper I could hear them breathe
> Lightly, through their white swaddlings, like an awful
>   baby —

is closely prefigured in the journal entry she makes while waiting for her operation: "A helpful inmate in a red wool bathrobe brings the flowers back, sweet-lipped as children. All night they've been breathing in the hall, dropping their pollens, daffodils, pink and red tulips, the hot purple and red-eyed anemones."

Perhaps these findings help us to understand her work better. But even the most patient and sympathetic reader of these journals will not be gratified to find these germinations of important poems as much as he will be appalled by the furious discipline that went into the making of the poet herself. For more than ten years Plath flays the impossible out of herself. The journal is her endless series of proposed regimens and marching orders. She will work, and thereby she will — must — succeed in making herself a writer:

> This summer I must do gallons of reading in psych, philosophy — English: I have a colossal list of books. Why, oh, why, in all those camp and social summers, didn't I read more purposive lasting books instead of the young girl's novels?

Three summers later, while on her honeymoon with Ted Hughes in Spain, she proposes for herself a week of writing short stories "along with chapters in my new novel that might do for articles for *Harper's*; also an article with sketches, on Benidorm for *The Christian Science Monitor*. Must learn Spanish and translate French too." A year later, trying to combine a heavy teaching load at Smith, her alma mater, with her un-slackening desires to write (or, more precisely, to pub-lish), she demands to know from her diary whether she'll get through the particular set of tasks she's set for her-self on the day she's writing: "Will it come and we do it? Answer me, book." Her emphasis is always on the quantitative — how many lines adding up to how many poems adding up to how many books: "Only 16 poems published in the last year."

She is frantic to find someone she can imitate. But everything she reads is a source of potential torment; to read a book is to realize she hasn't written it. Even her own perfectionism, when she's aware of it, must be coped with in a perfectionist's way:

> Talking about my fears to others feeds it. I shall show a calm front & fight it in the precincts of my own self, but never give it the social dignity of a public appear-ance, me running from it, and giving in to it. I'll work in my office roughly from 9 to 5 until I find myself doing better in class. In any case, I'll do something relaxing, different reading, etc., in the evenings. I'll keep myself intact, outside this job, this work. They can't ask more of me than my best, & only I know really where the limits on my best are. I have a choice: to flee from life and ruin myself forever because I can't be perfect right away, without pain & failure, and to face life on my own terms & "make the best of the job."

Not "right away" perhaps, but she's going to be perfect someday. Her diary is her goad, and she admits her dom-inant inclination to write in it when she is "at wits' end, in a cul-de-sac. Never when I am happy." On at least one frustrated occasion she assaults it: "Saturday exhausted, nerves frayed. Sleepless. Threw you, book, down, punched with fist. Kicked, punched. Violence seethed. Joy to murder someone, pure scapegoat. But pacified during necessity to work. Work redeems."

It is a particularly American notion, the redemption that can be earned through work. Plath, who relished *New Yorker* acceptances the way entrepreneurs light up at profits, was in many ways a Parnassian Jay Gatsby, who, in the back of a copy of *Hopalong Cassidy*, it will be remembered, wrote down, on September 12, 1906, the following regime for himself:

Rise from bed	6.00 A.M.
Dumbbell exercise and wall-scaling	6.15–6.30 A.M.
Study electricity, etc.	7.15–8.15 "
Work	8.30–4.30 P.M.
Baseball and sports	4.30–5.00 "
Practice elocution, poise and how to attain it	5.00–6.00 "
Study needed inventions	7.00–9.00 "

This is the document Gatsby's father proudly shows to Nick Carraway at his son's funeral: " 'Jimmy was bound to get ahead. He always had some resolves like this or something.' " What Mr. Gatz was showing Nick was a sort of man-on-the-move's diary — all Gatsby had to do was stick to that regime, and he wouldn't have to write another entry: every day would already be accounted for, down to the quarter hour.

Plath has Gatsby's discipline, but she is in the end a much less romantic figure. She dreams small; she knows what she wants early, never changes course, and always — until her explosive end — tries to get what she is after in the most practical, utilitarian manner. When she is a graduate student at Newnham College, Cambridge, she decides she will write her novel. In preparation for it, she will bank her observations and sensations in her journal: "*It's hopeless to 'get life' if you don't keep notebooks.*" This is a normal enough plan for a writer; but

Plath adds her usual obsessive arithmetic to it. Writing on
March 4, 1957, she decides she will have it done by the
end of May: "I will doggedly write my 3 pages a day,
even if my supervisors scorn me." It is a joyless, mechanical creation, and some part of her knows it. Moments of
true (as opposed to de rigueur and manufactured) self-
awareness are rare in Plath's journals, but one of them
surely occurs — in parentheses — on Saturday, July 19,
1958: "I dimly would like to write (or is it to *have* written?) a novel, short stories, a book of poems."

William K. Wimsatt, and Monroe C. Beardsley, two
of the architects of the New Criticism, once wrote that
a poem is like a pudding; one asks that it work. Plath
would have pleased him: never has poetry (except in her
amazing last months) been closer to cookery. On Thursday, February 19, 1959: "A misery. Wrote a Gran-
chester poem of pure description. I must get philosophy
in." There is a particular reason she must put that extra
ingredient, like nutmeg, in: "Until I do I shall lag behind
A.C.R. [Adrienne Cecile Rich]" She senses how she tries
to validate the fact that she is living by seeing her name
in print ("Rejection of my Johnny Panic story without
a note from *The Yale Review*: all my little dreams of
publishing it there vanished: so writing is still used as a
proof of my identity"), but this self-knowledge is intermittent and tenuous. When Plath takes a job typing case
histories in a psychiatric hospital in Boston in 1958, she
quite rightly marvels over what magnificent material this
will bring her way as an incipient novelist. And yet she
doesn't notice some of what she types as an extreme version of her own woes. She transfers a capsule summary
of the case of "Edson F." to her journal: "Produces a
number of documents to indicate his existence. Birth
certificate. Poll tax papers and naturalization papers."
Here is her own need writ large and crazy.

In the *Writer's Diary* abridgment of Virginia Woolf's
journals Plath seeks identification and solace: "Just now
I pick up the blessed diary of Virginia Woolf which I

bought with a battery of her novels Saturday with Ted. And she works off her depression over rejections from *Harper's* (no less! — and I can hardly believe that the Big Ones get rejected, too!) by cleaning out the kitchen. And cooks haddock & sausage. Bless her. I feel my life linked to her, somehow." But Woolf was, inevitably, competition as well. Plath records her admiration of the last fifty pages of *The Waves*, and immediately thereafter demands that she herself write something surpassing them: "I underlined & underlined: reread that. I shall go better than she. *No children until I have done it.*"

Plath's gruesome death — her head in a gas oven in a flat near Primrose Hill one February morning in 1963 — ensured that her poems would exert a grim biographical fascination beyond any literary one. Her journals, however much they illuminate her imaginative capital and artistic drive, inevitably fascinate us in the same guilty way. There is a sort of prurience in knowing so much about a person capable of such enormity against herself, but to recognize that is not the same as to resist it. In the journal, one day in 1958, Plath records how she and her husband were unable to nurse an injured bird they had found back to health. Eventually, after taking a walk outside with it, they decided they had to put it out of its misery:

> I resented the hale, whole birds in the tree. We went home: the bird peeped feebly, rallied to peck at our fingers. Ted fixed our rubber bath hose to the gas jet on the stove and taped the other end into a cardboard box. I could not look and cried and cried. Suffering is tyrannous. I felt desperate to get the sickly little bird off our necks, miserable at his persistent pluck and sweet temper. I looked in. Ted had taken the bird out too soon and it lay in his hand on its back, opening and shutting its beak terribly and waving its upturned feet. Five minutes later he brought it to me, composed, perfect and beautiful in death.

Surely she remembered that bird on the morning she killed herself. Certainly no reader of her diaries can fail to imagine her remembering it.

On April 8, 1862, the Goncourts note with a mixture of contempt and admiration that Victor Hugo "always has a note-book in his pocket and that if, in conversation with you, he happens to express the tiniest thought, to put forward the smallest idea, he promptly turns away from you, takes out his note-book and writes down what he has just said. He turns everything into copy or munitions. Nothing is ever lost: it all goes into some book or other." The Goncourts did not use their own journals so relentlessly as mere means to artistic ends; their diaries were meant in and of themselves to be accounts of their age. But even so one can find in them the germinations of novels like *Les Frères Zemganno* and *Soeur Philomène*. The ample and catholic genre that D. H. Lawrence called "the one bright book of life" has been appropriately abetted by the most varied sorts of diaries and notebooks, books which have housed everything from interesting anecdotes to meticulous first drafts and details meant for garnish — although the novelist may not yet know how or when such details will be useful.

The three notebooks Dostoevski keeps during the making of *Crime and Punishment* (a book, incidentally, he considered writing at least partly in the form of a diary), are memoranda about how to do it more convincingly ("N.B. In giving it artistic form, don't forget that he is 23 years old"). They also contain a number of outtakes: Raskolnikov, for example, does not in fact shoot himself in the novel, but that's only because Dostoevski decides to take away the gun he had ill-advisedly given his character. The notebooks show the novelist paying tremendous attention to the small details of psychological plausibility, but they are also the place in which he can paint the big picture for himself: "N.B. His moral development begins from the crime itself; the possibility of

such questions arises which would not have existed previously." It is a little unsettling to see novelists writing
such descriptions; it's as if they were students sitting
down to write bad, reductive term papers about their
own masterpieces. But then one remembers that this is
what came *before*. The sentences above don't represent
a novel that's been boiled down; they represent one that's
about to be detonated, given the big bang that will transform it from an abstract black hole into an expanding
galaxy of people, voices, smells, and colors.

There could hardly be a more bizarre combination of
the abstract and the concrete, of conception and detail,
than the projection of *To the Lighthouse* Virginia Woolf
makes in her diary on Thursday, May 14, 1925: "This is
going to be fairly short; to have father's character done
complete in it; and mother's; and St. Ives; and childhood;
and all the usual things I try to put in — life, death, etc.
But the centre is father's character, sitting in a boat, re-
citing, We perished, each alone, while he crushes a dying
mackerel." Two months later she is drawing the book's
shape more definitely: "(I conceive the book in 3 parts.
1. at the drawing-room window; 2. seven years passed;
3. the voyage)." The following spring, when she has finished the first part and begun the second, she uses the
diary to record her doubts: "Is it nonsense, is it bril-
liance?" At other points she clucks with satisfaction:
"Dear me, how lovely some parts of the *Lighthouse* are!
Soft and pliable, and I think deep, and never a word
wrong for a page at a time." The more practical consid-
erations of writing also fly in and out of the journal: Is it
going fast enough? What will the reviewers say? Will
The Common Reader and *Mrs. Dalloway* make her
enough money to add a bathroom to the house?

F. Scott Fitzgerald, who was publishing *The Great
Gatsby* as Woolf was envisioning *To the Lighthouse*,
kept notebooks not for the casual sort of recreation she
usually found in them, but with the deliberate purposes
of a young Jimmy Gatz. Fitzgerald's notebooks are full

of overheard scraps of conversation that he would drop like candies onto his characters' tongues. "He wants to make a goddess out of me and I want to be Mickey Mouse": where he first heard this remark is apparently not worth noting; what counts is preserving it, so that it could be uttered in the story "On Your Own." Some of his own aphorisms and observations are in the notebooks, too: "Debut — the first time a young girl is seen drunk in public"; "There are no second acts in American lives." These are lines we think we remember from Fitzgerald's fiction — in fact, they are notebook fragments that were still waiting for their stories when their author died on them. These books, like dresser drawers waiting to be weeded and organized, also contain some of Zelda's thoughts ("The bad things are the same in everyone; only the good are different"); apparent warnings to himself ("Sending orchestra second rate champagne — never, *never* do it again"); and traces of his own discernings of the essential features of his work: "Reporting the extreme things as if they were the average things will start you on the art of fiction." This is the method of much of *Gatsby* itself, after all: "Snell was there three days before he went to the penitentiary, so drunk out on the gravel that Mrs. Ulysses Swett's automobile ran over his right hand. The Dancies came, too."

Fitzgerald succeeded for a time, Malcolm Cowley once said, partly from a "double personality" that let him approach the world he wrote about as both participant and observer. It is this same sort of vision Albert Camus describes in his notebooks: "I am happy to be both halves, the watcher and the watched." Camus's *cahiers* contain some personal material and recorded emotion, but mostly they are the testing ground for the creative work to be done elsewhere. He uses the notebooks both to muse on truths ("Civilization does not lie in a greater or lesser degree of refinement, but in an awareness shared by a whole people") and to collect the particular sights and voices in which he would embody them in novels and plays. It is in one of his notebooks that one can find what may be the clearest explanation of a philosopher's turning to fiction: "Feelings and images multiply a philosophy by ten." The notebooks not only warehouse bits of conversation, in the manner of Fitzgerald, but also contain extended drafts of actual material. The opening sentences of *The Stranger* ("Today, mother died. Or it might have been yesterday, I don't know") appear, without any scoring or revision, in one of the *cahiers* from the late 1930s, beneath the notation "2P." This and other hints in the book have led Camus's editors to wonder whether the opening of the novel was originally intended to be its second part, preceded by a depiction of a pre-absurd Meursault.

Graham Greene kept journals he later used in writing the two novels he set in Africa, *The Heart of the Matter* and *A Burnt-Out Case*. Like Dostoevski's notebooks they contain the big picture as well as squirreled details and anecdotes. His "Congo Journal" from 1959 shows that *A Burnt-Out Case* was almost mystically conceived: "All I know about the story I am planning is that a man 'turns up,' and for that reason alone I find myself on a plane between Brussels and Leopoldville." But once the imagination's fire has been lit, the journal helps to scuttle in some of its small, single coals: "*Remember*: the dog at Mass. The captain sitting in the verandah doorway, the dog behind him, chatting to the black crew below." In a footnote made in the journal after *A Burnt-Out Case* had been finished, Greene is amused by his methods: "The economy of a novelist is a little like that of a careful housewife, who is unwilling to throw away anything that might perhaps serve its turn. Or perhaps the comparison is closer to the Chinese cook who leaves hardly any part of a duck unserved."

In 1947 the English novelist Jean Rhys finds herself unable to write at all; a diary seems the only hope of unblocking herself. So she begins one: "This time I must not blot a line. No revision, no second thoughts. Down it

shall go. Already I am terrified. I have none of the tools
of my trade. No row of pencils, no pencil sharpener, no
drink. The standing jump." She conducts a mock trial of
her values and achievements in the diary, answering an
italicized inquisitor in her own voice:

> *You are aware of course that what you are writing is
> childish, has been said before. Also it is dangerous
> under the circumstances.*

> Yes, most of it is childish. But I have not written for
> so long that all I can force myself to do is to write, to
> write. I must trust that out of that will come the pat-
> tern, the clue that can be followed.

> . . .

> *All right, but be damned careful not to leave this book
> about.*

A few decades earlier Katherine Mansfield makes her
diaries serve many different functions: prophet ("I've
re-read my diary. Tell me, Is there a God?"); punching
bag ("What a vile little diary!"); and votive candle for
the brother who was killed in the First World War: "If
I write every day faithfully a little record of how I have
kept faith with you — that is what I must do." She uses
them to exhort herself toward her art, and to plan some
of her stories' settings. She is also aware, as many writers
of fiction come to be, of the diaries' possibilities by themselves, as more than just the scaffoldings for other imaginary towers. On January 22, 1916, when she is mo-
mentarily considering the alternatives to fiction she
might use to make New Zealand "leap into the eyes of
the Old World," she concludes: "Lastly, I want to keep
a kind of *minute notebook*, to be published some day.
That's all. No novels, no problem stories, nothing that is
not simple, open."

But six years later she is dying, and using the journal
to enumerate the reasons she has for trying to stay alive:

Now, Katherine, what do you mean by health? And what do you want it for?

Answer: By health I mean the power to live a full, adult, living, breathing life in close contact with what I love . . . Then I want to *work*. At what? I want so to live that I work with my hands and my feeling and my brain. I want a garden, a small house, grass, animals, books, pictures, music. And out of this, the expression of this, I want to be writing.

Even in the most deliberate of notebooks, such as Dostoevski's, the artist's personality is found raising its head from beneath the blueprints. And this juxtaposition of the artist's self and his work is, finally, nowhere more startling than in the diaries of Kafka. (He is given to alarming juxtapositions in any case: August 1, 1914: "Germany has declared war on Russia. — Swimming in the afternoon.") If one reads the journal he kept at the beginning of the First World War, one finds him recording illnesses, contemplating suicide, and searching for alternatives ("Leave your job?") even as he makes preliminary sketches for "The Castle" and makes himself resume *The Trial*. The diaries show the same gift for expressing mental captivity in grotesque physical terms that one finds in those books: "There is no doubt that I am hemmed in all around, though by something that has certainly not yet fixed itself in my flesh, that I occasionally feel slackening, and that could be burst asunder." He comes to regard the diary as useful evidence of what he is ("Leafed through the diary a little. Got a kind of inkling of the way a life like this is constructed") — but not exactly a solution to his rather extreme predicaments: "New schedule from now on! Use the time even better! Do I make my laments here only to find salvation here? It won't come out of this notebook, it will come when I'm in bed and it will put me on my back so that I lie there beautiful and light and bluish-white; no other salvation will come."

Asking personal or artistic salvation from a notebook is an unreasonable request for any human being, let alone Kafka. But novelists have used these books to edit and psychoanalyze themselves, to create and abort, since the novel was invented. In many ways one would expect this particular species of diary to be the least intimate, the one a reader should be least shy to inspect: after all, the book on the workbench seems less vulnerable than the one on the night table. And yet, we may have to take the most care of all in reading these books; because they are written by men and women whose words we are used to judging, we tend to put them to an aesthetic test we spare most of the other diaries in this book. Lest we extend that test to their authors' preliminary musings, perhaps we should remind ourselves of what Henry James wrote in *The Art of Fiction*: "We must grant the artist his subject, his idea, his *donnée*: our criticism is applied only to what he makes of it." In reading a writer's journals we must content ourselves with the luxurious sensation of invading a creative privacy, and stop short of inventing an aesthetic of notebooks. With our current Texas-sized appetite for archives we may be in danger of doing that. Because of our growing mania for collection, writers are already, as Elizabeth Hardwick has pointed out, "chatting away in a bugged universe." They are increasingly aware of it, and some of them, like Auden, are increasingly ill at ease.

When one moves away from the fiction shelves and into another part of the library, seeking a glimpse of the diaries of painters, the first thing one is struck by is that these books don't seem like diaries at all. These huge reprints, so heavy, so full of plates, so full of edges that pierce one's ribcage on the way to the circulation desk: What place do they have in this intimate, ruleless genre? If one takes down *The Notebooks of Edgar Degas*, for example, one quickly finds the editor's assurance that Degas's notebooks "were also his diaries" — But *how*?

one asks, flipping through the sketches and watercolors and washes of landscapes and horses and ballerinas and boulevardiers. Lots of draftsmanship here, but not much penmanship: just those occasional jottings in the margins. Are they what Mr. Theodore Reff is talking about?

They are; and quite properly, too. An inquiry into the word-filled edges shows them snowflaked with accounts, addresses, timetables, biblical and literary quotations, detailed notes about color and light, jottings about physiognomy, reminders of projects to be attempted. These notebooks are a serious workshop, and the words that fleck them are a revealing guide to the premises: "Nothing is as beautiful as two varieties of the same color side by side"; one reads this and finds oneself considering those pictures of girls in rehearsal halls where the blues so often and so satisfyingly are next to, well, other blues. There are also, beside these conceptual entries, some how-to reminders as well: "Mixing watercolors with glycerine and soda one could make pastel-soap potash instead of soda." And Degas does not neglect to let one feel immediately present at the creation; next to a sketch of a sunset at Tivoli is the note: "It will be night in ten minutes. Tivoli 5h 10 — 10 Nov 57."

The further one ventures into Degas's notebooks the more one senses a shyness, a scrupulousness, that makes moments of revelation, when they do come, all the more compelling. He does not want the clamorous fame that is sustained by ignorance: "There is a sort of shame in being known especially by people who don't understand you," he writes. In 1856 he worries about how easy it would be to get seduced by the quick rewards available to painters at a time when their medium is undergoing a revolution that aestheticians have found apt and viewers have never ceased to find likable:

It seems to me today that if one seriously wants to create art and make a little original corner for oneself, or at least keep for oneself the most innocent of per-

sonalities, it is necessary to strengthen oneself in solitude. There are too many scandals. One could say
that paintings make themselves like stock-market games
by the meddling of people eager to gain a profit. One
thus has as much need to predict the disposition and
plans of one's neighbor in order to create as these
business people need others' funds in order to gain a
sou. All this commerce sets one's spirit on edge and
warps one's judgment.

Degas is so shy of writing about his own romantic
life that when he does the entries are really fragments of
fragments. Near the sketch of a girl's head in Notebook
6 is a note that has undergone much crossing out and
erasure. This is what is left: "I wouldn't know how to
say how much I love this girl since she . . . Monday
April 7. I can't refuse to . . . to say that it is shameful
. . . a girl without protection. But I will do it the least
possible." Clearly Degas did not seek sexual favors with
the droit du seigneur with which we stereotype painters'
behavior toward their mistresses. In a notebook kept
twenty years after the one just quoted, he is still passionately reticent: "One night I put my hand on her shoulder
— in an embarrassed way. I didn't know what I was
doing. Then I felt her knee, which she'd leaned against
her shoulder and that all of a sudden touched my hand."
The obliqueness of these entries remains attractive a
hundred years later; in their own day they were also
prudent. After all, one wouldn't want to expose one's
heart too obviously to some of the artistic acquaintances
one was likely to make in Paris in the 1870s. There is, for
example, the following address marked on page 85 of
Notebook 31: "De Goncourt / 53 Boulevard Montmo-
rency / Paris-Auteuil."
What Degas was, with paint, to the exquisite ballerina,
Edward Weston was, with a camera, to the magnificently
dumpy pepper. His *Daybooks* from the late 1920s and
early 1930s record his photographic mission of "making

the commonplace unusual," clearing "away the haze of a futile romanticism" and showing the imaginative implications of simple objects by representing them just as they are: "If a soul be unaware, and a camera be used to copy an apple, the result can be no more than a record of an apple: but give the same camera and apple to one who sees more than said apple's surface and edible qualities, who understands the apple's significance, — then, the result will be — more than an apple!"

Weston knew that there was plenty of imaginative energy to be inferred from a green pepper, so long as that pepper was served up without any photographic gimmickry. Weston's peppers sometimes seem like magnificent nudes, or modern civic sculptures by Henry Moore, but they are always peppers, too. He found that the way to reach visionary ends was first to serve literal ones, and the proof that he never lost sight of his peppers' pepperness, even after they had taken him on flights of implication and association, was that he still knew they were first and foremost meant for the dinner table: "It has been suggested that I am a cannibal to eat my models after a masterpiece. But I rather like the idea that they become a part of me, enrich my blood as well as my vision."

The *Daybooks* record the methods, accidents, excitements, and distractions of his creative hours in Carmel, California:

The glorious new pepper Sonya brought me has kept me keyed up all week and caused me to expose eight negatives: — I'm not satisfied yet! These eight were all from the same viewpoint: rare for me to go through this. I started out with an underexposure — by the time I had developed the light had failed, and though I tripled my time again I undertimed! Again I tried, desperately determined to get it because I could ill afford the time. Giving an exposure of 50 minutes at 5:00 I timed correctly, but during exposure the fire siren shrieked, and promptly the fire truck roared by followed by every car in town: the old porch trembled, my wobbly old camera wobbled, the pepper shimmied, and I developed a moved negative. Next morning I went at it again: interruptions came, afternoon came, light weak, prolonged exposures necessary, — result, one negative possible, but possible also to improve upon it.

I tried the light from the opposite side in the next morning light, — brilliant sun through muslin. Better!

Weston's war between artistic experiment and commercial survival is chronicled with alternating exasperation and triumph. On April 17, 1930, he notes that he "sat down and drafted a 'manifesto,' announcing that I would no longer retouch my professional portraits. This is a drastic move! Dare I put it into effect? Will I gain or lose? — I mean my bank account?" He cannot afford precipitousness or hubris, he knows ("I don't care — but my family —"), but he is sickened by the irony foisted upon him by "the class of unhealthy parasites I detest: I lost a sitting (this came to me after) because I only charge $40 — instead of $500 —! this is tragedy."

The *Daybooks* show him, unlike Degas, prone to a sexual arrogance that seems to let him think of women as the perks of genius. But they also show his contemptuous refutation of other clichés about the nature of the artist. Writing about his son, the photographer Brett Weston, on December 29, 1929, he complains: "Brett loses everything he touches, breaks things right and left, is forever hurting himself. All symptoms of a disorderly mind. And art is based on order! The world is full of sloppy 'Bohemians,' and their work betrays them."

Although Weston sets considerable store by his notebooks, he is never really certain why he is keeping them: "I always sit me down to write when I have something disagreeable to groan over," he writes one day, aware, like Mary Shelley, of the diary's consequent distortion of his personality. Elsewhere he says he's "more inclined to write when in a period of exciting work." But after a gap of more than ten years, he decides, on April 22, 1944, that he has "not had much time, nor necessary aloneness for keeping an intimate journal." The chief point to be salvaged from all this apparent contradiction is that to Weston the *Daybooks*, however useful, always come second. They are servants of his art, never ends in themselves. He uses them to purge himself of "psychological headaches or heartaches," the sloppy emotionalism he wants to keep out of his photographs. And he uses them as "a way of learning, clarifying [his] thoughts." On March 12, 1929, he recalls destroying his notebooks from 1920 to 1923, because he was embarrassed by what they revealed of his immaturity during a dramatic and emotional "period of growth." He regrets this action now: "My desire to destroy was natural, — to look back over immature thoughts and excess emotion was not pleasant, — but I should have locked the books away — to reread them was too much. The same will happen to this period. I pray for strength not to destroy."

We can only be glad, of course, that he did summon up the strength to preserve the *Daybooks*, which are a rather remarkable aesthetic document. In them Weston lets us see his false starts as well as his victories, and one comes away from the experience feeling properly grateful — without coming around to the feeling that absolutely every last scribble or splotch of an artist should be preserved. Weston has a great moment on December 3, 1930, when he plans an after-Christmas bonfire to destroy all but his very best work. In doing so, he is hoping to serve posterity, not deprive it: "If I am indiscriminate, the public will be." For all the notebooks' excitement and interest, the reader should put them aside and go back to the galleries to look at the photographs, for they were the notebooks' raison d'être. An artist with such a clear sense of means and ends that he could eat his own models would quite rightly deplore any sentimental lapse of proportion by even the most avid reader of diaries.

When it comes to means and ends, there are those older architects who claim that in recent years their profession has taken a crazily Platonic turn by honoring architects for buildings they manage to conceive but never quite construct. (For a long time Michael Graves was more renowned for buildings he drew than ones he built.) But for the most part in architecture, as in the other arts, notebooks are content to remain the messengers between inspiration and object. Le Corbusier is said to have taken great care in cataloguing and preserving his, but, as his posthumous editor Maurice Besset reminds us, he did not lose sight of the fact that "these sketchbooks were basically a working tool."

Still, posterity has a way of letting its archival impulse go reverentially crazy. The multivolumed *Le Corbusier Sketchbooks* have required three organizations to get them together: the Architectural History Foundation in New York, the MIT Press in Massachusetts, and the Fondation Le Corbusier in Paris. On the table of contents pages are photographs of thirteen of the books, most of them the sort of spiral-bound books that students call "assignment pads." They are spread out in rows, giving a certain suggestion of religious relics or exhibits in a criminal proceeding. Each page is photographed inside the volume, even if that page is inhabited by only a few halfhearted swirls or half a faint-hearted phrase. The reproduction seems horribly slavish at first, and yet after a time a reader of the sketchbooks grudgingly finds the inclusiveness instructive. To see one visionary thought separated from another by hundreds that are mundane or have been crossed out and contracepted gives one a sense of the sporadic visitings of creativity. Le Corbusier's sketchbooks are like the lengthy printout of a brain scan, and if the needle doesn't jump every few minutes that is fine; a certain realism is preserved, and our excitement remains ready for the sudden storms. One page of Sketchbook A2, from 1915, says only: "Cities which stifle // [cities which are] clogged." Fourteen more pages, which include musings on French toilets, plans for dividing profits, and a note about flooring being put on asphalt to foil humidity, go by before clutter makes way for revelation: "Architecture will no longer be with endless details but with broad organic lines . . . It will be Roman." The inspired notes also share tenancy of the notebooks with small pencilings that will remain forever cryptic. What, for example, can one make of the note "with archipelago in . . . London, March, 1953," which can be found added to a book of sketches from a South American trip made in 1929?

Genius, of course, is prone to its own sentimentality, and it may be a good thing that the need to jot down practical reminders cut off too many outbursts like this one in a notebook kept in 1931 during a trip to Spain, Morocco, and Algeria: "Watch out for Electricity — progress: destroyers of a people who are in a state of sublime equilibrium unique in the world today." Fortunately, the important sketches manage to cling to their space in the overflowing archive. In Notebook D13, written partly aboard the Liberty ship *Vernon S. Hood* between Le Havre and New York in December 1945, is a crude sketch of his quarters. The figure drawn therein seems to be giving a "Hi, Mom!" sort of wave, and it is annotated with the words: "It was in this freighter cabin on the way to New York that I invented the Modulor symbol" — what Françoise de Franclieu, subsequent annotator of the annotator, explains as "a measurement based on the human body and on mathematics, a creative tool for order and harmony . . . a numbered scale encompassing the human figure as the determining factor in filling space." What better place to come up with such an idea than in a cramped ship's cabin? Making the captioned sketch is Le Corbusier's way of putting a plaque on the floating workship where he arrived at what was perhaps his most important discovery. So here the notebook gets used by the artist not just to prod himself toward his creations, or to map them out, but to commemorate them as well.

A decade ago Martha Graham intended to publish her memoirs, most of which she had tape-recorded; her notebooks were given to her publishers only to be of assistance to them in editing the autobiography. But the means looked even more interesting than the historical end they were serving, and the *Notebooks* were published by themselves.

They impress a reader mostly with their velocity. They show creation hurrying on to fulfill itself, too busy to stop for conventional punctuation and vaulting over dashes instead. Graham's thoughts come very fast, and her transcriptions of them end up being cryptic and abbreviated even to someone familiar with her dances. Alongside hurried abstractions and meditations on the symbolism of what she is about to make lie the more material and definite traces of craft: specific stage directions ("Chorus on stage — massed — / Jocasta backs in — / Turns to face chorus / Throws arm over face — stands as tho' struck / The Chimera of Desire — The Mockery of Desire"); notes from books, like Péguy's *Joan of Arc*, used in her research; even library call numbers of volumes for future reference (291/F54 *Myths & Mythmakers* — Fiske).

The notebooks are a great gathering of scraps that will soon be melted down and set dancing. Graham is aware of her imagination as less purely creative than assimilating: "I am a thief — and I am not ashamed. I steal from the best wherever it happens to me — Plato — Picasso — Bertram Ross — the members of my company never show me anything — except you expect me to steal it." She forges what she pilfers, and she keeps talking in front of the fire:

There is no nobility in the choice — not even courage —
  There is only necessity for freedom —
  freedom
    from what . . .

Here she is incarnating Joan of Arc one more time, trying
to figure out what she has on her own mind. Sometimes
she won't even know what that is until after a work is
already on the stage. One night during a performance of
Deaths and Entrances she suddenly apprehends the meaning of witchcraft and realizes what the ballet she has
already made actually means: "This . . . is what D & E is
about — only I did not know enough to quite see it
through." The notebooks echo with the phrases "what
has to be done," "that which must be done," "what I do
must be done." As much as any other artist's notebook,
Graham's permits the reader to see accident becoming
necessity, the chance observation turning into the inevitable vision.

It is a smug commonplace, especially among the slack-
bodied, that dancers are the most deeply stupid of all
artists. Allowances are made for their intense physical
regimen and how little time it leaves for the reading of
books, but a certain snickering still goes along with the
utterance of the cliché. Even Toni Bentley, a corps
member of the New York City Ballet, admits: "I think
too much, far too much, to dance." But it was perhaps
her greater cerebration, and the use of a book, that got
her through a crisis in her career not long ago. Worried,
as she approaches her twenty-third birthday, about her
commitment to her art and the apparent stagnation of
her career, she decides to keep a journal for one *Winter
Season* of the NYCB: "I began on November 21, 1980,
and finished on February 15, 1981. I was lonely; I was
sad. I had decided to be alone, but I had never decided
to be lonely. I started writing on a yellow pad. I wrote,
and I smoked. Every page was covered with a film of
smoke."

The journal that came out of those three months is instructive to the nondancer about such dancers' difficulties as obsessions with mirrors; "neurotic eating"; ignorance of money; fears of early retirement; and loyalty to each other versus devotion to the late George Balanchine: "We are the greatest ballet company in the free world because we live under a total dictatorship. We are all there for one reason and one man — Balanchine is our leader, and we are his subjects. For us to strike for our rights would be going against the only reason we are here at all." Less momentously, the nondancing reader learns how corps members cope with such difficulties as the roach that wanders onstage during Act 3 of *Coppélia* and the snowflakes that lodge in one's cleavage during *The Nutcracker*.

For a time during this winter season Toni Bentley loses the drive to go on with her art, but in some manner her journal sustains her: "I had a nightmare last night about Balanchine. He told me I danced like a Biafran — no substance. I awoke with a great fear and knew I must go and dance before him. My faith in dancing is gone, but my faith in life cannot be, or else I would not be here writing this page."

Feeling "starved" for a life outside the one lived in the rehearsal rooms and theater, and discouraged about the possibility of loving people and dancing simultaneously, Toni Bentley goes through a dark, but finally useful, season in her career and life. Only after taking a leave of absence, she notes in an epilogue, does she realize how much she needs to return to the art she has temporarily abandoned: "I found myself 'selling Balanchine' to everyone I encountered, spreading the gospel I had betrayed." Having given life a chance to compete with dancing, she finds the former lacking, and regains the prideful sense of distinction dancers make between themselves and earthbound mortals. Her diary helps her to find the way back to her art.

*

There are diaries that have helped creators discover — not just return to — their life's work. When Charles Darwin left Christ's College, Cambridge, he could have had little idea that he would one day give the biggest blow to man's pride since Copernicus had a few centuries before told him that the world, quite literally, did not revolve around him. Cambridge didn't do Darwin much more good than it did Wordsworth. His time there, he wrote in his *Autobiography*, was "worse than wasted. From my passion for shooting and for hunting and when this failed for riding across country, I got into a sporting set, including some dissipated low-minded young men." But he was fortunate in getting enough of a reputation as a beetle collector to be a credible respondent in 1831 to Captain FitzRoy's offer "to give up part of his own cabin to any young man who would volunteer to go with him without pay as naturalist on the voyage of the *Beagle*." If Darwin didn't know what would ultimately come out of this, still less so did FitzRoy; the latter's suicide many years later is thought by some to have been connected to his guilt over the assistance he provided Darwin in gathering the data that would eventually lead to his irreligious assault on man's belief in his splendidly complete debut as Adam.

But that would all come later. When Darwin begins writing the *Beagle* diaries he will send back to England, things are not exactly auspicious. On December 30, 1831, "wretchedly out of spirits and very sick," he is despairing his way across the Bay of Biscay: "I often said before starting that I had no doubt I should fervently repent of the whole undertaking." He looks forward to the time when he can just look back on it all. "Oh, a ship is a true pandemonium, and the cawkers who are hammering away above my head veritable devils." When the voyage is over several years later, Darwin will rewrite and edit the diary into the famous *Journal of Researches into the Geology and Natural History of the various countries visited during the Voyage of HMS Beagle round the*

World, and the early nauseated intimacies of the original will be shaped up into a more suitably impersonal and august opening:

> After having been twice driven back by heavy southwestern gales, Her Majesty's ship *Beagle*, a ten-gun brig, under the command of Captain FitzRoy, RN, sailed from Devonport on 27 December 1831. The object of the expedition was to complete the survey of Patagonia and Tierra del Fuego, commenced under Captain King in 1826 to 1830; to survey the shores of Chile, Peru, and of some islands in the Pacific; and to carry a chain of chronometrical measurements round the world.

Even in the more private and personal diary, Darwin has to be careful of an uninvited public; it has been suggested that the surprising lack of reference to his shipmates shows a wariness of prying eyes in close quarters.

However circumspect, the journals give us clear sightings of Darwin with the gauchos of Argentina; meeting with General Rosas, exterminator of the country's Indians; bemoaning the "poor wretches" living on Tierra del Fuego; braving an earthquake in Chile; and riding the giant tortoises of the Galapagos Islands. The theory of natural selection doesn't come to him with eurekan suddenness; it only begins to evolve as a slow geologic rumble over the course of the nearly five years the *Beagle* is at sea. And it is in the journals that one hears the tremors. Pondering, while in Argentina, the disappearance of such creatures as the megatherium, Darwin realizes the extreme slowness with which species die out:

> To admit that species generally become rare before they become extinct — to feel no surprise at the comparative rarity of one species with another, and yet to call in some extraordinary agent and to marvel greatly when a species ceases to exist, appears to me much the

same as to admit that sickness in the individual is the prelude to death — to feel no surprise at sickness — but when the sick man dies, to wonder, and to believe that he died through violence.

In the Andes, increasingly aware of the grinding, inexorable, almost imperceptible movements of the earth, Darwin wonders "at the force which has upheaved these mountains, and even more so at the countless ages which it must have required, to have broken through, removed, and levelled whole masses of them."

He was the ultimate inductor. With a mind he called (in his *Autobiography*) "a kind of machine for grinding general laws out of large collections of fact" he went to work, after his return to England, on "the chief work of [his] life," *The Origin of Species*. It took him twenty years, and during that time notebooks, just as they had been on the *Beagle*, were the workshop in which he collected his facts and ground them up:

My first note-book was opened in July 1837. I worked on true Baconian principles, and without any theory collected facts on a wholesale scale, more especially with respect to domesticated productions, by printed enquiries, by conversation with skilful breeders and gardeners, and by extensive reading.

The minute particulars of the notebooks will not be much looked into by the nonscientist; it is the majestic plausibility of the general theory that will arrest and abash him. After more than a century, Darwin's work still strikes most men with more reality than they want to bear. We haven't really gotten over the shock to our collective pride, even as we revere Darwin and keep his portrait above the High Table of the college where he was such an indifferent student. So it seems fitting to reopen his journals and find him capable of giving fresh offense. If even the Church of England has made its

peace with Darwin, the men at Her Majesty's Ministry
of Defence have new reason for feeling annoyed at him:

> After the possession of these miserable islands had
> been contested by France, Spain, and England, they
> were left uninhabited . . . The theatre is worthy of
> the scenes acted on it. An undulating land, with a
> desolate and wretched aspect, is everywhere covered
> by a peaty soil and wiry grass, of one monotonous
> brown colour.

This is his description of the Falkland Islands.

His voyage to agnosticism was slow and not entirely
pleasant. A century before Darwin made it, Voltaire was
taking his own ontological trip to deism and perhaps
beyond: his commentators are still not entirely sure
where he ended up in regard to God's existence or the
lack of it. But his own busy existence as playwright,
philosopher, historian, and court savant was sufficiently
varied to require at least the dozen complete notebooks
(or sets of them) listed, along with sixty-one fragments,
in the table of contents in his complete works. The contents of any one of them may be as brimmingly varied
as the reflections in his published works. One of the
printed Paris notebooks, for example, lists the item:
"There are 10,000 public prostitutes in Naples"; on the
facing page lies the fact: "It was Rudolf Hapsburg who
introduced the use of the German language into public
acts." There didn't need to be any relationship between
one datum and another. They simply had to be there —
privately kept facts waiting to be polished into public
aperçus. Another of the Paris notebooks — "Extracts, and
memorandum with reflections on various subjects" — is
loaded with small bits of information and nascent hy-
potheses flagged for further consideration. "Notice," "It
appears that," "To know whether," "Compare," "See,"
"To remember that," "NB," "To show," "It is believed
that," and "Consult" are the imperatives and suppositions
one sees him committing to paper as he harvests the facts

that will help him alchemize religion into rationalism: "There must be in the Chinese character a spirit of moderation that is hardly in other men, since there has never been a religious war or fanaticism there."

Generally unbedeviled by any foolish consistency, Voltaire felt less reason than ever to practice it in his notebooks. When we see him reflecting in the second Paris notebook that "animals have a great advantage over us; they can foresee neither troubles nor death," we are immediately signaled by his percipient editor, Theodore Besterman, to move to one of the Piccini notebooks, where we will note Voltaire seeing things a different way: "Man is the only animal who knows that he must die. Sad knowledge, but necessary, since he has ideas. There are therefore miseries necessarily attached to man's condition."

What a life of detection these notebooks draft the scholar into! Besterman is off and running with the very first entry in the very first notebook he prints, the "Small Leningrad notebook," written between 1726 and 1728. The entry — written in English — reads: "England is meeting of all religions, as the Royal exchange is the rendez vous of all foreigners." This is not just any hypothetical caterpillar destined to become an intellectualized butterfly; it is, according to the editor, the tadpole that turned into Voltaire's very bravest prince of thought: "This phrase," the footnote tells us, "is the germ of an important passage in the sixth of the *Lettres philosophiques* . . . Indeed, it marks in a sense the beginning of that movement of thought in Voltaire which led to his intellectual revolt against intolerance."

Besterman is never off the job for a moment. In 1968 he edited an enormously expensive facsimile edition of *Voltaire's Household Accounts, 1760–1778*, and defended his enterprise in a preface by asserting that where a man of Voltaire's eminence is concerned, "anything and everything connected with him is precious, though we must not make the mistake of treating every detail as equally important." He talks of "the little details of everyday life which are at the basis of all history," and says that while he would rather know whether Voltaire believed in God than what he paid for linen, such details as the latter help us understand the circumstances in which this man pondered ultimate questions. So he goes ahead: "We now know, for instance, that on 24 October 1765 he gave 60 francs 15 sols for eighteen white handkerchiefs."

In cases like this not the sky, but the bottom of the barrel, is the limit. T. S. Eliot supposed that if Shakespeare's laundry lists were ever discovered a critical genius put them to some exegetical use, and he no doubt supposed right. Any biographer whose mind has been loosened or heartbeat quickened by the sight of his subject's diary will agree. But perhaps it is best that Shakespeare's diary — and laundry bills — remain undiscovered. The hunger for such records may finally do more good in exciting our minds about their supposed keeper than could any particular news they might give us about the price of handkerchiefs for whoever was playing Desdemona.

If you are an arranger not only of words, but of shapes and rhythms and systems as well; if you interest yourself in painting and sculpture and aviation and optics and anatomy and botany and geology and a great many other things besides, then your notebooks will rather likely be quite full and also quite difficult to organize. Leonardo da Vinci, before whom all the preceding creators seem paltrily gifted, kept notebooks for roughly forty years, from his days in Florence to his royal service at Amboise. His manuscripts run to five thousand pages and are left in various places. He never got around to publishing anything while he was alive, and it's no wonder. For all the evidence of revision in his notebooks, for all the emendations that show he was bent on seeing his treatises printed up and passed around, he seems to have been far more concerned with thinking about everything avidly than anything finally. When you are, after all, interested in everything, distractions come easily. The manuscript in the British Museum (Arundel 263) is described by its author as "a collection without order, made up of many sheets which I have copied here, hoping afterwards to arrange them in order in their proper places according to the subjects of which they treat."

The notebooks, like mere commonplace books, contain passages copied out from Leonardo's reading; they also contain records of his dreams, philosophical speculations, plans for painting, and nascent dissertations on most of the subjects yet conceived by man. Where the art of painting is concerned we find the specific:

> One who was drinking has left the glass where it was and turned his head towards the speaker . . . Another is speaking in his neighbour's ear, and he who listens turns towards him and gives him hearing, holding in one hand a knife, and in the other the bread half cut through by the knife. Another, as he turns round holding a knife in his hand, has upset with his hand a glass which is upon the table.

But this highly particularized portion of the guest list for *The Last Supper* was composed by a painter who was also more theoretically angry at those writers who classified painting as one of the mechanical arts: "If you call it mechanical because it is by manual work that the hands represent what the imagination creates, your writers are setting down with the pen by manual work what originates in the mind." Edward Weston, recalling Leonardo in his *Daybooks*, made similar defenses of his own art against criticism brought against its automated nature: a case of one notebook propelling another. Considering his negative of a juniper tree, Weston wrote: "It has exciting rhythms plus exquisite detail which no painter could record, — or if attempted must appear niggling, while in the photograph — an exact transcript of Nature and therefore exactly true — it is honest, convincing." Leonardo would have had something to say about this, too, one supposes, but certain inventions were not fully anticipated, even by him.

In one of his notebooks Leonardo worries about wasting time, doing too little and doing it so badly that no impression of himself will be left. This reflection shows him, too, to be the prey of the diarist's calendar-consciousness: "We have no lack of system or device to measure and to parcel out these poor days of ours; wherein it should be our pleasure that they be not squandered or suffered to pass away in vain, and without meed of honour, leaving no record of themselves in the minds of men; to the end that this our poor course may not be sped in vain."

The artists here have ultimately been most concerned to let their final creations, rather than their notebooks, do their talking to posterity. But now, after Leonardo, a ne plus ultra if ever there was one, it is time to turn to those diarists — the apologists — whose private books were quite deliberately addressed to unborn readers whose attention they craved and whose good opinion they courted. Like all the diarists already met, they lean toward the long view. Their distinctive feature is that they lean toward it at a higher volume.

5

Apologists

*"Hey world! Come here! I wanna
talk to ya!"*

—ARTHUR BREMER
May 6, 1972

ON THE MORNING of August 9, 1974, Richard Nixon
resigned the office of President of the United States,
having made the bad mistake of letting his enemies get
hold of his diary. An extraordinarily long and unusual
diary it was, whose existence had come to light the previous summer when Mr. Alexander Butterfield, a Nixon
aide, explained to Mr. Fred Thompson, minority counsel
of the Senate Watergate Committee, that recording de-
vices had been installed in the White House and Execu-
tive Office Building "for historical purposes, to record
the President's business." Every uttered belch and pro-
nunciamento, every syllable of state, every scrape of the
presidential chair or throat was automatically taken
down. Technology had solved the diarist's perpetual
problem of having to sit down to record the events of a
busy day just after it had been lived. In fact, Richard Nixon
literally could not stop keeping this diary. Short of asking
that the whole system be shut down, he could not himself
prevent the wheels from turning and turning; he was
nowhere near the buttons. Buying new notebooks? Keeping track of filled diaries? These traditional duties of the
diarist were also of no account. As Mr. Butterfield ex-

plained, "The Secret Service are highly trustworthy. It was their responsibility to change the tapes . . . and to store them."

Whether it was the comic-opera uniform he approved for the White House police, or his reference to a rather dull revenue-sharing formula between the federal and state governments as a "New American Revolution," Richard Nixon imagined everything connected with his presidency on a Mount Rushmore scale. His huge electronic diary was going to be, he thought, a vast assortment of raw materials for a heroic collection of memoirs. It was actually just one more case of his having an ordinary political impulse hopelessly swollen: the wish to explain, to justify, to plead a case before history. Statesmen more ordinary than Nixon, opposition leaders both loyal and revolutionary, free and imprisoned, have all felt the need not only to make history but to write it as well — or at least to get their versions on the record. To this end they have often written diaries, sometimes as personal notes for the orderly histories they intend to write when they have retired from the field, and sometimes to be served up to posterity whole. The apologia is as much a part of written political history as the diplomatic cable, the parliamentary *Hansard*, or the *Congressional Record*.

But politicians cannot lay sole claim to this chapter. The apologia has been used by other sorts of men and women who wished to make the world sit up and take notice of their suffering or simply of their existence: unappreciated artists; nebbishes turned killers; those denied their dreams because they were the wrong age, or the wrong sex, or just in the wrong place; those trying to lead upright lives when their nations were on sprees of violence. It is in this chapter, too, that we find the lovers, spurned and scornful, hurt and bewildered, proud and defiant. They do not really make such strange bedfellows with politicians — after all, few things make us as self-justifying as our principles and our partners.

*

Richard Crossman, who served as a cabinet minister and Leader of the House of Commons in the first Labour government of Harold Wilson (1964–1970), had been an author, educator, and journalist before turning to politics in middle age, and the instincts of his earlier vocations convinced him that he might eventually turn his new political experience into a book about the workings of English government as seen from the inside. Toward this end, for six years he kept a diary, which he dictated each weekend into a tape recorder. Like Nixon's tapes, these were to be the notes for a work of thoughtful political literature. But like the Supreme Court, Crossman came to decide that the tapes themselves were most worth hearing for " 'a daily picture of how a minister spent his time.' " So the actual diary, rather than the sort of memoir-textbook he anticipated, was the book that got published.

It was a good decision. For one thing, by presenting it in all its hugeness, Crossman saves glimpses of as yet unknown significance from the editorial wastebasket. (On October 25, 1966, there occurs the only reference to a Conservative member from Finchley: "The debate [on a prices and incomes bill] had dragged on until there wasn't adequate time for Frank Cousins before nine o'clock, when Mrs Thatcher was due to get up. So the Whips did a deal under which she started a quarter of an hour late. She made a good, professional, tough speech and sat down just after 9.45 instead of at 9.30.") For another and more important thing, he shows the workings of government more truly and revealingly than he could have in a book that merely abstracted his diaries. The government Crossman describes proceeds with fair amounts of good will and decency, bruised ego, bumblings, tedium, and bits of imagination, all of which can be captured most fairly if captured in their dailiness. Even its Prime Minister's days are spent in "endless fixing and arranging" rather than Churchillian rallyings of the populace.

We see that Wilson's men, if not exactly visionaries, are no Nixonian gangsters. They can be interested in their own smooth sailing — "Jimmy Marjach said to me, 'Thank God, if Martin Luther King hadn't been murdered the Sunday papers would have concentrated on tearing Wilson to pieces for failing to carry out the Mark II Cabinet as he said he was going to" — but they can be selfless, too. During the cabinet shuffle mentioned just above, Crossman, to keep the right egos caressed and things going smoothly, puts himself in the background and helps get Barbara Castle (also a political diarist) made First Secretary of State. His decision here is taken not because of some Machiavellian scheme, but as a result of, first, his feeling that the cabinet truly needs revitalization, and second, a sudden notion he gets strolling home from work: "While I was walking home I suddenly wondered why I should be so defeatist, changed my mind and walked across the park to No. 10. Harold was in and I went in there and had what was a not-unimportant talk." In other words, a couple of history's gears shifted not as the result of great political and economic forces, but because Richard Crossman's spirits perked up during a walk across the park, and because Harold Wilson hadn't left the office yet. Had Crossman written the political science book he originally intended, the stroll across the park would probably have been edited out. Crossman's volumes are salutary reading for those who think history churns only from enormous imperatives and petty conspiracies.

Still, ego is never deeply submerged in politics, and Crossman is made of flesh and blood. Just after the magnanimous gesture recounted above, he has to confess to "a sense of let-down. I saw a news flash on the tape saying that the one certainty [in the impending cabinet shuffle] is a really big promotion for me, and I began to wonder whether I haven't given my future away and been too generous." Most politicians are blends of opportunism and sacrifice; those elements were mixed in more noble proportions in Crossman than in others, but both remained present, and their continuing coexistence is what makes his diary so much better a political legacy than any one prices and incomes bill or cabinet shuffle. He shows government to be a good deal less mysterious, and rather more human, than we had imagined. And when he gets around to making one of his own self-justifications to history — on Easter Sunday 1968, when the world was going through a spring of student rebellion — it is an unusually sober and modest one. Just as a good poem can usually be recognized by a certain tension in ideas and language, an honest man can sometimes be known by the quality of his doubts:

> All over the world this revolt against the establishment is like a volcanic eruption destroying the structure of the countryside over which it pours. It's made my main philosophy of life appallingly out of date. I've always worked on the assumption that you can make democracy work by education and communication: by enabling people to be not merely formal voters but active participants, settling their own fortunes, taking part in collective decisions. But in this country people don't want to take part in collective decisions. In the W.E.A. [Worker's Educational Association] we failed completely, just as we failed completely in the *Daily Mirror*, to get anything approaching mass participation. Indeed, throughout my adult life I've seen participation decline . . . I now accept that the settled and just management of society by a progressive oligarchy is probably the best we can hope for.

Few figures could better exemplify a just oligarchy than Sir Harold Nicolson, whom Virginia Woolf — at least on July 5, 1924 — found so "trusty & honest & vigorous." Diplomat, writer, and partner to Vita Sackville-West in a successful if unusual marriage, Nicolson

retired from the Foreign Service in 1930 and went into
the British Parliament several years later, becoming a
National Labour member and a foe of Munich who
counseled military preparedness and resistance to Hitler's
demands in Europe. During this time and through much
of his later life he kept a diary. He would type it up, or
sometimes dictate it, after breakfast; it eventually ran to
three million words, many of which were edited and
published by his son Nigel, who in 1964, along with his
brother, asked Sir Harold

> why he had kept it day after day for over 34 years.
> "Oh, because I thought I would," he replied. "Come,"
> we said, "that's not good enough. You didn't write it
> for publication?" "No, that never entered my head."
> "You never showed it to anybody?" "Never." "You
> never re-read it yourself?" "Very, very rarely, when
> I wanted to check a name or a date." "Then why did
> you take such trouble?" "Because I thought that one
> day it might amuse you and Ben." And that was all
> that we could get out of him. Six months later, lunch-
> ing alone with him at Sissinghurst [the Nicolsons'
> castle], I repeated my question. He replied that the
> diary became a habit. "Like brushing your teeth?"
> "Exactly."

But Nigel Nicolson realized, as will anyone who reads
the diary, that his father's motives were more complicated: "His diary received the fantasies of his ambition
and the dregs of his despair. In it he would talk to himself, reassure himself, scold himself, take stock of what
he had become and hoped to be." Statesmen can be like
other diarists in claiming that they write only for themselves, and that they hardly ever read their diaries, but
more often than not the careful secretarial and custodial
regimens they devise for them belie their protests, which
may be coy, or may be necessary self-delusions allowing
for greater candor and more natural prose. Like Nicolson,

they usually agree to publish when asked. Thriving on their senses of history and self-promotion, most politicians can't resist the opportunity to use their journals as posthumous press releases.

Harold Nicolson seems to have been a modest man by most standards, let alone a politician's, and although his diary has its share of records of his own successes at speaking and persuading, and occasional jibes and thrusts (measured ones) at his opponents, it reflects a man who is secure enough by circumstance and temperament to see beyond the fate of his own reputation. He has that rare quality of knowing which things deserve worry and which things don't, and it is in periods of genuine crisis that his diary functions most remarkably. When one is forced to live in dread, a day or moment at a time, writing a diary, which can stop dead at any point, makes better sense than a book which needs the retrospection events may never permit. In the days before September 1939, Nicolson takes to making entries on an almost hour-by-hour basis. His account of parliamentary sessions held in blacked-out chambers, of gas-proofing his home, of false alarms and reprieves, is as absorbing as any that can be found. By then his journal has become more than the self-defense of a single statesman. It has become an apologia for what seemed to be a submerging civilization. On December 29, 1938, he tries to find reasons for his depressed and anxious condition, and writes: "Is it loathing of the thought that this evil *Mein Kampf* theory, this vulgar violence, may triumph over the gentle elegancies which we and France have evolved? Or does my depression come from the fact that I have no power and so little influence? That my lack of combative instincts make me merely write comments upon statesmanship without being able to influence or to grasp it?" A few weeks later, imagining the sort of world that would be left for his sons and nephew, he prophesies: "All the truthfulness, all the outspokenness, all the easiness of life

will have gone. They will never know *la douceur de
vivre*." Diary-keeping must itself have seemed an activity
that was seeing its last days.

In the thirties Nicolson became acquainted with Charles
and Anne Lindbergh. He wrote the authorized biography
of Dwight Morrow, the diplomat who was Anne's father,
and for two years the Lindberghs rented Long Barn near
Sissinghurst from the Nicolsons, occasionally visiting
with them. Both men, in their public lives and diaries,
viewed the approach of the Second World War with
alarm and sorrow, but with wholly different ideas about
whom to blame and how to respond. (When in 1939 he
came upon an article by Nicolson attacking his isolationist
radio speeches, Lindbergh would recall in his diary that
Long Barn had been rented "at a very adequate price.")
Charles Lindbergh knew his own version of *la douceur de
vivre*, an American one, more homespun and taciturn
than the life Nicolson had in mind, a small-town existence
he had seen in his youth and one that remained his idea
of a life worth living. The possibility of that life ended
for Lindbergh with his 1927 flight to Paris and the later
kidnaping and murder of his infant son. The press
devoured his privacy with an almost unbelievable feroc-
ity, and he came to see the newspapers, with their exclu-
sives, circulation wars, Winchells, and flashbulbs that
endlessly exploded in his face as the vanguard of all the
modern forces undermining him. Anne Morrow Lindbergh's diaries show how she managed to maintain a
lovely and delicate percipience toward the world in the
face of this tyranny of publicity. But Charles Lindbergh's
story is different — it is the tale of Tom Swift hardening
into Coriolanus.

The Wartime Journals of Charles Lindbergh, published
in 1970, show just how much pain his celebrity inflicted.
He describes, without false modesty, his 1927 solo flight
and landing as being "really one of the most interesting
times of [his] life," but a decade later he suffers almost

physically from being reminded and reminded of it. On April 6, 1939, he attends a party at the American Embassy in Paris:

> Probably forty people there, including some of society's greatest bores. They will *never* get over talking about the time I landed at Le Bourget in 1927, and they all seem to have done the same thing: start to Le Bourget from Paris, get stuck in the traffic jam, see me ride by somewhere in an automobile, and meet me at a lunch at the embassy which Ambassador Herrick invited them to. And they usually want to hold my hand while they tell it all.

To read Lindbergh's words after a train ride to New York in August 1941 — "What wouldn't I give to be able to ride on trains and go to theaters and restaurants as an ordinary person" — is curiously moving; it is to see someone suffering from a strange disease few of us are ever likely to contract.

One way in which he sought relief was his mental flirtation with nazism. One of the many shrewd remarks Harold Nicolson makes in his diary is that Lindbergh's sympathy with Nazi "theology" is "all tied up with his hatred of degeneracy and his hatred of democracy as represented by the free Press and the American public." It was as if he could escape the proportions imposed on him only by standing beside something even more bloated with myth. After becoming involved with the effort to keep America from fighting Germany, serving the America First group as, ironically, its most public figure, he was even willing to cooperate with interviewers from the Hearst papers if that would advance the cause.

His *Wartime Journals* show a proud man who becomes a victim of too stiff a rectitude and too great a naiveté. He can actually conclude after addressing an America First rally in Cleveland that "no sensible person can attend these meetings without realizing that public opinion is *not* ready for war." That such a rally would attract the already converted does not seem to occur to him; and in those converts he takes dubious satisfaction. Two months after the Cleveland rally he is at another in Madison Square Garden: "I studied their faces carefully while I was sitting on the platform, and they were *far* above the average of New York. Those people are worth fighting for." Hitler remained a tragic figure to him, as late as 1945 and after his own useful World War II service as a colonel in the Air Force. In May 1945, on an inspection tour of Germany, he stands in the Führer's ruined mountain retreat office at Berchtesgaden, lamenting Hitler's failure to use his power for good, but also picturing him in this spot a few weeks before, "where I am standing, looking through that window, realizing the collapse of his dreams, still struggling desperately against overwhelming odds."

Lindbergh, like Nicolson, claimed that he never gave a thought to publishing his journals at the time he was keeping them. But the diaries from the early forties reveal the careful precautions he took to deposit them (along with Anne's) at Yale, lest they be damaged by the approaching war. They were to be his eventual answer to the press that had made him its captive and the political detractors who had questioned his loyalty. On July 19, 1941, he wrote: "Anne and I are not ashamed of the way we have lived our lives, and there is nothing in our records that we fear to have known. I wonder how many of our accusers would be willing to turn their complete files and records over for study in the future." In his introduction to the journals the publisher William Jovanovich recalls how he once asked Lindbergh to read what he felt was a sympathetic and reasonably meticulous biography of himself: "Soon afterward I received from him a document of seventy-six typewritten pages in which he listed the factual inaccuracies of the book, whose author had naturally depended mostly upon newspaper sources." The huge deliberateness of such refutation is disturbing. The *Wartime Journals* are sad reading,

but they were inevitable. A man who can privately respond to a biography with seventy-six pages of correc-
tions will not be content to reply to his critics in sum; he
will want the evidence of hundreds of days set out one
by one.

If one had wished to give Lindbergh an antidote to his
romantic view of the Nazis, no more jolting dosage could
have been provided than the journals kept by Joseph
Goebbels during the final months of the Third Reich.
They are a bizarre blend of cruelty, delusion, and only
occasional awareness that the end is approaching. They
read like the chart of a patient slipping in and out of a
high fever; most of the time a delirium of thought and
language is the rule. Throughout these bomb-drenched
last days Goebbels can be found correcting the proofs of
a new book, still duly noting who is up and who is down
in bureaucratic favor, and making sure his own contribu-
tions to the regime are made plain. On March 22, 1945,
as his countrymen are starving, and either submitting to
or openly welcoming the enemy, he records: "My war
propaganda is now being eulogised quite openly in
London. It is being said that it is the most exemplary of
all the war efforts being made anywhere today and that
it is primarily responsible for the fact that German
resistance is so much in evidence, even though on a
reduced and enfeebled scale." The familiar diction of
the Big Lie, the soporific idiom of any tyranny, has
almost entire possession of Goebbels's tongue. When he
reports a successful holding action, he must intone it:
"Violent Soviet attacks in East Prussia once more failed
against the unflinching resistance of our defences." He
hopes to seduce history with the same voice he shouted
into the microphones; it doesn't matter that the amphi-
theater is empty or that he's left with a simple diary
instead of thousands of broadcast megawatts. He cannot
turn himself off.

Even when a cause is noble it is an unsettling thing to
see a man become an idea; exhortation can pulverize

nuance in the speaker and the audience. Even though Leon Trotsky insisted that a man must live in the service of "a great idea," and that he took up a diary in his French and Norwegian exile because it was the only forum he had left, and even though he felt guilty when he let the texture of personal routine and reflection creep into it — "All this is trivial detail compared with the realization that the fascist reaction is moving closer every day" — enough of that personal detail manages to find a place in his book to make it not just an apologia for his dissident Marxism, but a human portrait as well. That a diarist would try to suppress his personality, the quirks of circumstances and mentality that make him what he is, seems the oddest kind of ambition given the sprawling allowances for self-indulgence the genre permits. But that is what Trotsky, like many other apologists, vexes himself with, and his book sometimes comes alive only in spite of his wishes, during his lapses.

In most places the voice of the true believer and propagandist is present, whether it is directed toward the brutalities of Stalin, the timidity of the French premier Léon Blum, or the hucksterism of Lourdes, but Trotsky's nature and diction are hardly the mad mix of a Dr. Goebbels. He can still see the moment for the millennium: "It's spring, the sun is hot, the violets have been in bloom for about ten days, the peasants are puttering around in the vineyards. Last night we listened to *Die Walküre* from Bordeaux until midnight. Military service extended to two years. Rearmament of Germany. Preparations for a new 'final' war. The peasants peacefully prune their vines and fertilize the furrows between them. Everything is in order . . . And yet this order has hopelessly undermined itself. It will collapse with a stench." It is easier to trust a man's future visions when, as here, he retains a sharp eye for the present moment. The finest passages in Trotsky's book concern his wife, and show how their marriage was not just one of minds and causes, but of spirit and romance, too. On March 27, 1935, he records how she suddenly had to sit and rest when they were out on their walk:

> What a pang of pity I felt for youth, *her* youth . . . One night we ran home from the Paris Opera to the *rue* Gassendi, 46, *au pas gymnastique*, holding hands. It was in 1903. Our combined age was 46 . . . N. was probably the more indefatigable one. Once, while a whole crowd of us were walking somewhere in the outskirts of Paris, we came to a bridge. A steep cement pier sloped down from a great height. Two small boys had climbed on to the pier over the parapet of the bridge and were looking down on the passers-by. Suddenly N. started climbing toward them up the steep smooth slope of the pier. I was petrified. I didn't think it was possible to climb up there. But she kept walking up with her graceful stride, on high heels, smiling to the boys. They waited for her with interest. We all stopped anxiously. N. went all the way up without looking at us, talked to the children, and came down the same way, without having made, as far as one could see, a single superfluous effort or taken a single uncertain step . . . It was spring, and the sun was shining as brightly as it did today when N. suddenly sat down in the grass.

Trotsky soon calls an abrupt halt to this reflection on youth and age, knowing that he must get his book back to the serious business of politics: "Perhaps all these thoughts come to mind because the radio is playing Wagner's *Götterdämmerung*." This excuse doesn't ring very true, and even it is made possible only by a diary's love for the immediate moment.

Retaining his sense of the absurd is one of the ways the banished man of the opposition retains his humanness. Jayaprakash Narayan, leader of the "JP" movement for a new nonviolent revolution in India, was imprisoned for 139 days during Indira Gandhi's 1975 state of emergency.

The *Prison Diary* he kept is certainly a brief for his revolutionary programs, but his book is so full of quiet, gentlemanly ironies about Mrs. Gandhi's betrayal of her country and political birthright that its author often sounds like one of the shrewdly soft-spoken friends of Dr. Aziz in *A Passage to India*. We hear a good man, one whose heart and voice have not been engorged with fanaticism, despite the thorough cultural transformation his movement seeks. Pondering whether he should request parole to help in administering relief after terrible floods in his home state of Bihar, he lets sorrow and jest accompany his anger at having to make such a plea to the daughter of Nehru: "I recall that at the time of the great earthquake in 1934, the British released Rajen Babu from the Hazaribagh jail — not on any request from him but on their own. But Mrs. Gandhi is not so human or weak, if you will, as the British imperialists!" Like a good diplomat who keeps his eye on his mission even when he would like to indulge in the luxury of anger, Narayan maintains restraint.

Veljko Mićunović, who kept a diary when he served as Tito's ambassador to Moscow during the 1950s, shows almost biblical patience as he navigates the Orwellian tunnels of Russian-Yugoslav relations during the Cold War. No matter how often or instantly history is rewritten, he fills his pages, as he seems to have filled his meetings, with quiet point-by-point refutations of slander and bullying and false flattery. To a reader of his diary he becomes a trusted Virgilian guide through a frosty version of hell. On November 6, 1956, while flying between Belgrade and Moscow, he notes how three days before, Soviet troops had been preparing their invasion of Budapest even as Khrushchev and Tito held talks, at Brioni, that were supposed to settle the Hungarian dispute. Khrushchev and Malenkov, he reports,

behaved in an extremely cordial manner, as never before. This was a premeditated gesture intended to

influence our talks and our whole attitude toward
them, because it is simply impossible to behave otherwise toward people with whom one has recently been
exchanging kisses as with the closest of friends. As I
am writing this I still seem to feel Malenkov's fat
round face, into which my nose sank as if into a half-
inflated balloon as I was drawn into a cold and quite
unexpected embrace.

And that is as strident as he ever allows himself to become.

Men like Trotsky and Narayan and Mićunović spent
lifetimes pleading their causes. Their revolutions were the
stuff not of seasons but of epochs. But when the sixties
came, that time when it was said we could all be famous
for fifteen minutes, methods of promotion — of oneself
and one's cause — changed. It was a time of sunshine
revolutionaries, of heroes and villains quickly created and
quickly eclipsed. And it was a time when a number of
diaries became published instant replays. One of them,
The Strawberry Statement, is the journal of James Simon
Kunen, a student who took part in the April 1968 up-
rising at Columbia, the university George Templeton
Strong helped build. With its vignettes of library sit-ins
and street demonstrations, and its gee-whiz political phi-
losophizing, it is a charming book for stretches, but too
aware of its own freakish birth not to be a little embarrassed by it. *New York* magazine encourages Kunen to
keep this diary, so he does, and on May 21, 1968, he
writes: "As a result of the proliferation of my diary in
New York magazine, I am now a qualified spokesman for
the Columbia strikers, the international peace movement,
and everyone in the world younger than thirty." A couple
of months later he muses:

> This ego-blast book I'm writing fits well into the anti-
> hierarchy scheme, it seems to me, because I am not an
> author, nor will I be an author once having written a
> book. This seems altogether fitting and proper. Why
> should only book writers write books? Who cares

about them? They're not where it's at. Let everybody write so that no one is a writer.

While few would argue with the diary's being among the most democratic of all literary forms, a generous forum to the dispossessed, its offer to be the effortless "ego-blast" of those seeking a joy ride with history is perhaps its least attractive potential. That period of instant fame and instant books, which Kunen flagged down and Richard Nixon presided over in part, gave us some gruesome shotgun marriages of the diary and history.

To see Richard Nixon's televised awkwardness, even when he was at the height of his foreign policy achievements and popularity, could be painful, embarrassing, or delicious, depending on one's own politics and personality. But few would deny his odd lack of a self-image. For thirty years he sheepishly begged an identity from history's hands, a sense of who he was that he could not only project but recognize as himself. Nightclub impressionist David Frye used to get his biggest laugh by saying, "I *am* the President" in Nixonian tones with shaking jowls and V-waving fingers, and one can almost believe that Nixon's lack of a sense of self was so huge that he needed the very presidency to give him just the minimum identity a man needs in order to live. In a sense he was saying, "I am the President, therefore I am." The President is, after all, assured of having his existence confirmed by history. And so is his assassin. To enter history you can become a President or you can kill one; the attention is guaranteed. Whenever the President is in public view he is followed by news cameras — just in case the unthinkable should happen, it will be on film. White House reporters know it is a death watch; the reels of their cameras spin as endlessly as Nixon's own tape recorders. It is a fact to fixate the man who would quickly shoplift an identity from history. Arthur Bremer, a twenty-one-year-old unemployed virgin busboy shot and paralyzed George Wallace in Laurel, Maryland, on May 15, 1972. The "Manuscript

Found in Bremer's Vehicle," 113 pages that were introduced as evidence at his trial (another 148 pages were
buried, and discovered years later, near his furnished
room in Milwaukee) showed that Wallace was Bremer's
second choice. Richard Nixon had been his first.

With some savings from his last job, and the certainty
that assassination would make people pay attention to him,
Bremer stalked the President across the Canadian border
when Nixon made a state visit to Ottawa in April 1972.
"Speed limit — 70 m.p.h. I did over 90 once or twice —
danger gave me an erection," he notes on his arrival in
Canada on April 21. Two days later he waits for Nixon
outside the American Embassy, intending not only to kill
him, but to do it nonchalantly:

> I wanted to shock the shit out of the SS men with my
> calmness. A little something to be remmered by. All
> these things seemed important to me, were important
> to me, in my room.
> I will give very little if ANY thought to these things
> on any future attempts.
> After all does the world remember if Sirhan's tie was
> on straight?
> *SHIT*, I was stupid!!

Here Arthur Bremer forgets his business for a moment.
He interrupts his speech to posterity with a little repri-
mand to himself. But this is just a pause; his book is
clearly not a memorandum written to its author. It is his
address to the hundreds of millions who are going to
have to watch — again and again, slow motion, instant
replay — what he, Arthur Bremer, is going to do. His
apologia is as important to him as the approaching deed
itself. On April 24 he is "thruorly pissed off. About a
million things. Was pissed off befor I couldn't find a pen
to write this down. This will be one of the most closely
read pages since the Scrolls in those caves. And I couldn't
find a pen for 40 seconds & went mad. My fuse is about
burnt. There's gona be an explosion soon. I had it. I want

something to happen. I was sopposed to be Dead a week & a day ago. Or at least infamous." He needs his book as much as his target; his homicidal and literary enterprises are one.

Bremer is an astute observer of the mass media. When he fails to get Nixon and begins to go after Wallace, he understands that his new course will incur him less notice. This annoys him:

> SHIT! I won't even rate a T.V. enteroption in Russia or Europe when the news breaks — they never heard of Wallace. If something big in Nam flares up I'll end up at the bottom of the 1st page in America. The editors will say — "Wallace dead? Who cares." He won't get more than 3 minutes on network T.V. news. I don't expect anybody to get a big throbbing erection from the news. You know, a storm in some country we never heard of kills 10,000 people — big deal.

But he shoots him anyway. Wallace was paralyzed; Bremer's blond crew cut and sunglasses impressed themselves for a brief time on hundreds of millions of minds, and then he went to jail. He is still there. His diary was published by Harper's Magazine Press. Near the end of his manuscript Bremer had written: "© copyright 1972 Arthur H. Bremer entire contens pages 1–248 inclusive or parts or portions there of may not be reproduced without the written consent of the author."

Harding Lemay, who wrote the introduction to the published edition, finds Bremer "pitiful and oddly touching" and his copyright notice "a heartbreaking plea." If it is heartbreaking, it was also perfectly sensible — Harper's indeed had to indicate that their edition was "© 1972, 1973 by Arthur H. Bremer." Bremer understood the vehicle he would ride into history. He succeeded: if not quite the Dead Sea Scrolls, his diary was published, read, and reviewed. He did what all apologists wish to accomplish; he made history prick up its ears and take notice, however briefly. Mr. Lemay presented

Bremer's diary more or less as a document that indicted us all for his act. We were sociologically responsible for Arthur Bremer; in some way his crime was our fault. This is a familiar argument about murder, political and otherwise; it may even have some merit. But for the reader to take responsibility for the impulse of Arthur Bremer to be heard through his diary is to try to assert control over too basic a part of the human make-up. Arthur Bremer's need to be noticed was a human one, however haywire it had gone; as long as men live in history, and can imagine both an audience and a future, Bremer will happen again and again. Changing society would not prevent more of him; only changing the nature of man could have a chance at that.

Lee Harvey Oswald chose "Historic Diary" as the name for the journal he wrote in Moscow. His 1959 defection to Russia was the first way he chose to be noticed, and he was determined to record his act for all the world to read. When it seemed, several days after his arrival, that he would not be permitted to stay, he attempted suicide. He later made this entry for October 21, 1959:

> I am shocked!! *** I have waited for 2 year to be accepted. My fondes dreams are shattered because of a petty offial, *** I decide to end it. Soak rist in cold water to numb the pain, Than slash my leftwrist. Than plaug wrist into bathtum of hot water. *** Somewhere, a violin plays, as I wacth my life whirl away. I think to myself "How easy to Die" and "A Sweet Death, (to violins) ***

Like Bremer, Oswald seems to have read just enough books to remember and occasionally approximate the "literary" tone appropriate to dramatic happenings to the hero. Both assassins present themselves to posterity in tacky rhetorical finery, and they are determined to be let in. Their choice of a diary as the written counterpart of their action is especially sensible, given the high-risk nature of their occupation (consider Oswald and Jack

Ruby); the assassin knows he may not get the chance to write his memoirs.

Most men and women don't seek to burst upon the world's notice with an insane and momentary flare. They look for a living, a niche, a measure of honor and security. When these hopes and expectations are thwarted, then, in the words of Willy Loman's wife, attention must be paid. Diaries, in these cases too, have served to present demands for recognition — as well as stiff upper lips — to the world that has abused their writers. Every century offers its examples.

Simon Forman was an enterprising man, even for an Elizabethan. He flamboyantly combined his skills as an astrologer and sexologist — a kind of Ur-Californian — into a London consulting practice that attracted such prominent customers as the sea voyager Sir Thomas Shirley, earned him a mention in *The Devil Is an Ass*, and inspired no less a play than *The Alchemist*. He left behind casebooks that are now treasure chests of Elizabethan sexuality and superstition. He also left behind a small diary, which records the struggles of his noble occupation against such finicky guardians of public order as Giles Estcourt, Justice of the Peace:

> The 12th of June [1579] I was robbed and spoiled of all my goods and books first dwelling in Fisherton parsonage, and was committed to prison, where I lay sixty weeks before I was released. I had much trouble and defamation without desert by that cursed villain, Giles Estcourt . . . This year I did prophesy the truth of many things which afterwards came to pass. The very spirits were subject unto me; what I spake was done. And I had a great name; yet I could do nothing but at adventure.

These are not false protests; Simon Forman was not by nature a complainer, just a man who grew weary with the law's restraint of his innovative trade. By 1587 he seems resigned to living as best he can in the face of continuing harassment by justices and sheriffs: "This year I had much trouble and imprisonments. I practised magic, and had much strife with divers that I had in suits of law; but I thrived reasonable well, yet I lost much. Thomas Eyre sent me to prison the 6th of March."

One likes Simon Forman, as one likes most Elizabethans; they never surprise us when we discover them stumbling onto new continents and making poems of matching magnitude. To move to the English eighteenth century, with all its gouty politicians hunting for places in fractious Parliaments and writing aggrieved poems to settle their literary and political scores, is to sigh with a sense of diminution: too many coughing Whigs and too few Tom Joneses. George Bubb Dodington, keeper of one of the century's most copious political diaries, was, alas, one of the century's representative men. His eye never strayed far from the sight of a warm plush chair waiting for his girth and influence to sink into it, and his diary records, with a staggering lack of insight into his own motives, his every maneuver in its direction.

He attached himself to Frederick, Prince of Wales, at a time when the Prince was having one of those protracted and tiresome eighteenth-century kinds of quarrels with his ruling Hanoverian father. But Dodington always did his best to keep a door open back at the main palace, too, and soon after the Prince unexpectedly died in 1751, he sought a way to return to the government. On May 5, 1752, he records his conversation with Henry Pelham, First Lord of the Treasury, with a smarmy exactness of such length that we can only admire his endurance:

I said that as to quitting the King's service [originally], I did not do it by any compact with the Prince, that it was full four months after, before his Royal Highness made me any offers, and then did it in such a manner that left me no room to refuse, without offending him for ever. That Mr. Solicitor-General Murray knew this, and I had living and written evidence to prove it uncontestably. Since I came into the service, I could appeal to him, whether my behaviour was not entirely calculated to soften, rather than inflame: even to the loss of my favour; whether, when the little incendiary system prevail'd, by which alone many of those about his Royal Highness could ever be of any significance, since I could not stop it I did not absent myself from the House, rather than take part, or countenance it. But however, I desir'd the King should know that I would not justify with my King, and my master, and submitted myself to think I was to blame, since he was displeas'd and therefore begg'd his pardon, which was all in my power to do except by my future services to show him that I deserv'd it. That this with the interest I could, and was willing to center towards his service, I thought might be sufficient to remove objections, that had really no foundation: especially, when convey'd through so able, so powerful, and I trusted, so friendly a canal.

Uriah Heep could scarcely have held this note longer.

Pelham, unfortunately, also died, and Dodington lost this chance for rapprochement, but he did not retreat from the political wars. In April 1754 he campaigned for the parliamentary seat from Bridgewater against the Earl of Egmont. The days before the election he records having "spent in the infamous and disagreable compliance with the low habits of venal wretches" — such is the politician's lot — only to lose the election "by the injustice of the Returning Officer. The numbers were, for Lord Egmont 119, for Mr Balch 114, for me 105. — Of my good votes, 15 were rejected: 8 bad ones for Lord Egmont were receiv'd." ("Never complain, never explain" was not stitched into the Dodington family crest.) The next day, he records, he "left Bridgewater — for ever." Here it is not perhaps irrelevant to note an entry in the diary of Lord Egmont's father, made twenty years before, recounting a conversation with Horace Walpole, brother of the Prime Minister: "He described Doddington as the vilest man, vain, ambitious, loose and never to be satisfied. He wants now to be a Lord, and when he is that, he will want to be a Duke."

Benjamin Haydon, born into the next century in Britain, a time when the various reform bills were only beginning to pry the Dodingtons of the country from those plush chairs, spent much of his hugely ambitious, productive, and debt-stalked career attempting to convince the rulers of his country that they should be commissioning paintings of Britain's heroic past rather than supporting the painters of ladies and lap dogs sheltered by the Royal Academy. It was a grand struggle against Philistinism, slander, and privation that Haydon carried on, and he recorded most of it in twenty-six volumes of journals forever to rank with the greatest diaries of complaint and self-promotion. A huge, hearty, boiling stew of a man, witty, paranoid, bathetic, and glorious, Haydon details his fight for a living and a cause in journals that could hardly be more rich, rough, and fortifying to read. The volumes read like a lifelong harangue from Speakers' Corner in Hyde Park, the complainant never pausing long enough to catch his breath or take a sip of water. What he writes on July 16, 1830, a few days before one of his trials for debt, can be considered the keynote of the speech:

> The most difficult people in the World to rouse are the English, and they are the most terrific when roused.
>
> Nothing moves them so soon as injustice, and I will venture to say that my treatment if fully detailed, would rouse them as much as any of their great political questions.
>
> Every real Friend of the Arts would rejoice to see these jackdaws [viz., creditors and solicitors] stript of their corporate importance, and sent, unplumed, about their business.

Sixteen years later, in the last months of his life, he is still fighting off bill collectors and the indifference of his countrymen. As his exhibition of *The Burning of Rome by Nero* and *Banishment of Aristides* fails, he writes: "They rush by thousands to see [Tom] Thumb. They push, they fight, they scream, they faint, they cry help & murder, & oh & ah. They see my bills, my boards, my caravans, & don't read them." And yet, working on his last great historical canvas, *Alfred and the First British Jury*, he finds that not even the mental confusion brought on by his dangerously increasing debts can long keep him from his painting:

> Came home in excruciating anxiety, not being able to raise the money for my rent for the Hall, & found a notice from a broker for a Quarter's rent from New-ton, my old landlord for 22 years! For a moment my brain was confused! I had paid him half, & therefore there was only 10. left. I went into the painting room in great misery of mind. That so old a Friend should have chosen such a moment to do so gross a thing is painful. After a hour's dullness, my mind suddenly fired up, with a new background for Alfred. I dashed at it, & at dinner it was enormously improved. I make a Sketch tomorrow, & then begin to finish with the Saxon Noble.
>
> But what a struggle is High Art in England!

Only after the struggle becomes too painfully fierce, on June 22, 1856, does he make his final entry:

> God forgive-me — Amen.
> Finis
> of
> B. R. Haydon
> "Stretch me no longer on this tough World" — Lear.
> End —
> XXVI Volume.

He left the diary open, and then he shot himself.

It may be ironic that one of Haydon's great artistic legacies is his aggrieved diary, but it still can't be denied that he at least got the chance to struggle in his vocation in a society whose gate toward professional fulfillment was very strait indeed. Thousands of men and women went to quiet graves after being so flatly denied the opportunity to begin pursuing their ambitions that they would have craved even Haydon's setbacks. One of these sad and brave souls was Ellen Weeton, who grew up in the village of Upholland near Wigan. As a young woman she kept a school and worked as a governess to help support her mother and further the ambitions of the selfish and scheming brother she mistakenly loved. She recorded her sacrifices by keeping copies of the letters she sent, as well as a journal proper, in a series of books which were not rediscovered until nearly a century after her death. They tell the story of a highly intelligent woman whose talents for learning and writing were thwarted by sex and circumstance. In 1810 we find her at Dove's Nest, serving as governess in the family of Edward Pedder, who reminds a reader of Thackeray's Sir Pitt Crawley:

> The comforts of which I have deprived myself in coming here, and the vexations that occur sometimes during the hours of instruction with a child of such a strange temper to instruct, would almost induce me to give up my present situation, did not the consideration which brought me here, still retain me. O Brother! sometime thou wilt know perhaps the deprivations I have undergone for thy sake, and that thy attentions have not been such as to compensate them . . . I will be patient — I will be resigned, and — with the help of the Power around me, I will persevere.

In 1814 she marries Aaron Stock, a widower, partly because that, too, is to her brother's financial advantage. Stock abuses her physically and mentally and then forces

her out of their house, depriving her of their daughter,
Mary. From this time on the copybooks are not kept for
any generalized idea of posterity, but for the girl who is
growing up without her mother. Miss Weeton spends the
years of her daughter's youth bewildered and resentful
at her abandonment, and mystified by society's counte-
nancing of it. In June 1825 she meets another deserted wife
who is on her way, with her child, to seek aid from the
parish she grew up in: "How frequent are these instances
of cruelty to wives! What hard hearts men have, and how
little punishment they meet with for this description of
profligacy. If they steal a sheep or a horse, they are
pursued and hung; to desert a wife is a thousand times a
greater crime; yet no police pursues him for this." We
see her travel alone through London and Wales, timidly
venturing into Vauxhall, curiously approaching a Welsh
slate quarry (but afraid to come closer to it than two
hundred yards because of the men there), walking dis-
tances that make a twentieth-century reader's feet ache
in his house slippers. She is wary but resourceful, an enforced blend of Jane Eyre and Moll Flanders. Condemned
to a wanderer's existence, she is baffled and angry at her
fate, but dignified in the face of it:

> The solitary life I lead, is not from choice; I see no
> way of avoiding it. In lodgings, I have hitherto found
> it unavoidable; and I have found no family to board
> with, who would take me on such terms as I can
> afford — such a family, I mean, as I could wish to
> reside with; for I could not be comfortable to mingle
> continually with people of coarse manners, vulgar, and
> illiterate. I appear to be condemned to solitude for
> life. I am naturally of a lively, social turn, and to be
> often in the company of such as possess highly gifted
> and highly cultivated minds, would be a gratification
> to me, superior even to books. But! God has said "Set
> your affections on things above, and not on things of
> the earth." — and therefore appears to have specially

deprived me of all those things on which I could have set my affections. Thy will be done! I see Thy mercies and Thy Graciousness in this, and am thankful.

The diarists we've just met were dispossessed by the traditional blind spots of their civilizations. Others, ordinarily content, have become internal exiles only during periods of national history so unusually dark that they were ashamed to be living in them. Their diaries have been written to let outsiders and future countrymen know that there was a saving remnant of the citizenry that kept its head and decency even when the prevailing Zeitgeist went berserk.

Lady Augusta Gregory, Yeats's artistic partner in the Irish literary revival early in this century, usually filled her diary with the literary news and movements of her time. But during the Irish rebellion and civil war her book became an explanation of those caught between their Irish patriotism and their hatred of violence; she wished to be a "Republican 'without malice,'" an impossible affiliation. Lady Gregory was an aristocrat, the owner of the house at Coole that Yeats was to celebrate as a sanctuary of beauty in this especially nasty century in history's cycles. She spent the years of rebellion wondering if the house would survive to be passed on to her heirs. Between 1919 and 1923 her diaries react to the miseries of terrorism, executions both official and partisan, and the brutality of the Black and Tans — which gives way only to the cruelty of the Republicans after the British withdraw in 1922. "'Wasn't it a woeful time!'" she quotes the Kinvara oysterwoman as saying about one of the bad winters in this era, and for periods her own pen is so immobilized by doubts about means and ends that she cannot do much more than utter similar sighs. For all her many friends on the different sides of the violence, Lady Gregory is forced to endure this period in a state of fearful indecision: "I told Father O'K[elly] one should no more be angry with Government or Re-

and loss on paper is an open question: putting love in writing has, after all, cost men and women everything from embarrassment to money to jail terms. But the compulsion is strong, and the diary stands with the sonnet and the letter as a place where great love can be immortalized, apparent mismatches defended to the world, and revenge — immediate or posthumous — sought against the faithless.

Marie Jenney Howe wrote that when that amazing French protean George Sand "was normal she did her work. Whenever she lost her poise she wrote a journal." One of those poiseless periods occurs when she is overthrown by the quixotic creator of *Fantasio*, Alfred de Musset. The journal she keeps in November 1834 shows how love can make the most sublime fool out of even the shrewd and proud. It is as messy and unfocused as George Sand herself was that fall. Huge in her blame of both, she uses some entries to address Musset and some to address herself; in others she talks to God. She uses the journal alternately to torture and cure herself, and above all to make Musset *understand*.

She is justifiably indignant at the gap between her strong intelligence and her weak flesh: "Am I not thirty years old and in full possession of all my powers? Yes, God in heaven, I feel that I am. I am still able to make a man happy and proud if he is willing to help me. I need a steady arm to uphold me, a heart without vanity to receive and sustain me. If I had ever found such a man I should not be where I am now. But these masterful men are like gnarled oaks whose exterior is repellent." She is trapped by her preference for the frailer Musset. "You were too suave, too subtle. When I tried to draw near, you dissolved into air before my lips could touch you. You are like those blossomy shrubs of India and China that bend with the slightest wind. From their frail stems we never obtain strong beams with which to build homes. We taste their nectar, we grow heady with their perfume, under their influence we fall asleep and die."

publicans than with different sections of one's own mind, tilting to good or bad on one or the other side, in many questions besides this." She wonders "what Christ would do were He here now."

The diary of Friedrich Percyval Reck-Malleczewen, a German aristocrat and philosopher, records, on October 30, 1942, observations that Lady Gregory's friend Yeats would recognize as bizarre symptoms of "The Second Coming" he prophesied:

> For the last nine years, since the coming of Hitlerism, the summers have been concepts on a calendar, only, and have drowned us in rainfall like the original Flood. Year after year, the vintages have failed. The botanists say that certain plants which normally bloom in the fall now come up in spring, while there are spring-blooming plants which now emerge in late fall. I have heard from zoologists on the Eastern Front, in the northern Caucasus, that tropical snakes formerly native to India are now to be found in the vicinity of the Volga, on the threshold of Europe. Thus, everything is out of joint, the usual order of things has been overturned.

These notations are addressed to "you, future reader," who can still open the journal Reck-Malleczewen kept until he was arrested by the Gestapo and killed at Dachau: "Night after night, I hide this record deep in the woods on my land . . . constantly on watch lest I am observed, constantly changing my hiding place." The line that occurs again and again, snapping posterity to attention, is: "Thus we live in Germany today." Reck-Malleczewen was a well-born East Prussian, a stern and conservative man appalled by the shrill transformation of frustrated mailmen and schoolteachers into Nazis. His diary records their tyrannies, both petty and enormous, as part of the rise of modern "mass man," a formless and godless creature oozing onto the saddle of civilization. Reck-

Malleczewen sustains himself in this dark time by hating the "vegetarian Tamerlane" who leads them:

> I have hated you in every hour that has gone by, I hate you so that I would happily give my life for your death, and happily go to my own doom if only I could witness yours, take you with me into the depths. When I let this hate free, I am almost overcome by it, but I cannot change this and do not really know how it could be otherwise. Let no one deprecate this, nor fool himself about the power of such hatred. Hate drives to reality. Hate is the father of action. The way out of our defiled and desecrated house is through the command to hate Satan. Only so will we earn the right to search in the darkness for the way of love.

If these animadversions seem to prefigure Solzhenitsyn's calls for a religious cleansing, they also make Reck-Malleczewen an heir to Dostoevski, whose own angrily prophetic journal he quotes: "And what are the words, 'The end of the world is at hand,' which Dostoevsky wrote in his journal seventy years ago, but a presentiment of the apocalyptic horsemen now thundering down upon us, and a prophecy of how utterly lost we have become?"

When history is made by fiends it will be officially recorded by slaves. That is why private men like Reck-Malleczewen, at the risk of their lives, have turned diaries into the only truthful chronicles of whole people and generations. What such diary-histories lack in statistics and documents they make up for with the passion of the single human voice, one man standing for thousands. Chaim A. Kaplan, who ran a Hebrew elementary school in Warsaw and was to die at Treblinka, kept, in Hebrew, a diary of his life in the ghetto — partly to unburden his sorrow, but mostly in the service of history. He worries about the inadequacy of his book in the face of the enormities it is charged with preserving, but he knows his record has its own special methods and truth:

> I risk my life with my writing, but my abilities are limited; I don't know all the facts; those that I do know may not be sufficiently clear; and many of them I write on the basis of rumors whose accuracy I cannot guarantee. But for the sake of truth, I do not require individual facts, but rather the manifestations which are the fruits of a great many facts that leave their impression on the people's opinions, on their mood and morale. And I can guarantee the factualness of these manifestations because I dwell among my people and behold their misery and their souls' torments.

Like Reck-Malleczewen, he is urged to give up his task as being too hopeless and too dangerous. He understands the risks, but chooses to take them. On June 27, 1942, he writes: "These lines are being written after midnight, and out of the silence of the night, the rumble of the wheels of the cars hurrying on their way to Pawiak, the house of slaughter, reaches my ears. A ray of light showing through the window would endanger my life." His diary becomes his "sacred task," and he continues to write even when he has gone for days without food. The last line he writes, on August 4, 1942, is a question: "If my life ends — what will become of my diary?"

The answer is that his attempt to smuggle it out of the ghetto was successful; it would be discovered years later in its hiding place — a kerosene can.

Until now we have been looking at people serving or opposing things larger than themselves — causes, tyrannies, revolutions, obsessions, anonymous prejudices, armies, and secret police. But most of the battles we fight, aside from those within ourselves, are fought for and against the individual beings we know best. The diaries launched by love travel with more passionate velocity than most, and their courses are usually the most erratic of all. Whether or not one should put the record of love

She gets advice from Liszt, Sainte-Beuve, and Delacroix. The last tells her: " 'Let yourself go . . . When I am in that condition I have no pride. I was not born a Roman.' " "Go" she does indeed. Restraint is rarely the hallmark of the love apologia, and it certainly has no place in these pages of George Sand. "Last night I dreamed that he was beside me, that he embraced me. I awoke swooning with joy. What a dream, my God! This death's-head beside me, and this gloomy room where he will never set foot again, this bed where he will sleep no more! I could not keep from crying out. Poor Sophie [her maid], what nights I give her!"

One likes to imagine Sophie's diary.

Sand's, with its complete lack of inhibition, probably did her some good. By the time we reach the point at which she contemplates suicide and the reaction her son and daughter would have, we are certain she has no intention of doing anything as silly as that. The words she turns upon herself are punishment enough: "Preach your big words, then, and make your phrases. Make some yourself, unhappy woman. You who write, unconscious of what you are writing. You who know nothing, nothing, except that you love enough to die of love." (She would live another forty-two years.)

Perhaps we keep telling ourselves that this journal must have been healthful for her because we feel a bit guilty reading it — we get too much entertainment from it at the expense of its author. We don't want her to stop putting down all these words, as beautiful, lush, and silly as opera. Here, at only thirty, she has something of the aging film star or croaking diva about her. Her torment is a little too gorgeous to take seriously, and yet, in the end, we feel pain for her, because we know that she sent this journal to Musset, that he ridiculed it, and that his brother published some of it. We admire but cringe at her crazy courage — as we leave her to Chopin, whom she would meet two years after that distracted November.

Laurence Sterne's *Journal to Eliza* is not, like Sand's,

the record of an early engagement in a lifetime spent
fighting love's wars. It is the record of one last debilitat-
ing campaign. During his last year Sterne composes a
journal recording his love for Mrs. Eliza Draper. It is
necessitated by Mrs. Draper's absence in India; it is made
convenient by Mrs. Sterne's absence in France. The journal is meant to be sent to Mrs. Draper as a day-to-day
record of Sterne's activities and affections. The parts
of it that were actually sent to her (as well as the one she
kept in counterpoint) have disappeared, but a fragment
of Sterne's, from April 13 to August 4, 1767, survives. It
is a remarkable production to have come from the creator of *Tristram Shandy*, the book of whimsy and ab-
surdity that managed to burlesque the novel almost before
the novel was invented. *Tristram Shandy* is a universe of
tricks, a Joycean castle of jokes and dreams. But love
and anger and sickness reduce its creator to almost a
single note of complaint in his diary. Whereas George
Sand berates herself as much as Musset, Sterne too often
just crabs. One can't believe his friends were as solicitous
of him in his trial as he says; he talks too much of how
he must turn them away, refuse their invitations. We
simply don't trust him after a while. But his book is still
more than, to use Robert Fothergill's phrase, "the written equivalent of a Moan." There is, for example, the
following entry from July 27, 1767:

Arrived at York. — where I had not been 2 hours
before My heart was overset with a pleasure, w.ᶜʰ
beggard every other, that fate could give me — save
thyself — It was thy dear Packets from Iago — I cannot give vent to all the emotions I felt even before I
opened them — for I knew thy hand — & my seal —
w.ᶜʰ was only in thy possession — O tis from my Eliza,
said I. — I instantly shut the door of my Bed-chamber,
& ordered myself to be denied — & spent the whole
evening, and till dinner the next day, in reading over
and over again the most interesting Acc.ᵗ — & the

most endearing one that ever tried the tenderness of
man — I read & wept — and wept and read till I was
blind — then grew sick, & went to bed — & in an
hour calld again for the Candle — to read it once more
— as for my dear Girls pains & her dangers I cannot
write ab.ᵗ them — because I cannot write my feelings
or express them any how to my mind — O Eliza!

Strip this passage of its rhetorical extravagance and you
will still be left with a moment of real drama, one made
possible more than anything else by the nature of a journal. No written medium may adequately convey antic-
ipation — Betsey Wynne's wait for Fremantle comes
to mind — but by the time he reaches this entry a reader
has witnessed months of Sterne's anguish and months of
his waiting for news of Eliza. Just as the passage does
not have to be weakened by retrospection, it has gathered
power from all the entries that have come before it:
Sterne has no way of knowing on what day this news
and emotion will burst, and neither does the reader.
When it does break he feels its force, and we can forgive
much of the whining that precedes it. (Also, he might
keep in mind what George Sand herself wrote: "First love
is the most ideal — and last love the most real and
inescapable.")

The diarist aching for love almost always claims that
he will go mad if his love is not reciprocated or restored.
Madness is the hyperbolic stock-in-trade of the apologist
for the heart. (Werther's friend Wilhelm published only
Werther's letters, but we also know that there was a
diary showing "how [he] got into all this, step by step.")
But when madness is terrible and real a man may turn
to his diary as the last hope of getting his story out
before he is locked away. In the winter of 1918–1919
Vaslav Nijinsky — his greatest dancing triumphs behind
him, his loyal wife Romola by his side, and the shadow
of the sanatorium before him — is at Saint Moritz and
going mad. He begins a diary with a zealousness that

frightens Romola: "He wrote feverishly for hours and hours, day and night. I tried to stop him, as I feared he would be exhausted. I felt that slowly, mercilessly, he was being drawn away from his art, his life, and me by an uncanny, invisible power." The document that is created claims to be a divinely inspired revelation to mankind. It is a brief for the poor, for vegetarianism, against war, and against the primacy of reason over feeling.

It is a strangely beautiful book (rediscovered fifteen years after he wrote it, when Romola searched some old trunks for costumes for an exhibition), sweet-souled with the guilelessness and logic of the mad. And it is a terrible book, an awful cry from a man who once leapt higher than any other man and who now buckles under the weight of his feelings of persecution. He writes: "I told my wife that I would destroy the man who would touch my notebooks, but I will cry if I have to do it. I am not a murderer." There are not many entries in the journal, and it hardly seems like a diary in any usual sense; it more resembles a long petition or a huge suicide note. But there is a scary immediacy surrounding Nijinsky's driven words that justifies the title by which his book has always been known: *The Diary of Vaslav Nijinsky*. At one point he writes: "My wife is telephoning. Thinking that I have gone for a walk she is having a heart-to-heart talk with the doctor. My wife loves me, she did not say anything nasty about me." People come up the stairs, into the room, threaten to interrupt his prophecy, make him afraid. His uncertainty as to his audience makes for moments that are comic as well as heartbreaking. He qualifies an attack on his mother-in-law with a brief mention of her kindness, and then says: "I talked of her kindness because I do not want people to think that I am nasty." Real freedom and perspicuousness have left him now; he will be costumed as Petrouchka for the rest of his life.

But one story of flesh and blood simmers beneath the surface of these visions and commandments. The story of Nijinsky and Diaghilev makes the diary the story of a man who suffered not from abandonment but suffocation by a lover. How the impresario tried to make him not only his performer, but also his creature, is the real story in this diary, the one the reader knows Nijinsky will keep returning to, the fuel of the volcano. After writing of politics and the First World War, he suddenly notes: "Diaghilev is a terrible man. I do not like terrible men, but I will not harm them. I do not want them to be killed. They are eagles. They prevent small birds from living, and therefore one must be on one's guard against them." Woven among reflections on justice, peace, poverty, and God are passages about Diaghilev's lust, his hair dye, his legal battles, his jealousy: "I practiced my dances and composed ballets alone. Diaghilev did not like this. He did not want me to do things alone, but I could not agree with him. We often quarreled. I used to lock my door — our rooms were communicating — and would let in no one. I was afraid of him. I knew that all my life was in his hands." Nijinsky asks for mercy upon his former possessor, but it is not Diaghilev who needs it. In fact, in a cruel and strange way Diaghilev has, long after abandoning Nijinsky, achieved his object: Nijinsky is utterly his, will never be apart from him, never free of the attentions of his memory. Still, Nijinsky tries to free himself, and the weapon he picks is his diary — if he can get Diaghilev to read it, he will have his revenge:

> I do not like wicked people. I have written down the name of Diaghielev, etc., etc., because it is easier for people to notice these names. I purposely made a mistake just now in writing the word Diaghilev because I want him to see that I have forgotten how to spell his name.

As it does in the case of the words against the mother-in-law, the diary, with the fond and incomplete cleverness of a child, reveals the trick as soon as it plays it. Immediately below the lines just quoted, Nijinsky adds: "I wanted to continue to write on the previous line, but God does not wish me to go on writing on the line where the name of Diaghilev is written. I have noticed my mistake, I had written the name of God and of Diaghilev with a capital. I will write god with a small letter because I want no similarity." But it is too late for such a wish. God and Diaghilev have been too long conflated for anything to be done about it now. Indeed, it is easier for Nijinsky to demote God to the lower case than Diaghilev.

Love, it is said, may be blind; but, it is duly noted, the neighbors aren't. What of the man or woman who is part of an arrangement the world deems wrong for him or her, but who, unlike Nijinsky, seeks to defend that match? Where does he or she find comfort and self-justification? Often, like the deserted or abused lover, in a diary. Dora Carrington, a confused young painter of some talent who stumbled onto the fringes of the Bloomsbury circle, spent the last half of her short life living with and keeping house for the biographer Lytton Strachey. Strachey, who turned clever dismissal into historical art, was powerfully educated, prematurely decrepit, fiercely witty, and thoroughly homosexual. Carrington, as she was always known in Bloomsbury, was none of these things, but she joined with Strachey in creating a household built of jokes and teasing, English nonsense, sexual safety, and true devotion. At times they appear to have been like a father and daughter, at others like a mother and son, and, more often, like children huddled in a Hansel-and-Gretel cottage.

In 1917 Mark Gertler, the painter, tried to break off his own relationship with Carrington because he couldn't comprehend her new attachment to Strachey. Carrington records the rupture, which occurred one April eve-

ning on Percy Street in London, in her diary, recon-
structing Gertler's words to her: "To think after all
these years in 3 months you should love a man like
Strachey twice your age (36) and emaciated and old.
As I always said life is a crooked business." Carrington
notes that she "walked back to Gower St and Mrs
R [eckes, the housekeeper] opened the door, and Alix
talked to me, and they did not know what a difference
there was, as if my nose had been cut away."

This is not to be the last of Gertler, and later there
will be Carrington's relationship with Gerald Brennan,
but from now on Strachey is to be the home of her emotions. It is a delicate life, something of a toy world, that
she makes with him, a world to which they can retreat
from periods of passion and turmoil with other partners,
one in which he gently educates her and she worship-
fully nurses him. Late in the spring of 1919 she writes:

> I saw Lytton writing on the lawn and out of sheer
> reverence did not dare disturb him so sent back the
> dinner three times. Finally cut mine off, and started
> eating it as I was so hungry. Lytton came laughing
> in and said "I have been waiting for you to call me" —
> and I had thought he was having inspirations and had
> not dared interrupt him! We roared with laughter
> most of lunch over it. Minnie was absolutely awed
> by reverence for the great author! And asked what
> time he would take tea! I painted most of afternoon.
> Interesting conversation at tea about Peterloo, Trades
> Unions, and Cooperation. Lytton has promised to read
> me the first part of [his biography of Queen] Victoria
> tonight — I am excited.

Strachey's death from cancer on January 21, 1932, leaves
Carrington despondent. A few weeks later she tries in
her diary to recall their odd symbiosis, but realizes that
it can neither be recaptured nor made clear to those outside the cottage walls:

No one will ever know the special perfectness of Lytton. The jokes when he was gay. "The queen of the East has vanished!" . . . Sometimes I thought how wasteful to let these jokes fly like swallows across the sky. But one couldn't write them down. We couldn't have been happier together. For every mood of his instantly made me feel in the same mood. All gone. And I never told him or showed him how utterly I loved him. And now there is nobody, darling Lytton, to make jokes with about Tiber and the horse of the ocean, no one to read me Pope in the evenings, no one to walk on the terrace. No one to write letters to, oh my very darling Lytton.

Exactly a month after making this entry, on March 11, 1932, Carrington shot and killed herself.

These have been extraordinary cases, people for whom love was or became all. If we recognize their passions, we may still be rather daunted by the scale on which they felt them. With most of us it is not often like that. Love, perhaps to our regret, is one of the things we are likely to experience in moderation. Most men and women will fall in love, be loved, fend off, pursue, and be rejected not so many times after all. Human continence and wariness are actually more remarkable than human wantonness. For most men and women love will be in the course of things, a part of the whole, and their diaries, like their lives, will fall into another chapter of such a book as this. To the hearer there are cries for real and cries of wolf. Whether he chooses to listen or turn a deaf ear will depend on the patience he's been endowed with, the ethics he's learned or chosen, and what kind of day it has been. But most human beings would rather receive attention than pay it, and unless the circumstances of the apologist with a diary are genuinely woeful, or his cause tremendously just, a reader is likely to shut his book like a vaudeville manager who hooks and drags a tiresome act off the stage. The autobiographer who seeks to justify a life on the whole or in balance can usually win our sympathy or at least our hearing. But the diarist who hits the stride of daily self-justification — and once hit it is not easy to break — may arouse our suspicions and eventually our disgust. Ad infinitum usually means ad nauseam.

But where there is real suffering there can be no better way to understand it than to see it unfold in its daily wretchedness. It is one thing to hear of a man who has spent ten years in prison for a crime he didn't commit; it is another to be taken into his cell and shown the three thousand lines he scratched on the walls to count off the days. Real horror, like real suspense, is best built gradually. Probably no book can build it more effectively than a diary. In the summer of 1979 the bones of Tammy Mathre, a twenty-year-old college student from Knoxville, Iowa, were found scattered in the mountains of Wyoming. A year before, after a period of emotional and religious disturbance, she had left home, telling her family that she was taking " 'a long vacation.' " A year later a diary, written in her checkbook, was found with her bones. She talked about its being "God's will" that she was going through the suffering of being lost and exposed, but she also wrote about the planes that flew overhead, hoping they might be looking for her.

> "But nobody knew she was there," said Johnson County Sheriff Paul Redden, who theorized that she had injured herself in a fall and was unable to leave . . . "She talks a little bit in the diary about how her feet are swollen and red, and how if she got out they may have to be amputated . . . Exposure and starvation got to her. She died a pretty horrible death."*

The last entry, made on August 31, 1978, recorded that she had not eaten in a month. Tammy's mother, Opal

* *New York Times*, July 6, 1979.

Mathre, "refused to disclose the [exact] contents of the diary, but said, 'At least we know where she's at.' "

Our troubles are usually less catastrophic than Tammy Mathre's. But in one degree or another we are likely to feel the need to litigate with the world and the future. It is then we realize that our diaries, aside from whatever else they may be, can be our depositions.

6

Confessors

> *Some of the craftiest scoundrels that*
> *ever walked this earth, or rather — for*
> *walking implies, at least, an erect posi-*
> *tion and the bearing of a man — that*
> *ever crawled and crept through life*
> *by its dirtiest and narrowest ways,*
> *will gravely jot down in diaries the*
> *events of every day, and keep a regu-*
> *lar debtor and creditor account with*
> *Heaven, which shall always show a*
> *floating balance in their own favour.*
> *—*DICKENS, *Nicholas Nickleby*

HAD BASIL HALLWARD NOT ACCEPTED, one November night late in the nineteenth century, an invitation to read his friend's diary, he might have made it to Paris, his announced destination, instead of being forever detained in London by the knife that got put in his skull. The friend was Dorian Gray, and Basil had been begging him for assurance that the charges of his depravity circulating through the city were falsehoods:

> Dorian Gray smiled. There was a curl of contempt in his lips. "Come upstairs, Basil," he said, quietly. "I keep a diary of my life from day to day, and it never leaves the room in which it is written. I shall show it to you if you come with me."

The diary in question was, of course, the famous portrait of Dorian Gray, which Basil himself had created with no idea that it would become such a gruesomely literal example of Art's imitation of Life — the very aesthetic the creator of them all, Oscar Wilde, was always complaining of. We have already seen examples of diaries that are not kept with pen and paper, but Dorian Gray's was nothing so benign as Fräulein Schroeder's carpet. After seeing it Basil had to be killed; and, later, when Dorian tried to destroy it, he would be destroyed instead.

Wilde kept no diary that we know of, but he was fascinated by the idea of a double life, or what he called Bunburying in *The Importance of Being Earnest*, a play that contains a good deal of talk about diaries. Both Gwendolyn Fairfax and Cecily Cardew keep them, the latter "in order to enter the wonderful secrets of my life. If I didn't write them down I should probably forget all about them." Gwendolyn never travels without her diary: "One should always have something sensational to read in the train." As in so many of Wilde's writings — and one would expect this from a man who kept half his life under wraps — there is more here than meets the eye. Gwendolyn is actually showing the English audience what had happened to the diary in their country during the preceding two hundred years. Having been brought to life partly by the dour Puritans of the seventeenth century as a place in which the faithful might privately expiate their sins, the diary had become, by the late nineteenth century, more typically the place in which they could savor them. Pepys would have been pleased. The opening words of the minister in *The Book of Common Prayer* are, "The Scripture moveth us, in sundry places, to acknowledge and confess our manifold sins and wickedness." But by Cecily's day the diary was often the answer to Saint Augustine's prayer to God to make him pure, but not too soon. By unburdening one's soul on paper, one could have one's sins and remember them, too. Confession was still good for the soul, but now it could be a positive delight to the eyes as well.

The confessional diary can announce, "I was wrong" with as much insistence as the apologia proclaims, "I was right." The latter is frankly directed to posterity; the former may be, but it is just as likely to be a matter between the writer and his God or the writer and some other elusive embodiment of conscience. The diary is a very pliable priest: a writer can make his book as tough or forgiving, as Jesuitical or Franciscan, as he wishes. His book may have the Puritan's tortured sincerity, or it may be worthy of La Rochefoucauld's skeptical observation that we "confess to little faults only to persuade ourselves that we have no great ones." One can always have things as one wants them in a diary; it is easy to believe that one's own authorized version and the truth are the same thing.

"Bless me, Father, for I have sinned": this is how the Catholic penitent begins his confession. He kneels, in darkness, behind a curtain, waiting for the priest to slide back the screen in front of his lips with a delicate scrape. The sinner murmurs what wicked thoughts and deeds have been his since he was last before the open screen, is absolved, and makes an Act of Contrition. The priest sends him forth with some comforting words — and then slides the screen back once more. It is not too unlike the opening and closing of a book, and the penitent's Saturday afternoon cleansing is not so very different from the confessional diarist's nightly one. Both ritual unburdenings are conducted with the promise of secrecy. The priest has taken vows never to disclose what he hears in the confessional box, and the diary cannot unlock itself.

This secrecy, this conspiracy, is what animates the confessional diary beyond all others. A young girl is presented with a lockable diary on Christmas; she addresses it as "Dear Diary" or even by a particular name: Anne Frank's diary was her "Dear Kitty." Millions of such diaries survive in shoeboxes along with elementary school autograph books; millions of others have perished in late adolescent *Kinderdämmerungs. Oh, my God, how could I have written this?* the seventeen-year-old cries, and off into the wastebasket goes her book. Twenty years later, when shame over youth's inanities has been utterly overpowered by the simple desire to have back youth itself, she wishes she had kept it.

The generic *he* gives way to *she* in these paragraphs, because the secret-keeping adolescent diary is, or certainly has been, pre-eminently a female genre. We are still not likely to give boys diaries at Christmas. Later on, when they're suitably professional and significant, they can start them; then they will be important "records." But to write in one's "secret friend" on all the ordinary days of childhood is not seemly for a boy: inner lives are for little girls; baseball is for their brothers. A subtle, even unconscious, indoctrination has probably always been going on in the presentation of these diaries to girls (those with locks still sold in the five-and-ten never carry a boy's picture on them; it's always a girl's). The little girl is being trained to appreciate dailiness, and ordinariness: her lot in life is the quotidian; her brother will do whatever transcending there is to be done.

But the bright little girl soon enough recognizes that the cultivated inner life can be a much more powerful and dangerous weapon with which to repel intruders than any baseball bat. It may be in her diary that she discovers how to keep part of herself back, and to take revenge on those who have wounded what part of her has been exposed. She learns things about herself faster than her brother, and when he tries to read her diary — and of course he will — it will not be just to torment her with the news that he's done so, and not just out of animal curiosity, but also because he's jealous. No one likes anything to be kept from him; and certainly no one likes to be talked about without the chance to reply. Parents have often regretted the harmless or "improving"

little books they've given at Christmas when, a few
months later, they realize they're among the principal
themes. In the 1941 movie *Kathleen*, a teenaged Shirley
Temple plays a headstrong girl who accuses her governess of snooping in her diary when she is able to quote
the way her charge has characterized her. The governess
replies: "If you were a nice girl with a nice clean mind
you wouldn't keep a diary."

A friend of mine, a minister's daughter who grew up
in the Midwest in the 1950s and 1960s, not long ago
presented me with the diary she kept between the fifth
and eighth grades. It is a wonderfully typical example
of the genre. On its vinyl cover is the cartoon of a girl
(in sweater and pearls) seated at a desk, mooning over
an open diary and the picture of a boy. Hearts swirl
around her head. The lock is missing and the owner has
written "STEVE & ME" in ballpoint across the vinyl,
thereby identifying the diary's main plot interest. The
diary is the five-year kind, but little attempt has been
made to keep the entries, which are messy and sporadic,
to their allotted inches. They were made between 1961
and 1963, when the author matured from eleven to
thirteen. Only two public events are mentioned in the
book: John F. Kennedy's inauguration and his assassination.

Before Steve come Ricky and Dennis, with minimal
ecstasy, trauma, and remorse. But with Steve the writer
has finally

> experienced ½ way Lepalzerade. Are you at all inter-
> ested in that word? I hope cuz I'm gonna explain it.
> Each letter stands for somethin
>> L ove
>> E motion
>> P assion
>> A nticipation
>> L Violence
>> Z eal

E Heat
R ousing
A nxiety
D evotion
E xasperation

Well it means the feeling of an adolescent (girl) before
during & after ALOP (lip o press) or just when she's
very near a boy!
    I sure felt it!

Many of the entries are signed with "Love." P.S.'s
are sometimes included. She worries that she's boring the
diary, but also pities its poor papery inability to feel
what it's like to get it "OTL" (on the lips); and she asks
it rhetorical questions: "Have you noticed a change in
Steve? Boy I have!! Oh, its wonderful I'll tell ya!"
Amidst the copied-out lyrics of Connie Francis songs,
and the tales of romance at basketball games, problems
are pondered: "What am I gonna do? Gordy R. . . . likes
me & I've gotten myself into a 'se terible predicamente.'
I've acted like I like him & I do, but not romantically cuz
he just ain't the type. He's not real cute but he's sweet &
considerate. Well anyway tonite at the homcomin game
we tied Lima Central Catholic 20–20." Fantasies are also
played out: "Then he pulled me around & held me in his
arms (boy I wish it really did happen this way!)"
Mother is a problem; she simply doesn't understand
and has the occasional whole entry devoted to her mis-
apprehensions. Still, the diary helps the daughter to forgive with the perspective provided by time. An entire
page (five years' worth of December 9s) is covered with
"I hate my mother I hate my mother I hate my mother."
But a penitent hand subsequently writes, "This was long
ago" in a large diagonal across the page. Similarly, one
of the lists of pre-Steve boyfriends later receives the mature annotation "SILLY GIRL . . . STEVE ISN'T EVEN
ON THERE." Other lists of early attractions have been

scratched out for fear of their discovery by the diarist's older brother.

Actually, the treachery of a younger sister is the subject of the very last entry in the book, an embarrassed cri de coeur:

> Oh damn damn damn damn damn damn damn damn damn damn damn damn it. C . . . got into my diary and read it. And then she went down and told the whole family what it said. Of course they all laughed but I wish they'd go to hell! What I write in my diary is my own personal stuff and I don't like people to get into it. When is she gonna grow up! None of my other friend's brothers and sisters ever do stuff like that. Skip K . . . may be a brat but he doesn't ever do that.

The book had survived a previous invasion by the older brother, but this discovery by the whole family breaks the spell and dissolves the habit. Note how "Dear Diary" has become just an object now — "my diary" — like a doll that's ceased its sorcerer's dance and gone back to being wood and cloth.

The adolescent girl's diary has been so much a genre unto itself that in 1980 an anthology of them, called *Heart Songs*, was published. It contains excerpts from Anaïs Nin, Marie Bashkirtseff, Selma Lagerlöf, and others, including "Gretchen Lainer," the pseudonymous author of *A Young Girl's Diary*, which was published by Dr. Hermine von Hug-Hellmuth in 1919 and praised by Freud as "a little gem . . . It has never before been possible to obtain such a clear and truthful view of the mental impulses that characterize the development of a girl in our social and cultural stratum during the years before puberty." There has been some suspicion that the unknown donor of the diary to Dr. Hug-Hellmuth first jazzed it up a bit, but the book certainly seems believable enough when held against similar works, and has been studied by more than one psychoanalyst since Freud himself.

Gretchen began the diary at eleven, in Vienna, near the turn of the century. She and her friend Hella decided to keep diaries in order, at least in part, to record what they were learning about sex. Virtually everything in the diary relates in one way or another to that amazing set of secrets: menstruation; a flasher; a couple seen making love without shutting the blinds; speculation about how babies arrive in the world. Gretchen has a confidential crush on not just Professor Wilke, the natural history teacher, but a beautiful girl ice skater as well. The diary is driven by an exuberant obsession with knowing, telling, confiding, not being able to bear knowing and telling, and then bursting forth with the secrets anyway. Her older sister, Dora, also a diary-keeper, insists that Gretchen should not keep one until she is older, because "little children . . . will write such a lot of nonsense." But Gretchen ignores this advice and shows herself capable of contempt for Dora's supposedly more mature secrets:

> I've had a frightful row with Dora. She says I've been fiddling with her things. It's all because she's so untidy. As if her things could interest me. Yesterday she left her letter to Erika lying about on the table, and all I read was: He's as handsome as a Greek god. I don't know who "he" was for she came in at that moment. It's probably Krail Rudi, with whom she is everlastingly playing tennis and carries on like anything. As for handsome — well, there's no accounting for tastes.

It's true: for all our curiosity, no one else's secrets ever turn out to be quite as interesting as our own.

The psychoanalyst Karen Horney grew up in Germany just a few years ahead of Gretchen Lainer. No doubt the diaries she kept (published not long ago as *The Adolescent Diaries of Karen Horney*) were good training for someone who was to become a professional listener

to secrets. At fifteen and sixteen she reveals in her book
that the bane of her adolescence is not, as in the case of
my friend, a mother, nor, as with Gretchen Lainer, an
older sister; rather, the villain of the pages is her father,
who frowns on the ambition that will eventually take
her so far. She is determined, despite him, to be a doctor.
So definite are her plans that on December 26, 1900, she
writes: "You see, dear diary, Fate will have an easy time
with me, for I prescribe everything for him."

Her crushes are, of course, frequent, intense, and varied.
Fräulein Banning, her French teacher, and Herr Schulze,
her professor for history and religion, receive her warm-
est thoughts and sentences. Poor Herr Schulze tries to
explain Christ's personality and the "divine spark in every
human being" to Karen without realizing that she is
taking his as her own secret holy spirit: "Well, it was
heavenly, and he was heavenly. It's so touching, how he
responds to all my questions. He is my inner God. I am
afraid that when I no longer have him as a teacher, I may
go astray. In any case I shall be *very* grateful to him for
what he was, is, and, I hope, still will be to me."

There is actually remarkable perspective here for a
fifteen-year-old; she is interpreting the experience even
as she lives it. Just three weeks later she is able to write:
"I think I shall always and always be fond of him, even
if other crushes command my emotional energies." One
can hear the girl turning into the doctor right at the
comma. She learns that to master experience one must
allow oneself to feel it but not to exaggerate its effects.
In September 1901 she tells her diary of her disappointing reunion with her friend Tuti; she had thought their
friendship special, but is saddened by how little she now
feels: "I would almost like to say with Lenau, 'I bear a
deep wound in my heart.' The affair isn't quite so tragic
after all, but still so similar. To you, my dear diary, I
will confide it. To you alone. You're probably preparing yourself for a love story?? No, nothing of that sort."
Just, in fact, a disappointment. From here on she has

trouble confiding one of her "eternal crushes" to "Kitten" without suspecting the diary of laughing at her. She even goes so far, when her medical ambitions are temporarily thrust aside by a passion to be an actress ("nourished by the glorious declamation lessons with Herr Schrumpf"), as to invent rebuking dialogue for the diary: " 'You're telling me all sorts of plans, and I don't understand anything about it. How have you arrived at this?' " She is already, in fact, talking herself out of it, but letting the book do some of the dirty work of balloon-bursting.

Although they are still unlikely to receive them as presents, and have to show a more unusual initiative in starting them, some boys have of course kept diaries, and some of them have found their way into print. About a dozen years ago, Jean-Jacques Larrea, a New York City paper boy, kept a diary, recording his revenges against delinquent and unfriendly customers and identifying them by their house numbers. One December 18 he "put styrofoam shavings in an extra paper and threw it into 82-58's open window . . . She is stupid, saying that she owed me one week, when her daughter even said it was two." He displays the same youthful tendency to give life to the diary ("Guess what!"), signing his entries with experimentally varied forms of his name, as do the girls already mentioned. His mother took his diary to an editor and it became an illustrated children's book (with a few too-good-to-be-true embellishments, one can be certain: ten-year-olds, however precocious, do not talk about an "apothecarian concoction").

As a Manhattan teenager, Jim Carroll, the rock musician and poet, saw some of his *Basketball Diaries* appear in the *Paris Review*. Kept between 1963 and 1966, when he went from being twelve to fifteen, they are the story of an aspiring punk. High school basketball, sex, drugs (heroin before grass; codeine highs in Grand Central), petty theft, and screwing around are the mainstays of the action. Desperate to be a tough guy, a scholarship kid who eventually winds up getting busted for possession,

he is an agonizingly hip and humorless diarist who confesses to few fears other than the atomic bomb. That
dread sweats out of the entry he makes after being trapped
in a subway car during the great Northeastern blackout
of November 1965:

> Listen here: I got out of basketball practice at five,
> then made a quick take to the subway with Lang. We
> just catch the last car out of the 7th Ave. local and
> all is cool until we get out of the tunnel at 125th St.
> and the fucking bitch starts going put-put. It's that
> way on through the tunnel toward the 137th St. stop
> and finally, zapp, no movement, and no light, except
> for the dim battery-run jobs. Everyone is mumbling
> the usual blah blah about the fucked-up train system
> and due to rush hour that meant a lot of blah blah
> 'cause this train was packed ass to ass. Now, I waited
> in tunnels before for breakdowns but around this point
> it's getting to be half an hour and the place smells like
> a cattle car. Everyone, it seemed, took off their coats
> and jackets at the same time and rushes of stench al-
> most blew me down. I remembered I had been saving
> one last fiver of scag in my jacket lining and I figured
> if this shit's keeping up then I'm getting down. Lang
> and I were starting to goof in stage whispers, "Only
> ten minutes of oxygen to go," but now it's nearly an
> hour gone by and frankly the war-baby-blues were
> starting to unscrew me, like you don't break down an
> hour and more for no reason, and I figured if this tin
> can went plunk we'd at least be led out along the
> rails . . . plus the fact there were no tunnel lights on
> either made for more A-bomb paranoia.

There is of course no "Dear Diary" shit for this kid, but
some of the same confessional instincts of his demure
female counterparts apply. In Carroll's case confessional
habits first came from religion. One of his rock albums
is *Catholic Boy*, and his diary tells us: "I hated that fuck-

ing school and that whole religion worse than anything before with their tiny dark boxes you enter like they were phone booths to God." For all his scorn of the rite, his simile shows him susceptible to its appeal.

Post coitum omne animal may be *triste*, but whoever minted that line didn't sign his name to it. The author is still anonymous in books of quotations. And no wonder. Even when the epigram isn't true, it's an awkward time; most people would like to pretend those minutes don't exist. One is always looking for something to say or do during them. Some people reach for a cigarette, others for a bathrobe, and some for a pen. Few people are quite so coarse as to make journal entries while their partners still lie beside them, but before the first afterflushes of regret or pride have faded, many men and women have found an excuse to go into another room and jot down how it was. We've already looked at aggrieved lovers' apologias; the diaries we come to now are not so often concerned with unquenched torches as they are quite directly with sex, its sensations and stratagems. The love apologia has the urgency of a telegram; the sex confession often has a privately exquisite anguish and delight that make it the closest relative to the adolescent female's diary.

Once over their adolescent reluctance to keep journals, the men go on to write some of the best of this libidinous lot. Stendhal's diaries rank with the greatest and randiest of them all. Landing him in this chapter is a bit reductive, since his diaries are so wonderfully varied. At once brilliantly natural and utterly self-conscious, Stendhal is both delighted by life and disgusted by it; hard on himself and others, and yet generous, too. He is a great example of a man who sees through his own ruling passion — ambition — even as he revels in the way it drives him; and he is one of the few men ever endowed with what seems a constitutional incapacity for boring anybody — even on the subject of sex, the repetitions of which, after all, are a great deal more remarkable than the surprises.

From the summer of 1810 until the summer of 1811 Stendhal is mostly in Paris, newly successful as Auditor in the War Section and Inspecteur du Mobilier in the garish last years of Napoleon. Perfectly aware of the cheapness of Parisian pleasures even as he snatches at them, he seems always to be writing his diary on the fly and making it all the truer for that. He breaks off from French into English and Italian at will, stops writing when he misplaces the key to his book, admits his diary is written for "three or four friends whose character resembles his own" and then two paragraphs later writes: "*Don't go any farther, you bastards.*"

Angéline Bereyter, a pretty opera singer, has become his mistress, thereby bringing a balance to his hectic life: "The Minister of Love, who was about to be removed from office and who frequently diminished the happiness procured by the other Ministers, has finally redeemed himself." After receiving a series of his letters, "the amiable and gentle" Angéline finally allows him to visit: "Bereyter told me that, when I arrived at her home, I had tiny little eyes and a fatuous look. I must have seemed bashful. I kissed her tenderly the first day and possessed her at my apartment the second (January 29, 1811). I nearly missed her." This ability to record his lover's insults, her gentleness, and her flexibility continues during what for a time is a charming affair without illusions and certainly no great passion on his side. One sees them awaking happy, as on the morning when the Empress is delivered of a son: "I was sleeping with Angéline. The cannon woke her up at ten o'clock. It was the third shot; we counted the twenty-second with joy." (A mere twenty-one guns would have meant a girl; 121 were fired for a male heir.)

Angéline is Stendhal's pleasure in this period; the Countess Daru is his passion. From her he receives encouragement but finally no capitulation. The diary records his unsuccessful siege, but his yearnings for her never really obscure his concern with his first love — himself. When he includes in his diary the draft of a secret missive to his prey, he comments on it as follows: "I've toned down the outlines of this letter, there is more pride than love in it." (Eight years later, in a more self-critical mood, he annotates the annotation: "This man ought to have been thrown out the window.") When he finally gives up on her, he is pleased with the theatricality of his farewell: "I planned when I was leaving to say TO MY FAIR what I was thinking at the moment, but Corbeau left us only four or five seconds, which I employed IN SAYING, in regard to the cold, 'The cold is in your heart, etc.' This word wasn't bad, I squeezed her arm."

If there can still be a reader in the world who has a doubt that Julien Sorel was Stendhal, this passage ought to dispel it. But if he still demands more, he need just read the next entry (August 10, 1811), where he will find Stendhal consoling himself with the countess's niece:

During one of my trips (to Raincy), I found THE LITTLE π [Pulchérie Le Brun, niece of Pierre Daru]. I talked to her for want of something better to do. She hasn't much in the way of breasts and wit, TWO GREAT WANTS! Likewise for want of something better to do, I took a few liberties, there wasn't any resistance. So yesterday, not knowing what to do with myself, I got in my cabriolet and showed up at Villemomble. There were a lot of people there; I went out on the terrace, the little girl followed me, I took her arm and put mine around her a bit; later, in the salon, her knees and thighs. Her eyes thanked me by their look of love, outside that it was innocence itself. But, on the terrace, I became conscious of a great truth. Novelty is a great source of pleasure, you must give yourself up to it. I was sure of sleeping in the evening with the pretty Angéline, but I can only do anything with her now by making an effort, and by thinking of another woman. On the other hand, π, who is inferior in every respect, put me in a superb state.

Stendhal knows what a magnificent cad he is. He takes as his motto "Know thyself" and pronounces: "My means is this diary." Self-criticism can cover a multitude of sins, and no one sweeps them under more gorgeous rugs than Stendhal. So great are his diaries that by their end one would rather be him than read him.

Byron's moods and amours are, if anything, more complicated than Stendhal's, and he too finds his diary a way of disgorging his confusions: "This journal is a relief. When I am tired — as I generally am — out comes this, and down goes every thing. But I can't read it over; — and God knows what contradictions it may contain. If I am sincere with myself (but I fear one lies more to one's self than to any one else), every page should confute, refute, and utterly abjure its predecessor." The contradictions are, of course, the source of Byron's frequent exhaustion: to be a living oxymoron, a revolutionary aristocrat, a lord shunned by society, is more tiring than being, like Stendhal, merely a man on the make. But both take the same detached view of their indulgences, and are aware of the connection between the pleasures of the flesh and the food that feeds it. Pre-Angéline, Stendhal has a mistress with whom he sleeps just once a week: "I'm as chaste as the devil. As the result, I'm getting fatter." Byron's problem is rather the opposite: the more weight he puts on the more he wants to take it to bed: "I should not so much mind a little accession of flesh, — my bones can well bear it. But the worst is, the devil always came with it, — till I starve him out, — and I will *not* be the slave of *any* appetite. If I do err, it shall be my heart, at least, that heralds the way."

The spiritual never long conquers the glandular in Byron, but his diaries do show the peculiar force with which he could remember attachments that were purely mental. The intense love he conceived for Mary Duff when he was seven years old still perplexes him years later:

> How the deuce did all this occur so early? where could it originate? I certainly had no sexual ideas for years afterwards; and yet my misery, my love for that girl were so violent, that I sometimes doubt if I have ever been really attached since. Be that as it may, hearing of her marriage several years after was like a thunder-stroke — it nearly choked me — to the horror of my mother and the astonishment and almost incredulity of every body. And it is a phenomenon in my existence (for I was not eight years old) which has puzzled, and will puzzle me to the latest hour of it; and lately, I know not why, the *recollection* (*not* the attachment) has recurred as forcibly as ever.

But the journal, where love and all else are concerned, remains more a field of action than introspection. In Ravenna, January 5, 1821: "Clock strikes — going out to make love. Somewhat perilous, but not disagreeable." Enough said.

Herbert Hoover's America provides a less glamorous backdrop to a man of letters' lovemaking than Napoleonic France or Regency England, and Edmund Wilson's journals of the period show a seediness of spirit appropriate to the times and to his own low state. Shortly after the death of his wife, Margaret, he reluctantly goes to bed with a woman in a "horrid room on LaSalle Street" in Chicago, and the next morning, with a continuing lack of enthusiasm, obeys her request to beat her with a wire-bristled hairbrush: "First scraped, then spanked her with it. I found this rather difficult, perhaps because of inhibitions. She said afterwards that she had thoroughly enjoyed it, and explained that she thought she had wanted this because her husband didn't dominate her." The what-the-hell joylessness of the act is mirrored in the bored

and automatic style with which it is rendered: no Sten-
dhalian energy or anger brings it to life. But for all the
meaninglessness he associates with it, Wilson still feels the
urge to record this detail — and many more — about his
sex life, and to leave instructions in his will for their
publication. As Wilson's posthumous editor, Leon Edel,
says, "After a while, you're always writing for a public."
A while is probably no more than a sentence. The idea
that it can be longer than that is a diarist's convenient
fiction, an illusion that may keep him writing, but which,
in his deeper recesses, he knows is false. Wilson wanted
to be known and understood by what he put on paper;
it was his life, hairbrush and all, and it was put there for
others eventually to see. Byron may not have been able
to read his own diary once he'd written it, but he didn't
tear it up, either.

Wilson, Byron, and Stendhal were all unmarried as
they wrote the preceding entries; thus, they had no worries about immediate discovery. Of course, the intended
audience need not be anyone so particular as one's spouse,
but diaries can be uncomfortable third parties to marriages. In fact, they are much more at home in divorce
courts than in the drawers of end tables near the marriage
bed. Open a law book to *Parker* v. *Newman*, and you'll
find: "Plaintiff was properly allowed to state on redirect
examination that after she had seen the entry in her husband's diary, referring to defendant [in an alienation-of-
affections suit] and called her husband's attention thereto,
he changed or erased the entry."

Needless to say, he should have thought of that before.
But diaries often sneak up with unexpected nastiness on
spouse or widow. Carlyle, on reading her book, was
amazed to learn of his dead wife's unhappiness. In Virginia Woolf's story "The Legacy," a husband goes
through his wife's diary after she has been killed by a
passing car. The fifteen volumes finally tell him how she
went from adoration of him to boredom with their marriage; he is led to the conclusion that she stepped off the

curb to join in suicide another man she loved. In Graham Greene's *The End of the Affair*, a man has the opposite revelation on reading his married lover's journal. Expecting to find a record of Sarah's growing disaffection, he instead finds out — to his amazement and embarrassment — that she has continued to love him all along: "It's a strange thing to discover and to believe that you are loved, when you know that there is nothing for anybody but a parent or a God to love." Novelists are fond of diaries the way Elizabethan playwrights were taken with soliloquies. Not only do they give a character the chance to speak his mind without interruption, but the opportunity to speak from beyond the grave as well. In *All the King's Men*, Jack Burden finds the diary of his antebellum ancestor Cass Mastern, who caused his friend to commit suicide after he, Cass, had had an affair with his wife. The diary is used not to beg forgiveness from posterity, but as an instrument by which Cass can further punish himself: " 'I write this down . . . with what truthfulness a sinner may attain unto, that if ever pride is in me, of flesh or spirit, I can peruse these pages and know with shame what evil has been in me, and may be in me, for who knows what breeze may blow upon the charred log and fan up flame again?' "

But one man's horror can be another man's hobby. At the same time in which Cass Mastern supposedly lived, an anonymous gentleman on the other side of the Atlantic was keeping the diaries he would later use in the compilation of the apocalyptic sexual autobiography known as *My Secret Life*: eleven volumes, forty-two hundred pages, a privately published epic with thousands of climaxes. Steven Marcus, historian of Victorian England's pornography, outlines the author's meticulous compositional movement from diary entries to continuous narrative, a technique whose industry and persistence seem not inappropriate to a culture forever building railroads and managing subcontinents. So much a part of the author's life did his secret "memoranda" become that

Marcus is able to demonstrate that "the impulse to write [becomes] as urgent as his impulses toward sexual activity." In fact, the still unknown author says: " 'Writing indeed completed my enjoyment.' "

Printed anonymously during the 1880s and 1890s in Amsterdam by a typesetter who could probably not even read English (one somehow still sighs for him), *My Secret Life* was until recently a connoisseur's classic. In our own day, mass market paperback printing is the apt counterpart to our less stinting tolerance in things sexual. After a triumphal leap from repression to vulgarity in a single century, it is now possible to buy, for $2.25, the jointly published diaries kept by two people ("Antony Amato" and "Katherine Edwards") in the course of their secret affair. Tony is divorced; Kate is married, with children. They discover not only sexual excitement with each other (for six months in 1973 and 1974), but also the fact that they are both diarists. It comes to seem "as if our ultimate act of intimacy would be to show each other our diaries." After weeks of hesitation they manage to do this (while naked, incidentally); when the affair breaks up they decide to publish them. Whether *Affair* was a publisher's gimmick or merely an embroidered bit of actuality, it has, in the broad sense of the word, its "genuine" moments. At one point, for example, Tony looks for his passport and finds "a note in it I had written to myself three years ago. It said, 'Hiyo, Silver!' A little joke from me to me." This is, after all, the sort of joke a diarist would play on himself; he's feeling the same impulse that wants the past to talk to the present.

Kate makes entries that show her alternately pleased and appalled by herself. She is horrified by the prospect of discovery one minute ("I wonder if women with living mothers have diaries") and hopeful for it the next: "I hope you read this, Rolf Edwards. Read it and weep. For the TWO OF US." Her final phase of guilt, the one that will impel her to break the affair, begins when her daughter is in the hospital after an accident:

I went to my lover's.

When my child lay in the hospital, where did I go? I went to my lover's.

"I'll never leave you again," my lover said, and his words hung around my neck like a day-old doughnut.

To be frigid is to watch another person make a fool of himself.

I am coming down off a six-month high.

Really down.

My lover touches me and I feel my mother's dead clammy hands.

To be frigid is sobering.

To be frigid is a relief.

At least, Dear Diary, when I went to my lover's I had the bottom-line decency at least to be frigid.

A year later, rereading his diary of the affair, Tony writes: "Did I really feel that much? It is only a year and I am reading about a stranger, an obsessive, destructive stranger. That was not me. Thank God, that was not me." But of course it was.

A good deal kinkier — and probably a good deal less authentic — is 9½ Weeks, another recent pseudonymous work, by "Elizabeth McNeill." Half diary, half memoir, this record of a sadomasochistic affair is full of such homely details as what it feels like to watch "60 Minutes" while bound and gagged. But even in its likely fakery the book remains of some interest, for we find the author doubling her masochistic pleasure by having her tormentor read her diary in front of her: "Over, I thought, it's over, he knows me completely, there is nothing to hide, and sat down at the foot of the couch and watched him read."

Homosexual diarists have until recently taken special risks. The composer Ned Rorem may be able to make a second career out of publishing his sexually candid diaries, but in times past such books fairly begged for blackmailers. When the British government set out to convict

Roger Casement of treason for his part in the Easter 1916 Rising in Ireland, officials circulated the anatomically pre-occupied diaries he had kept for years of his homosexual encounters: Rio, February, 28, 1910: "Deep screw and to hilt. X 'poquino' . . . Mario in Rio — 8½ + (plus) 640$. Hospedario, Rua do Hospicio. 3$ only fine room shut window lovely, young 18 and glorious. Biggest since Lisbon 1904 and as big. Perfectly huge." Casement's entries have the same cryptic transparency as Pepys's ciphered dalliances. The poet Alfred Noyes, working in the News Department of the British Foreign Office, was allowed to see them for propaganda reasons. He told the *Philadelphia Ledger* (and thereby Casement's Irish-American sympathizers) that it "would be an insult to a pig's trough" to let the diaries touch it. There remain those Irish patriots who insist that the books were forged by the unscrupulous British authorities, but Professor B. L. Reid, in *The Lives of Roger Casement*, convincingly authenticates them. Not only, he argues, did Casement repeat his pleasures by writing them down, but also generally went through life "incapable of moving without leaving a trail of paper." Casement was in fact so aware of the controversial nature of his career as rebel and reformer that one can only conclude that not just the desire to recollect his delights motivated his keeping the diaries, but a desire for self-destruction as well.

Christopher Isherwood, who has lived to see the current tolerance toward homosexuality, has come to regret not the keeping of diaries about his love life, but their destruction. He says in his autobiography, *Christopher and His Kind*, that the books he kept during his years in Weimar Germany were used as raw material for the writing of fiction like *Good-bye to Berlin*. He then destroyed the diaries, telling his friends, with the swagger of the young artist, that he had done so because he had come to prefer the "more exciting fictitious past" he had created in his published work. As an old man, however, he admits that he destroyed the diaries because he worried that they might be gotten hold of by his enemies or the police. Now impatient with his old "arty talk," he would like them back so he could have his real past and not what has been refracted so often through novels, plays, and films that he is unsure of what actually happened. When it came time to write his autobiography he turned for information, with poignant irony, to the diaries of his mother, Kathleen, whom he had tried to cut off completely from his life in Germany: "Kathleen picked up scraps of news from friends who had visited him there and from his occasional grudging letters. I bless her for having recorded them."

The eighteenth-century biographer Roger North recommended journal-keeping to man as a useful "check upon all his exorbitancies . . . considering, that being set down, they would stain his reputation." If the diary fails to pre-empt vice entirely, it may still be of use in limiting it. Even the most formidable men and women beset by personal compulsions have often relied on their diaries for relief and discipline. Dr. Johnson could use his journals to upbraid himself for idleness, drinking, and a mind "clouded with sensuality," and whether Gladstone indulged in self-flagellation as a form of Christian humiliation or outré pleasure, his diaries from the 1840s and 1850s contain notations resembling whips under the relevant dates; similarly, his compulsive accosting of prostitutes on the street with a view toward reforming them — behavior he was more likely to exhibit during periods of stress, and from which his political allies tried to dissuade him — is marked in the diaries by "Saw one."

Evelyn Waugh's chronicles of the benders he went on when he and the century were in their twenties carried their share of self-disapproval, but made no attempt to preach to fellow inebriates. It was not so with Thomas Turner, an eighteenth-century resident of East Hoathly in Sussex, whose diaries are a constant record of drunkenness, chagrin, preachment, and relapse. In the course of

all these wash-and-dry cycles, they take on a drunken
rhythm of their own. On February 25, 1757, he notes
how he was an initially unwilling participant in a bac-
chanal with his wife, a couple of neighbors, and the local
parson, Mr. Porter:

> Up stairs they came, and threatened to break [the
> door] open; so I ordered the boys to open it, when
> they poured into my room; and as modesty forbid me
> to get out of bed, so I refrained; but their immodesty
> permitted them to draw me out of bed, as the common
> phrase is, topsy turvey . . . they gave me time to put
> on my wife's petticoats; and in this manner they made
> me dance, without shoes and stockings, until they had
> emptied the bottle of wine, and also a bottle of my
> beer.

It seems rather difficult to believe that Turner could have
been persuaded to dance in his wife's petticoats without
having helped to empty the bottles himself, but in his
woeful warning to the imagined readers of his journal
he chooses to blame the parson: "Now, let any one call
in reason to his assistance, and seriously reflect on what
I have before recited, and they will join with me in
thinking that the precepts delivered from the pulpit on
Sunday, tho' delivered with the greatest ardour, must lose
a great deal of their efficacy by such examples."

The diary is still alive as an aid to the conquest of
compulsions that in Turner's day would have been seen
as failures of the will or invasions of the devil, but in our
own receive treatment as medical problems. Diaries are
not only helping in those rather luxurious Progoffian
quests after our full "human potential," but in the treatment of physical affliction as well. Professor Angela
Barron McBride of the Indiana University School of
Nursing has lectured on her use of a journal in fighting
obesity. Through it she learned to find sympathy for herself and to stop using food as an instrument of gratification and punishment. On January 14, 1980, she wrote:

"Either everything is terrific or it's awful. I always say I was good today or I was bad today, and that makes food a moral issue. If food could only become just food, my problem would be solved."

A recently discovered diary has also become an important aid in the treatment of Tourette syndrome, a Job-like affliction that can cause a sufferer, suddenly and mysteriously, to break into any of about fifty movements, from twitching to tearing paper to shouting curses and grinding teeth. Joseph Bliss, a retired industrial chemist who must have been named in one of life's more cruelly ironic moments, was tormented by Tourette syndrome for decades before he knew he had an affliction with fellow sufferers and a name. He struggled to control his symptoms in private; sometimes at work he would have to hide in a stockroom or washroom dozens of times in a single day. In his thirty-five years of endurance and secrecy he kept diarylike notes of his symptoms. Even while some doctors dispute Bliss's notion that the movements are ultimately, if bizarrely, voluntary (and thereby finally capable of control), one expert in the field has praised Bliss's "35 years of intensive probing, a terrible persistence, and endless note writing . . . The aberration has been studied from a vantage point not available to the clinician — inside the host. It is as if the laboratory guinea pig could tell where and what it feels." However apt the comparison, it is rather cold, for Bliss's diary is at least as much a triumph of the spirit as it is a scientist's gold mine. As Bliss himself wrote during his secret struggle: " There are so many lovely things in the world to experience . . . And maybe even *yet* some soul-satisfying challenge to meet. But all of this will be dust if every thought and muscle is busy trying to hold back the blinking of an eye."

Go Ask Alice was a phenomenon of adolescent literature in the 1970s. The diary of a fifteen-year-old girl who died from a drug overdose (certain names, dates, places, and events were changed in order to accommodate her survivors), it sold millions of copies and became a required cautionary tale in many American schools. Its appeal was its authenticity. Alice, before her involvement with any drugs, buys her diary because Roger has asked her out; alas, a day later the romance is already punctured: "Yesterday I bought this diary because I thought at last I'd have something wonderful and great and worthwhile to say, something so personal that I wouldn't be able to share it with another living person, only myself. Now like everything else in my life, it has become so much nothing." Still, she and the book manage to make friends; it becomes a typical "Dear Diary" to which she confides adolescent loneliness, the fear of getting fat, and so forth. But when she begins taking drugs, the diary comes to occupy a truly privileged position: "I can't take a chance on anyone reading you, especially not now!" It becomes "Dear close, warm, intimate friend, Diary." Over the next year it receives the news of Alice taking drugs and having sex, selling drugs and selling sex ("Another day, another blow job"), her life as a runaway. It also gathers her swings of remorse, her returns home, her frightened and sentimental penitence ("I really have a great family!"), and resolutions for the future. In a hopeful moment she decides to buy a new diary: "I want to get a fresh new clean book when I get home. You, dear Diary, will be my past. The one I buy when we get home will be my future."

She does start a second diary, but soon runs into trouble again. By this time her relationship with the diary is so intimate that she asks it for help. Hospitalized after a bad LSD trip, she experiences a sort of delirium tremens symptom: she imagines bugs are crawling over her, and she tries to protect not only herself from them, but the diary as well: "I must get you back in your case because the maggots are crawling off my bleeding writhing hands into your pages. I will lock you in. You will be safe."

When she thinks she is on the road to comfort and normality once more, she offers the second book a loving valedictory:

> I used to think I would get another diary after you are filled, or even that I would keep a diary or journal through my whole life. But now I don't really think I will. Diaries are great when you're young. In fact, you saved my sanity a hundred, thousand, million times. But I think when a person gets older she should be able to discuss her problems and thoughts with other people, instead of just with another part of herself as you have been to me. Don't you agree? I hope so, for you are my dearest friend and I shall thank you always for sharing my tears and heartaches and my struggles and strifes, and my joys and happinesses. It's all been good in its own special way, I guess.
>
> See ya.

Three weeks after this entry was made she was dead from an overdose.

Go Ask Alice went before the United States Supreme Court as part of the "Island Trees" censorship case. The school board in that Long Island community had the book, as well as several others, removed from the school library because of its alleged corrupting influence. This particular school board (which lost the case) would no doubt be unhappy with *Jay's Journal* as well. This book, too, was edited by Beatrice Sparks, the editor of *Go Ask Alice*. It is the story of a sixteen-year-old boy who becomes involved in the occult, and, after a series of Alice-like boomerangings between blood-drinking and resolute wholesomeness, shoots himself with a .22 pistol. A true child of the late seventies, with all its new adolescent careerism, Jay sometimes comes across as a little Dale Carnegie warlock: "I'm going to use all the power I can get to reach the goals I've set for next year."

*

Some diarists have found confession so healthful to the
human spirit that they have generously taken it upon
themselves to confess not just their own sins, but those
of their neighbors as well. The tattling diary is the psychological complement of the confessional one. God
seems to have put a little bit of the secret policeman in
each of us, and it is not unusual to find someone who
keeps an honest book on himself keeping the book on
others, too. Freud's "Gretchen Lainer," so guileless about
herself, is just as ready to record others' delinquencies.
Indeed, she gets her first real knowledge of sex from some
empirical peeking through the drapes. One day in June
she and her friends

> went into Resi's room and from behind the curtain
> peeped into the mezzanine. A young *married couple*
> live there!!! At least Resi says people say they are not
> really married, but simply live together!!!! And what
> we saw was awful. She was absolutely naked lying in
> bed without any . . . clothes on, and he was kneeling
> by the bedside quite n—— too, and he kissed her all
> over, everywhere!!! Dora said afterwards it made her
> feel quite sick. And then he stood up and — no, I can't
> write it, it's too awful, I shall never forget it. So *that's*
> the way of it, it's simply frightful. I could never have
> believed it. Dora went as white as a sheet and trembled
> so that Resi was terribly frightened. I nearly cried with
> horror, and yet I could not help laughing.

She immediately applies her findings to speculation about
other adults she knows: "But just think if anyone is as
fat as Herr Richter or our landlord. Of course Herr
Richter is at least 50, but last January the landlord had
another little girl, so something *must* have happened."

Servants and masters are natural antagonists, and each
class has used the tattling diary to gain the upper hand
against the other. Richard Sackville, master of the great
estate of Knole during the reign of Charles II, is described

by his descendant Vita Sackville-West as having kept a
"Diary of Servants' faults":

	£	s.	d.
Henry Mattock, for scolding to extremity on Sunday without cause	0	0	3
William Loe, for running out of doors from Morning till Midnight without leave	0	2	0
Richard Meadowes, for being absent when my Lord came home late, and making a headless excuse	0	0	6
Henry Mattock, for not doing what he is bidden	0	1	0

It is rather embarrassing to see this lord of the manor
playing Saint Peter with shillings and pence instead of
fire and brimstone, but it seems to have confirmed his
sense of superincumbency.

Living below stairs, William Tayler, a footman in a
London household early in Queen Victoria's reign, is not
in a position to exact fines from his employers, but they
do not escape censure in the diary he keeps throughout
the year 1837. What is now a wonderfully sturdy document of servant life more than a hundred years ago gets
its start because Tayler wants a way to improve his bad
penmanship. It actually doesn't help very much, but true
to his resolution of January 1, 1837, he writes on the
following December 31: "I have at last finished the task
which I have been heartily sick of long agoe and I think
it will be a long time before I begin another of the kind."
Somewhat grudging but admirably reliable: as he is a
servant, so he is a diarist. But even if his book comes to
seem to him like one more dull chore added to his daily
fill of them, Tayler knows soon after starting his diary
that it is of potentially much greater significance than as
a help to his handwriting. After the relieved farewell
quoted above there is one more sentence: "Now all the

readers of this Book mite give an idea of what service is." Often slipping into the second person, Tayler clearly wants his unclear penmanship to be read.

On January 1, he tells us his routine of laying linen, clearing tables, opening doors, shutting shutters, and carrying candles: "All these things I have to do every day, therefore I have mentioned the whole that I mite not have to mention them every day." This admirable economy leaves Tayler the necessary space in which to scold and forgive his supposed betters:

> 19th [February, 1837]. This is Sunday, a wet boister-ous day. Been to church of course. Our old Lady is got quite well, thinks of little elce but playing cards and paying visets all the time. I was takeing in break-fast to the drawing room — she was talking about cards and who was good players and who was bad ones and choseing the people she should have to her next party and when it should be. When I went to take the break-fast away, she was fretting because her violets were all withered and had lost their smell. When I went to take lunch up, she was makeing matches or candlelights. When I took lunch away, she was reading a novel with the Bible laying by her, ready to take up if any body came in. She had a Lady to dine with them. During dinner, the conversation turned on wordly afairs — nothing relating to religion. At tea time, she was talk-ing about china, how much was broke in her house and what it would cost to replace it again. I think these were excelent ideas for an old Lady near eighty years of age on a Sunday, but for all this she is not a bad one in the end.

Tayler's diary runs to only sixty-three printed pages, but it is full of similar unselfconscious intelligence and charm. By that sixty-third page he is fully alive to a reader; the effect is as if one of the hundreds of servants who tiptoe through the great novels of Victorian England had suddenly sprung full-blown from a three-decker all his own.

The confession of others' sins rises from motif to raison d'être in the diaries of James Winston, the acting manager at the Drury Lane Theatre during the 1820s when it was leased by Robert William Elliston. Much of the diary is a prissy complaint about Elliston's drunkenness and the sexual excesses and arrogant ambition of the great Edmund Kean. On May 16, 1825, the following details are meticulously noted:

> Kean, about three o'clock in the morning, ordered a hackney coach to his door, took a lighted candle, got in, and rode off. He was not heard of till the Thursday noon when they found him in his room at the theatre fast asleep wrapt up in a large white greatcoat. He then sent for a potence, some ginger, etc., and said, "Send me Lewis or the other woman. I must have a fuck, and then I shall do." He had it. They let him sleep till about six, when they awoke him, dressed him, and he acted but was not very sober. After the play [we] got him to supper at Sigel's lodgings and got him to a bedroom and locked him up till the morning.

An acting manager's life no doubt has its trials, and each band of messily gifted revelers probably needs its Philostrate. Still, there is something perverse in the conscientiousness of Winston's book-keeping. He sometimes uses code for the names of places, persons, and sums of money, interchanging the numbers one through eleven and the letters in "King Charles." Perhaps that is done out of respect for the privacy of those whose failings he keeps track of. But it seems unlikely: the code probably just adds piquancy to his rereading of his records of espionage. (The choice of a decapitee's name for the cipher seems not insignificant.) Winston, however sorely tried by Elliston and Kean, enjoys his nightly executions.

They satisfy his instincts for retribution. It isn't as important to turn the diaries directly against any of their targets as it is for them to quench Winston's thirst for backstage drama. The diaries allow him to displace certain frustrations over his own less lusty life. In this way they are a kind of homemade pornography, all dressed up in dirt and rectitude at the same time.

This keeping of books on others is an act many diarists like to get in on at least from time to time. In his Hebrides journal Boswell mentions that Garrick kept a book recording the words of all those who praised and attacked him. And the Goncourts were not above putting down, in code, the latest news of the Emperor's amours.

Most mortals, and one hopes God Himself, are more ready to forgive a man's crimes against his own flesh than his crimes against another's. The diaries examined above are mostly instruments of their keepers' penitence or signs of their authors' awareness of the lustful pleasures to be had in retrospection: we can read them with a certain indulgence. But other diaries lead lives of crime in which the victims are unwilling ones. We read them with greater repulsion as well as greater perplexity — Why do real criminals write diaries at all? Aren't confessions, as defense lawyers always tell juries, extorted from tired suspects in the glare of interrogation lights, usually early in the morning and often after a beating?

Thomas Dangerfield (a.k.a. Willoughby and Field) was a late-seventeenth-century counterfeiter and confidence man who on different occasions made himself useful to Papists and Presbyterians in the wranglings and plottings over the then much-passed-about English crown. In late 1684 and early 1685, between stints at Newgate, his m.o. is to "borrow" money from people along the highway by claiming to be a gentleman who has just been robbed. He is very good at it. A diary he keeps during this period shows that:

Saturday, Dec. 13

I went from thence [Burford] through divers Villages with good Success, and most of 'em being near *Farringdon*; and after having spent the Day with much Pleasure, and handsome Profit, I return'd to my Inn at *Burford*, where I lay all Night.

Of a Farmer,	10s. 0	Receits
Of a Gentlewoman,	20s. 0	
Of a Miller,	6s. 0	
Of a Farmer,	6s. 0	
Of a Gentleman,	20s. 0	
Of a Dr. Of Laws,	15s. 0	
Of a Parsons Wife,	6s. 0	
Of a Widow Gentlewoman's		
Man Servant,	10s. 0	
Of a Farmer,	6s. 0	
Of a Farmer,	10s. 0	
	109s. 0	

1 refus'd 3,
5 refus'd me,

Spent at Dinner,	4s. 0	Expences
Spent at the *Bear*,	12s. 0	
Paid to the Gunsmith,	2s. 0	
	18s. 0	

One might say that like any man of business he had to keep books — that he was merely methodical. But one can't put it down to just that. The sums aren't sufficient to necessitate ledger-keeping, and the commentary shows a distinct self-congratulation: "having spent the Day with much Pleasure, and handsome Profit." When Thomas Dangerfield is pleased with himself he likes to take note of it: he records, for example, his attendance at church on Christmas and New Year's. He seems to have craved notoriety (he was charged with impersonating the Duke of Monmouth and claiming he could touch for the king's evil), and was probably delighted with the publication of his diary just before his death.

It was a just law that sent Dangerfield to Newgate, but it was certainly a very stupid one that gave rise, so to speak, to Joshua Naples's *Diary of a Resurrectionist*. Until the Anatomy Act of 1832 regularized procedures for the legal donation of human corpses to medical science, respectable hospitals in England had to resort to trafficking with grave robbers in order to obtain cadavers for their students. Joshua Naples was an accomplished supplier, and a typical entry from his diary reads as follows:

Seperated to look out, brought the F. from Barthol.[n] to St. Thomas, having not settled took from Hollis £ 1 0 0, afterwards met at St. Thos. & went to St. Jns, Ben not with us work'd two holes one bad, drew the C.[ns] & took the above to St. Thos.

The "F" means a female corpse; and, as Naples's editor, James Blake Bailey, B.A., Librarian of the Royal College of Surgeons in England, explained in the edition of the diary he published in 1896, the gist of the last sentence quoted above is that Naples and Co. "opened two graves; one body too decomposed to bring away, so they drew the canine teeth and sold them."

Naples's diary runs from November 28, 1811, to December 5, 1812 (there are no entries from May to July, when the anatomical schools were out). Beside the record of his gains he puts his frustrations: when bodies were too putrid to be sold, when members of his gang were too drunk or disputatious to do their work. He also mentions evenings he spent quietly at home.

Why did he keep it? Not, it would seem, for blackmail: it's too self-incriminating. As a business record? As with Dangerfield, there was too much needless risk in that, and it can't explain his editorial asides and embellishments. Two explanations suggest themselves. One is that he used it in a kind of plea bargaining: it is true that its usefulness to Sir Astley Cooper, an advocate of the new Anatomy Act, caused that man to intervene with the Secretary of State to save Naples further imprisonment after he had made an escape. But a better one involves ordinary bourgeois pride. Naples started out and ended up respectable. His father was a stationer and bookbinder; he himself had been a sailor on HMS *Excellent*, and thereafter a gravedigger. He stumbled into the grave-robbing business, naturally enough, from there. After the Anatomy Act was passed he became a dissecting room servant at Saint Thomas Hospital — rather like the Watergate felon who sells burglar alarms after doing his time. Actually, he was far less culpable than that recent species: all he had done was perform a necessary service that the law was too squeamish to condone. So why not keep a diary just as a nice respectable bookbinder might? Grave-robbing was, after all, a crime particularly suited to being viewed as mere commerce. From *A Tale of Two Cities* one will recall young Jerry Cruncher giving his father, a colleague of Joshua Naples, a proud moment when he exclaims: " 'Oh, father, I should so like to be a Resurrection-Man when I'm quite growed up.' " The elder Cruncher had not inaccurately described his work as being with " 'a branch of Scientific goods.' "

Newspapers are quite fond of "discovered" diaries (the *Times* of London will be a long time recovering from the Hitler fiasco of 1983), and those that have gotten themselves mixed up in murder and adultery, have added appeal. MAID KEPT LOVE DIARY OF SWINGING DIET DOC — this is how the *New York Post* told its readers of the "Everyday Book" kept by Mrs. Suzanne van der Vreken, housekeeper to Dr. Herman Tarnower, the Scarsdale physician who gained the closest thing to immortality our modern world has to offer by being shot by the headmistress of the Madeira School, Jean Harris. For years Mrs. van der Vreken, in a wicked combination of James Winston and

William Tayler, kept track of the number of times her employer entertained Mrs. Harris. The record shows not only a voyeurism somehow more sinister, in its mechanicalness, than Winston's, but also convincing proof of Mrs. Harris's declining stock with the diet doctor. As she came to be replaced in his slender affections by a younger woman (his medical assistant, Lynne Tryforos), she was offered his attentions on fewer and fewer occasions: 1977, 63 times; 1978, 49 times; 1979, 26 times.

The housekeeper's diary may have titillated readers of the *Post*, and it may have increased sympathy for Jean Harris from those who saw her as a sexual victim, but with whatever biases one reads it, Mrs. van der Vreken's diary is a grotesque. All those statistics of implied coupling and uncoupling give it the feel of a diary hoping for a crime to happen. But not all the diaries in criminal cases arrive on the evidence table so brazenly sure of themselves. Sometimes they are the poignant, almost embarrassed, traces of victims. They come into court with the sheepishness of clothes left hanging in a dead man's closet.

If Perry Smith and Richard Hickock hadn't slaughtered the Herbert W. Clutter family in the fall of 1959, Nancy Clutter, then not quite seventeen, would probably today be a Kansas farmer's wife in early middle age. She might still be keeping a diary, too, for she had acquired the habit with unusual order and method by the time she was in her mid-teens. As Truman Capote explained in *In Cold Blood*:

Before saying her prayers, she always recorded in a diary a few occurrences ("Summer here. Forever, I hope. Sue over and we rode Babe down to the river. Sue played her flute. Fireflies") and an occasional outburst ("I love him, I do"). It was a five-year diary; in the four years of its existence she had never neglected to make an entry, though the splendor of several events ([her sister] Eveanna's wedding, the birth of her nephew) and the drama of others (her "first REAL quarrel with Bobby" — a page literally tear-stained) had caused her to usurp space allotted to the future. A different-tinted ink identified each year: 1956 was green and 1957 a ribbon of red, replaced the following year by bright lavender, and now, in 1959, she had decided upon a dignified blue.

Her diary would help both to implicate and to exonerate in the investigation of her death. Because it made occasional mention of her father's opposition to any thought of his Methodist daughter marrying her Catholic boyfriend, Bobby Rupp, it helped draw attention to the possible "motive" of Rupp, who was an early suspect. But it also may have complemented the lie detector test that cleared him of suspicion; for Nancy was writing in her diary as Smith and Hickock were driving across Kansas to kill her: "Jolene K. came over and I showed her how to make a cherry pie. Practiced [a trumpet solo] with Roxie. Bobby here and we watched TV. Left at eleven."

Two months later, Perry Smith is keeping a haphazard diary of his own, in the Finney County jail, as he awaits trial for the murder of Nancy and her family: "Friday 15 January. Mrs. Meier [wife of the undersheriff] playing radio in her kitchen and I heard man say the county attorney will seek Death Penalty. 'The rich never hang. Only the poor and friendless.'" At least he has the decency to own up to his butchery, unlike two nineteenth-century diarists we know of, one an Englishman named Palmer and the other a Scot named Pritchard, who killed their wives and then faked uxoriously mournful journals with which to delude anyone suspicious. (At Balmoral on October 14, 1865, Queen Victoria shuddered to her diary: "After dinner Dr. [Norman] Macleod [who attended Pritchard in prison] gave us a long account of that dreadful Dr. Pritchard, and his interviews with him.

Never in his life had he seen anything so dreadful as this man's character and wonderful untruthfulness.")

That diaries should incriminate and exculpate seems likely enough, but the murder victim who writes a confession for his own killer is sufficiently uncommon. The recent history of the British theater, however, supplies us with such a rarity in the case of Joe Orton. In 1951 he and Kenneth Halliwell, both students at the Royal Academy of Dramatic Art, became lovers. Orton was eighteen and delighted to be escaping from his grim working-class background in Leicester. His diary from this period is full of ambition and elation (May 15, 1951: "Started at RADA O bliss!"). He is in love with the defiant career and sexuality he is choosing, and the last entries in his RADA journal, recalling the beginning of his relationship with Halliwell, are meant to tease anyone who might come upon them with the outlines of the whole story:

June 8
Met Ken. He invites us to live with him.
June 9
Went to the pictures.
Memo
I am puzzled.
June 10
Did nothing.
June 11
Must leave our digs.
June 12
Ken offers to share flat again.
June 13
I say No.
June 14
Ken offers again.
June 15
We accept because we must.

June 16
Move into Ken's flat.
June 17
Well!
June 18
Well!!
June 19
Well!!!
June 20
The rest is silence.

It almost was. For the next fifteen years Orton seems to have kept no diaries. Had he, they would have told a depressing story for most of that time. He and Halliwell lived a life of defeat in an English bedsitter, failing at writing novels, failing at playwrighting, and failing at a life of petty, if ingenious, crime: they spent six months in jail for wittily defacing the jackets of public library books with fake blurbs and obscenely incongruous photographs. Desperate for attention and success, they could find none — until the mid-sixties, when Orton at last began to make his name with plays like *Entertaining Mr. Sloane, Loot*, and *Crimes of Passion*. He and Halliwell continued to live together, but by 1967 Orton was writing a screenplay for the Beatles and Halliwell was unraveling. Having been the dominant partner in their years of obscurity, Halliwell was seen by Orton's flashy new friends as the playwright's increasingly pathetic appendage.

Orton wants to free himself of his lover, but can't bring himself to do it. During the early months of 1967 he resumes keeping the diary he had ceased to write after Halliwell had bedded him fifteen years before. In it he records his professional successes and worries, his troubles with the ever-more-depressed Halliwell, and the anonymous lavatory sex at which he has become boringly expert. On June 6, 1967, the night *Crimes of*

Passion opens in London, Orton picks up a man in Holloway Road and goes off to a furnished room for sex. The description of their time in bed is meticulous, graphic, and jaded. It ends so:

> I got dressed after washing my cock and kissed him goodnight and went home. I had to walk all the way back. Outside a newsagent, I saw a placard announcing ISRAELIS KNOCKOUT ARABS. So I stole it. As a souvenir and a reminder that, whilst I was having a first night and fucking an Irishman (the second more satisfactory than the first) the third War would have been averted. Got in at 2 and slept until 7:30.

These diversions presumably keep his mind off Halliwell, who is more and more accusing and desperate. On March 18 Orton writes:

> Exhausting wrangles over trivia. Kenneth, lying in bed, suddenly shouted "I hope I die of heart disease! I'd like to see you manage then." He talks a lot of *The Dance of Death.* "We're living it," he suddenly said. "This is Strindberg!" Soothed down the situation only to have it break out later. "You're quite a different person, you know, since you had your success."

On April 23:

> Dreary day, Kenneth in an ugly mood. Moaning. I said, "You look like a zombie." He replied, heavily, "So I should. I lead the life of a zombie."

There is not much that can be kept secret in a bed-sitter occupied by two people. Halliwell reads the diary, and no doubt Orton wants him to. It contains kind references to his continuing belief in Halliwell's talent, remarks that are perhaps impossible to speak face to face in their currently strained affair, wistful peace overtures in the psychological war of attrition Halliwell is losing: "Kenneth has more talent, although it's hidden, than [the producer] can flash if he had the reflector from Mount Palomar to do it with." But mostly the diary records Orton's own grievance over the scenes, and the recriminations and threats that are Halliwell's only real theater. Orton is playing to all of "swinging London," but Halliwell's lines just dissolve in the bedsitter's walls.

The neighbors didn't even hear him on August 9, 1967, when he delivered nine hammer blows to Orton's head. After the murder, determined to do away with himself as well, he seems to have decided that Orton's diary could provide the world with a fuller explanation than he has time to write. So he leaves a note on top of it:

If you read his diary all will be explained.
K.H.
P.S. Especially the latter part

The "latter part" Halliwell accomplished by taking twenty-two Nembutals with a glass of grapefruit juice; the coroner would later determine that he actually expired before Orton. Thoroughly eclipsed by his lover and victim, Halliwell even let him do the posthumous talking to the police. Instead of destroying Orton's humiliating version of their rotting partnership, he called attention to it. Like Benjamin Haydon, he gave his last thought to making sure whoever found the body found the diary — even if it wasn't his.

To be human is to feel guilty. One need not believe in Original Sin, or be in the throes of obsession, to be aware of one's daily misdeeds and failings. The opportunity to confess, be it to the bartender, priest, or diary, is seized like air; we should implode with our own remorse if we were denied it. In his book *Why Men Confess*, John O. Rogge reminds us that more than two hundred people owned up to kidnaping the Lindbergh baby, seventeen to the murder of the "Black Dahlia," and countless others to countless crimes uncommitted by themselves. These confessions are merely the psychotic extensions of an ordinary human need that has been thwarted. A man's fantasies may be so tightly reined in that it becomes easier to confess to someone else's killing than to admit them. A crazy psychological displacement takes place, and it no doubt brings an absurd sort of relief.

We all want to be the priest and the penitent, to hear and to tell. The very word *diary* excites us with the promise of guilty secrets to be revealed. Paul Klein, an independent television producer who was once head of programming for NBC, has said that for a television movie the "very best title you could ever come up with would be 'Diary of a Rape.' 'Diary' always works and so does 'Rape.'" If many of the diaries in this chapter are suspect — if "Elizabeth McNeill" faked her book, and if the diaries of "Gretchen Lainer," "Tony Amato" and "Katherine Edwards" were embellished — it is because the fabricators knew they could get an audience.

Less berserk than confessing to another's crimes as a way of lessening one's actual guilt is the use of the diary as a place where the *desire* to transgress is recorded. These are the diaries that contain the kisses unstolen, the freight trains unjumped, the revenges untaken; the ones kept by the men and women of the next and final chapter, those prisoners and invalids of one kind or another who must actually live their lives in their diaries — those men and women for whom the book becomes the world.

7

Prisoners

> *The paralytic on his couch can have*
> *if he wants them wider experiences*
> *than Stanley slaughtering savages.*
> —ALICE JAMES
> October 10, 1890

THAT BOOKS as ruminatingly undisciplined as mine can be published at all in 1984 shows that novelists, fortunately, are not infallible seers. Things are not nearly so bad for us as they were for Oceania's Winston Smith at the beginning and end of the book that memorializes his doomed rebellion against Big Brother. We contend more with the electronic explosion of information than its technological suppression. If books soon metamorphose entirely into tape and microchip, that transformation will be a matter of economic profit and (supposed) convenience rather than fearful extirpation. You may be intellectually ecstatic or aesthetically aggrieved at the idea of a Library of Congress in a cigarette pack, but fear is not really the appropriate reaction to this imminence. As for the place of diaries in all this: if they got written by candlelight, they can presumably get written in the green nighttime glow of the word processor.

For Winston Smith things were, of course, different. Starting the diary with which his rebellion begins is worth about twenty-five years in a labor camp. Winston is supposed to unwrite events, after all, not record them: his job at the Ministry of Information is the erasure and rewriting of "history." So high-tech an enterprise is it, too, that he has trouble at first managing the handwriting necessary when he switches to his own secret book: he is used to dictating most of his words into the "speak-write." Diary-writing is such a lost art in Oceania that aside from fearing to undertake it at all, he has very little idea of what to put down on the blank pages. He starts by pointlessly summarizing the plot of a propaganda film he has seen the night before. But then his pen, with what seems a will of its own, begins to print:

> DOWN WITH BIG BROTHER
> DOWN WITH BIG BROTHER
> DOWN WITH BIG BROTHER
> DOWN WITH BIG BROTHER
> DOWN WITH BIG BROTHER

This was the real purpose of buying the diary — rebellion — even though he hadn't known it when he found it in an out-of-the-way junk shop. What made him purchase the book was more impulse than focused intention. Its physical nature ("peculiarly beautiful . . . Its smooth creamy paper, a little yellowed by age") called to him.

Soon the volume presents itself to him as a space into which he can move. The apologists two chapters back wrote their books in order to explain themselves to the future, and Winston Smith certainly comes to have such a motive, but he is actually looking for something even more urgent: a place where he can come alive. In fact, writing the diary is feasible at all only because Winston's flat has a small alcove that was probably intended for bookshelves in the world that existed when the apartment house was built: "It was partly the unusual geography of the room that had suggested to him the thing that he was now about to do . . . But it had also been suggested by the book that he had just taken out of the drawer." The book joins the actual geography; it becomes Winston's secret room.

On the morning of the day he begins the diary, Winston is both attracted and repelled by a girl in the Fiction

Department of the ministry where he works. She carries a spanner and works on the novel-writing machines. Although she zealously affects the scrubbed genderlessness of the Junior Anti-Sex League, and is able to whip herself into an admirable fury during the daily Two Minutes Hate, she, too, is a secret rebel. This is Julia, and she and Winston eventually have an affair — in the telescreenless attic above the junk shop where Winston bought the diary:

> Now that they had a secure hiding place, almost a home, it did not even seem a hardship that they could only meet infrequently and for a couple of hours at a time. What mattered was that the room over the junk shop should exist. To know that it was there, inviolate, was almost the same as being in it. The room was a world, a pocket of the past where extinct animals could walk.

The same shop that provided the shelter of the diary's paper room now provides a real one. The diary is no longer needed, however generous a substitute it may have been for a while. Winston does not in fact require it during all the days of his erotic freedom. Only when he is broken by the Thought Police in the Ministry of Love must he again take up the book, this time as part of his "reintegration" into Big Brother's world. Subverting the exhilaratingly real arithmetic he had once confided to the diary, Winston now writes "TWO AND TWO MAKE FIVE" beneath one of Big Brother's most important slogans: "FREEDOM IS SLAVERY."

The hardest irony in *1984* is that the Thought Policeman who arrests Winston is Mr. Charrington, the man who sold him the diary.

During the last two years of his life, George Orwell, sick with tuberculosis, struggling to get *1984* written and then trying to prevent its being misunderstood, kept two "hospital notebooks" in which he recorded, with the detachment that is the hallmark of all his writing, such things as the side effects of streptomycin, dreams of death, hospital routines and noises, and the names of suspected Communists. He also noted the difficulties of thinking and writing when one is sick or convalescing. Eventually so weak that he had to be denied his typewriter, Orwell made some of his very last observations in his handwritten notebooks. But they were clearly a poor substitute for the urgent, and to him more real, writing he wanted to do and publish.

Substitution, sublimation, transference — these psychological phenomena are the sorts of things happening in the books in this chapter, where the diary is a wish world. The books kept by those we now meet — the imprisoned, the frightened, and the slowly dying — are by and large more inspiriting than depressing. For these people, diaries are not simply habits; they are attempts to create life, and if they sometimes fail, they retain the luster of heroism.

When Captain Alfred Dreyfus is taken to Devil's Island in the spring of 1895, he is issued some paper. Every sheet of it has a number and a signature on it; whatever use he makes of it will be strictly accounted for: "But what could I do with it? Of what use could it be to me?" The act of committing words to paper implies, except perhaps in the blindest alleys of postmodernism, some pact with purpose, but Dreyfus's circumstances threaten to overwhelm him as he tries to decide what to do. He makes attempts at apologia, but cannot sustain them: not only does he hear his cry vanishing in too literal a wilderness, but also the act of writing for him carries with it subliminal terrors — his conviction for treason was largely based on a piece of handwriting falsely attributed to him. The act of testifying in a paper court, after losing in a real one, is not enough to keep his spirit alive.

But he knows he must put the prison paper to use, just as he knows he must try to survive. So he struggles to keep his courage up on the numbered sheets before him. He remembers his wife and children:

> When will they discover the guilty one; when shall I know at last the truth of all this? Shall I live to know it? Doubt of it assails me: I feel myself falling into black depths of despair. Then I ask myself, what of my poor Lucie and my children? No, I will not abandon them. With all the strength that in me lies, so long as I have a shadow of vitality I will keep faith with those who belong to me.

He has decided the diary will be for his wife; in fact, it will be his marriage. Through it he will speak with her; with it he can move at least one other person into his cell. If he is condemned to hold out on one resource — "a perpetual companionship with my thoughts!" — he can try to keep those thoughts from dying out as mere echoes. At noon on Wednesday, September 2, 1896, he writes: "On the horizon toward Cayenne there hangs a pall of smoke. It must be the mail-boat." One day, he can hope, the diary will be on it, sailing to his wife not as apologia — he knows she believes in him — but as a substitute for the conversation and life together they are being denied.

But his torment is finally too much for the diary to relieve. He is constantly watched by the guards, but never spoken to. Not allowed to share his grief, he can't be alone with it either. And if there are thoughts that lie too deep for tears, there are also emotions too heavy for language to bear. On Bastille Day, 1895, he writes: "I have looked at the tricolor flag floating everywhere, the flag I have loyally served. My pen falls from my fingers." He often wonders what the use of keeping the diary finally is, deciding at least temporarily that it is better to live without thinking. On May 5, 1896, he records the latest variation on his torture: "Until the last few days the guards remained seated in their room during the night; I was awakened only every hour. Now they have to march without stopping, and most of them wear wooden shoes." More than two months go by before he feels strong enough to write another word. On September 10 the diary collapses irreversibly: "I am so utterly weary, so broken down in body and soul, that to-day I stop my diary, not being able to foresee how long my strength will hold out, or what day my brain will succumb under the weight of so great a burden." He ends it with an appeal to the President of the Republic, asking that it be sent to his wife.

This was not done. The diary was seized, along with his other papers, and Dreyfus was only able to regain it in 1899, at his trial in Rennes, where he was once again condemned. When he published the diary shortly thereafter, he included letters from his wife, further emphasizing its nature as a continuing proxy marriage, a simulacrum of communication and tenderness, one that kept breaking down in the face of circumstance.

What happened to Dreyfus prefigured the catastrophe that overtook the Jews of Europe a half century later, when one of the most indomitable — and ultimately most widely read — of all diaries was kept: by a young girl who first moved into a secret attic, and therein finding herself without enough space, moved into a book.

Anne Frank actually begins her diary before she and her family take up residence in 1942, with several other Jews, in the "secret annexe" of a house on Amsterdam's Prinsengracht Canal. She starts it as other young girls still start theirs, naming it ("Kitty") and promising it, on June 14, 1942, that "we're going to be great pals!" She introduces herself with a brief summary of her life, and is soon telling it school news, her problems with Mummy, her adoration of Daddy. She, like all those other girls, needs a confidante. But before long this diary will be no ordinary friend or refuge. Anne is about to be forced into a hiding place where there will be no chance to raise her voice in whatever little air there is to breathe. The diary is going to have to do a great deal more for her;

it will have to be windows and walks and a place where she can turn all her vitality up loud. Even the ordinary matricide of the adolescent female's diary has to take on larger proportions in Anne's: "Those violent outbursts on paper were only giving vent to anger which in a normal life could have been worked off by stamping my feet a couple of times in a locked room, or calling Mummy names behind her back."

Fully aware that she is reaping a whirlwind she has done nothing to deserve, it never occurs to her to do anything but live on inside it. She instinctively accepts the coexistence of individual human natures and historical enormity. Three days after the Normandy landing, "Mrs. Van Daan's grizzling is absolutely unbearable; now she can't any longer drive us crazy over the invasion, she nags us the whole day long about the bad weather. It really would be nice to dump her in a bucket of cold water and put her up in the loft."

For a few days in August 1943 Anne, like William Tayler, sets down the daily routine in the secret annex, so that she can get it into the diary once and have done with it. "*Half past nine*. Quickly into dressing gown, soap in one hand, pottie, hairpins, pants, curlers, and cotton wool in the other, I hurry out of the bathroom; but usually I'm called back once for the various hairs which decorate the washbasin in graceful curves, but which are not approved of by the next person." Life and conversation in the annex are maddeningly repetitive — she says that if one person began a story the other seven could finish it for him — but she remains on the lookout for whatever bits of uniqueness spring to life in the inhabitants' rooms. She uses the diary not only to give a picture of their dreary and dangerous reality, but, via selection, to make their lives seem more varied than they could actually have been. Whenever the world manages to secrete some of life's exciting normality through the shutters, Anne puts it down.

She is prodigiously funny. The diary is full of deft
comical sketches about peeling potatoes, losing her foun-
tain pen, listening to her father's relentless optimism. At
fifteen she can combine political astuteness and a bit of
swooning fantasy in an account of the day's big event:
"Super news! An attempt has been made on Hitler's life
and not even by Jewish communists or English capitalists
this time, but by a proud German general, and what's
more, he's a count, and still quite young." She knows
she is a gifted writer and will someday be a good one.
She thinks about becoming a journalist when the war is
over and is increasingly aware of the documentary value
of her diary as the war goes on. (She is conscious enough
of an audience to begin qualifications with, "Will the
reader take into consideration . . .") What is odd is that
she doesn't dream more about becoming a novelist. If
the requisites for that profession are wit, psychological
insight, and the ability to write stylish sentences, the
following ones certify her incipient skills:

> Mrs. Van Daan thinks I'm stupid because I'm not quite
> so lacking in intelligence as she is; she thinks I'm
> forward because she's even more so; she thinks my
> dresses are too short, because hers are even shorter.
> And that's also the reason that she thinks I'm knowing,
> because she's twice as bad about joining in over sub-
> jects she knows absolutely nothing about.

Anne can be as free with self-criticism as she is with her
prickings of others, and she is wise enough, when she
thinks she is falling in love with young Peter Van Daan,
to check herself with the hypothesis that she is deliberately conflating him with another Peter on whom she had
a crush in the days before they were all shut away.

She is not immune to despair ("I do talk about 'after
the war,' but then it is only a castle in the air, something
that will never really happen"), but her lack of self-pity

is fundamentally so great as to be staggering. On July 23, 1943, she records each of the clandestine tenants' wishes for immediate gratification once they are again allowed outside. Their fantasies run to hot baths, ice cream, coffee, and movies. As for herself: "While I should find it so blissful, I shouldn't know where to start! But most of all, I long for a home of our own, to be able to move freely and to have some help with my work again at last, in other words — school." If she is able to sustain these dreams through her moments of hopelessness, it is because she believes "in spite of everything . . . that people are really good at heart."

Living in a world where one is forbidden to cough and constantly asked to be sensible, she considers her book the garden of her dreams and more than once recalls the saying that "paper is more patient than man." Enduring in circumstances in which one's highest ideal is escape, she understands that "the brightest spot of all is that at least I can write down my thoughts and feelings, otherwise I would be absolutely stifled!" The diary is the only thing she has "for myself alone." When on Easter Sunday 1944 police come close to discovering the eight of them behind the cupboard, a period of still stronger precaution sets in. During it Anne impulsively declares that she will not agree to go on living without her book:

> "They will find Anne's diary," added Daddy. "Burn it then," suggested the most terrified member of the party. This, and when the police rattled the cupboard door, were my worst moments. "Not my diary; if my diary goes, I go with it!" But luckily Daddy didn't answer.

The very last words she writes in the diary show her awareness of it as the only place her heart can remain free to grow. In a world with only seven other souls in it, the ordinary frustrations of growing up are screwed tighter with repetition and ringed with terror:

Oh, I would like to listen, but it doesn't work; if I'm quiet and serious, everyone thinks it's a new comedy and then I have to get out of it by turning it into a joke, not to mention my own family, who are sure to think I'm ill, make me swallow pills for headaches and nerves, feel my neck and my head to see whether I'm running a temperature, ask if I'm constipated and criticize me for being in a bad mood. I can't keep that up: if I'm watched to that extent, I start by getting snappy, then unhappy, and finally I twist my heart round again, so that the bad is on the outside and the good is on the inside and keep on trying to find a way of becoming what I would so like to be, and what I could be, if . . . there weren't any other people living in the world.

The paper was more patient.

The secret annex was raided on August 4, 1944, three days after Anne wrote the words quoted above. She died at Bergen-Belsen the following March. Of the eight residents of the annex only her father would survive. The diary was resting in his briefcase when the Gestapo arrived. The arresting officer threw the book on the floor and used the empty case to cart off a Hanukkah candlestick and some silverware. When two of the Franks' protectors from the office beneath the annex — Miep van Santen and Elli Vossen — later picked it up, they could scarcely have known they would be carrying down the stairs one of the century's holy texts — and beyond any question its most famous diary.

To move from the diary of Anne Frank to that of Hitler's master architect, Albert Speer, may seem at first too perverse an illustration of the diary's indiscriminate availability, its willingness to lie down with anybody, victim or slaughterer. But a reader of *Spandau*, Speer's account of his twenty years in prison for the war crimes he admitted at Nuremberg, comes to see that the collection of notes he smuggled out for twenty years on scrap

paper, calendar sheets, box tops, and toilet paper has in
common with Anne Frank's book a persistent attempt to
create an alternative to the real world, the one from
which she was so insanely, and he so reasonably, sealed
off.

Unlike Anne, Speer was eventually allowed to reenter
it. He was released from Spandau in 1966 and went on to
publish the illicit scraps in the hope they would vouch
for his existence, prove he had continued to live during
the more than seven thousand days he had been locked
away. Meant to stand "in place of a life," *Spandau* is, he
writes, "all that has remained of my life between my
fortieth and my sixtieth years . . . Ultimately it is an attempt to give form to the time that seemed to be pouring
away so meaninglessly, to give substance to years empty
of content." Actually the twenty years were far from
meaningless. Speer knows it and the reader of *Spandau*
learns it as well. It is possible to begin Speer's diaries with
furious moral resistance but difficult to remain uncon-
vinced that during his just (indeed lenient) banishment
he failed to perform some sort of ethical regeneration,
to pass through a needle's eye of productive shame.

From a historical point of view the diaries will remain
valuable for the recollections of Hitler's private and
political inner circles; their musings on what passed for
entertainment and creative endeavor among Nazis; and
their reconstructions of Hitler's ability to talk himself
"into an auto-suggestive euphoria." A reader of the
diaries also sees those convicted at Nuremberg pointedly
being given the clothes of concentration camp victims to
wear in Spandau, and then either adjusting or simply proceeding to a new form of madness. In October 1946,
shortly before the transfer to Spandau is actually made,
Speer and his fellow prisoners have to clean the floor of
the room where Ribbentrop and others have recently
been executed: Hess sees what looks like a bloodstain on
it and salutes. Baldur von Schirach, head of the Hitler

Youth, drives Speer crazy by incessantly whistling "Lili Marlene." And when after ten years Admiral Karl Dönitz, Hitler's successor as Führer in the final days of the Reich, is released from Spandau, he laments that his career is ruined. Speer turns to him disbelievingly: " 'Your ten years here perturb you more than the fifty million dead. And your last words here in Spandau are: your career!' "

As for his own career, Speer recalls how when he was thirty Hitler "laid a world at [his] feet." This recollection occurs in his first year in prison. After four more he sees a ball of manure and recalls "how Hitler, while inspecting the models for new Berlin, ordered a globe of the world to be placed on the great dome as a support for the gigantic eagle. 'It ought to hold the globe in its claws,' Hitler said." And five years after this, reading a biography of Leonardo, Speer muses, without having to note the personal relevance, on the fall of the artist's patron, Duke Ludovico.

Speer allows himself to consider past glories, or what might have been, only infrequently. He tries to make use of the present by a variety of stratagems, some practical and some fantastic. He gardens, reads, and takes notes for a book on the architectural history of the window; and he imagines himself at the theater, gives himself semiannual vacations ("sleep cures"), and makes himself walk around the world. This last achievement is accomplished by measuring his steps in the prison yard perimeter:

It took 415 days for the 2,280 kilometers from Kunming to Peking, but that still makes a daily average of 5.4 kilometers a day. Since the beginning of my pilgrimage to the continent of Asia four years and ten months ago I have covered 14,260 kilometers . . . Now I have the distance from Peking to Vladivostok before me, and have requested books on that route.

These schemes help him fight off the occasional surges of despair, as well, as the "groundless panics."

But it is not his cleverness in passing the time that sets Speer apart from the Nazis with whom he is entombed. It is instead his willingness to assume guilt and believe in the possibility of his own deliverance. He undertakes a "moral reckoning," and since no other inmate is interested in helping him with it he uses his secret diary instead. It allows him to explore the nature and extent of his own culpability in a way that is prolonged, thorough, and subtle — in the good sense of that word. He is able to accept moral guilt first, and legal guilt only afterward, even though one would expect the latter to be the easier burden to pick up. The Allies' unpunished and "indiscriminate" air raids on Berlin and other German cities cast an ambiguous shadow over the laws used at Nuremberg, he feels, and it takes time for him to work through toward a sense of the statutory justice involved in his conviction:

> The moral guilt is undeniable. Up to now it has been hard for me to admit to legal guilt. But were not most of the verdicts based on the committing of such conventional crimes as murder and manslaughter, pillaging and coercion? If I recruited foreign laborers, the fact of coercion was implicit in that act. And that is punishable under the law.
>
> Who could survive twenty years of imprisonment without accepting some form of guilt?

That last rhetorical question: it is a point at which the eyebrows go up and the "aha's" come out. But Speer is himself aware of the temptation to assume guilt for reasons purely psychological and self-serving. After ten years of his captivity have passed he considers that his confessions at the trials were made from impulses suspiciously Nazi in nature:

Was my stand in court really an intelligent repudia-
tion of the high-flown bathos of those years? Was it
not rather only a different kind of blind self-sacrifice,
one more piece of romantic mania for self-surrender,
mindless youthful emotionalism? . . . Sometimes the
thought alarms me that Hitler, for all that I so strongly
disavowed him and all he stood for in court, would
have been keenly delighted by the role Albert Speer
played as a defendant.

He recognizes the "arrogance of the humbled" and that
he remains incompletely immune to fantasies about how
he "would have been one of the most respected men in
Hitler's world government." It takes years for the guilt
to soak thoroughly into his bones. He is honestly prone
to a kind of ethical recidivism and must take care not to
allow the years in prison to dilute what he has striven to
take in.

Still, he remains capable of human rage at his confinement: "They have physically and mentally destroyed
me. Ah, these spokesmen of humanitarianism! Only
twenty years! It has really been my life." But if he loses
the will to live, and to fight for his freedom, he will not
have enough mental energy and self-esteem to make his
engagement with guilt either possible or worthwhile. So
as late as August 24, 1960, he must accept a paradox:
"Will they ever be able to understand that I want to get
out of here and yet see a meaning in my being here?"
The sturdy intelligence so clearly at work in these diaries
provokes a reader to admiration — and plunges him into
lingering mystery. How could anyone of such apparent
sensitivity and scruple (who admits he had at least in-
klings of the worst horrors) have remained for so many
years at the side of barbarians? It is a genuine conundrum.
Speer finally illustrates not evil's banality, but its cen-
trality, its endless presence in people, its ability to fly
like bacteria into the blood cells of the high-minded,

breaking down their moral immunities and laying waste to their goodness. Somehow he makes a partial recovery. He comes to terms with himself at his trial and in prison, and he keeps on coming to terms with himself. His diaries demonstrate the ultimate justification for Nuremberg and for Spandau. One feels that his punishment took more than a quarter of his life, but finally saved his soul.

His diary-keeping is a suitable complement to the prison regimen. A chronic diarist and a prisoner share, after all, an extreme awareness of time. On October 3, 1946, Speer writes: "Out of seven thousand three hundred days, plus five leap-year days, nine have now passed." The accumulation of diaries might have provided him with some encouragement: as they mounted up, they would show that the number of days left on the calendar of captivity were dwindling, as if one pile of paper were being remade into another. But this comfort is denied him because of the need to smuggle out each entry: "I am sick of always merely observing and writing down and then getting rid of what I have written as fast as possible," he writes in his fifth year of imprisonment. "Nothing tangible remains." The brick garden he builds is at least there to be seen each morning. He reads the published diary of Goebbels; he sees the one Schirach is keeping get confiscated. The furtiveness of his own exhausts him. He often feels (like Dreyfus) that writing it is useless; gaps result. When he resumes it he must wonder whether his style doesn't sometimes indicate a spurious ironic mastery of his imprisonment, when in fact the humiliations keep stinging.

The diary becomes too much the instrument of his salvation to be completely abandoned. On April 29, 1966, only several months before his release, he writes: "When I think back on the twenty years: would I have been able to survive this time if I had not been permitted to write a single line?" He cannot stop in any case. He tries to, but he comes back to the clandestine pieces of paper; after all, "How does one conclude a thing like this?" He is able to stop writing it for about two months of the summer just before his release, and claims he doesn't miss it. But on July 22, 1966, he rushes back to its shelter to record a terrifying experience: "Last night I dreamed that I would never return home."

Spandau is a small piece of decency to be found amidst all the bones bleached and strewn by the Nazis. If indeed it stands "in place of" Speer's actual life, it will live with more purpose and lastingness than anything he made in the time he was free to live the supposedly real one. He came to understand this. The great innovations of his work for the regime had been, after all, in the realm of so-called "light architecture" — the achievement of eerie constructive effects through the use of giant floodlights, the sort of thing he did at the party rally in Nuremberg and the German Pavilion at the Paris World's Fair. Twenty years after the fall of Berlin, on July 9, 1965, he wrote in his diary that he felt "strangely stirred by the idea that the most successful architectural creation of my life is a chimera, an immaterial phenomenon."

Moving away from those imprisoned by and for enormity toward those jailed only by their own temperaments, we expect to feel a lower temperature of desperation. But this isn't necessarily the case. Whether they suffer from the freakishness of neurons, or a part of God's plan, those depressed and frightened in the midst of the world are free in only some legal sense of the term. Something has marked them out to live behind bars that don't exist, and their diaries are as likely to be tin cups to rattle against them as they were for the literal prisoners already encountered.

Poor William Allingham! To say that in his lifetime (1824–1889) he was a minor poet is to put it, as he put almost everything, mildly. To say that a hundred years since then he has ceased to be read at all is to tell the simple truth. An Irishman who toiled as a bank clerk and customs officer, he produced one poem whose title

"Laurence Bloomfield in Ireland" may vaguely resonate in minds swollen by study for Ph.D. oral exams, but his name is more likely to ring the doorbells to such minds as one recollected being "among those present" when Tennyson or Browning or the pre-Raphaelites sat down to dinner. Allingham wanted more than anything else to be one of the literary boys; the truth is he rather foisted himself on the greats. His diary records the crumbs of table talk he took home and struggled to content himself with. He was, it seems, a decent, lonely fellow who knew he was de trop, who longed for literary fame of his own but settled for making a not very good job of hanging on to that enjoyed by others. He was no Henry Crabb Robinson, that diarist of an earlier generation who could mingle with the Romantics at ease and with zest; Allingham seems to have suffered, through much of his adult life, from the certainty that he was the least-sought-after person in the room.

He worshiped Tennyson, who seems to have tolerated him with intermittent and tepid affection. On the evening of Sunday, June 28, 1863, Allingham confesses to a lonely mood and ponders his relationship to the Poet Laureate:

> I have lost the faith I used to have in people's wishing to see me — perhaps it is merely one of the signs that youth has passed away. But I feel a natural bond to him (I say it in humility) and to a very few others, and only in their company am better contented than to be with nature and books. With these persons I feel truly humble, yet at the same time easy. I understand and am understood, with words or without words. It is not fame that attracts me, it disgusts me rather. Fame has cooled many friendships for me, never made or increased one. Fame is a thing of the "World," and the "World" is a dreadful separator.

The logic here is more than a little confused; and it doesn't take much more reading of the diary to be sure that, at least where Tennyson was concerned, Allingham was more ignored than absorbed. When you feel "easy" with someone, you don't write "Hurrah!" after you've been invited to his dinner table — by a mutual friend, too — but that is what Allingham does the following October 3.

He is generally left alone and lonely, and maybe, he thinks, that is all he merits: "How many days of my life I pass without a word of conversation. But am I not as well off as I deserve to be?" When Tennyson, after a visit by Allingham on December 29, extends his guest the minimal courtesy of seeing him to the garden gate, it is almost too much: "When I went to T.'s room he said, 'Come whenever you like,' and as I went out by the garden he came after me and saw me through the gate. Truly friendly — a delightful visit!" One pictures Tennyson shaking his head as he goes back indoors.

Tennyson could, in fact, be positively churlish to his aging attendant. On July 22, 1866, when Allingham admits that he has felt "*intuitions* of Immortality," Tennyson refuses to believe him and accuses him of trying to compete with his own finer sensations. The following February the two of them are walking along a cliff, and Allingham confesses to being light-headed:

> T. tells of people who have fallen over, and at one place is a monumental stone to commemorate such an accident. I said (walking close behind him) "suppose I were to slip and catch hold of you, and we both rolled down together," on which T. stopped and said, "you'd better go first."

At first this anecdote seems, like most of Allingham's, just boring; but then one considers its psychological subtext and can't help but wince for him.

Allingham is devastated by Browning, too ("I always end by striking my breast . . . and crying out, 'O rich mind! wonderful Poet! strange great man!' "). When on one occasion in May 1868 Allingham "bashfully" con-

fesses to Browning how he has always believed in him,
the poet replies: " 'I am glad to believe that, for your
own sake among other things.' " And poor Allingham
doesn't see he's just been pushed off another cliff.

If Allingham's idea of participation in culture is our
idea of leeching, he can still worry that he isn't putting
enough of his behavior's results into the diary. He writes
a poem about the problem:

> A man who keeps a diary pays
> Due toll to many tedious days;
> But life becomes eventful — then
> His busy hand forgets the pen.
> Most books, indeed, are records less
> Of fulness than of emptiness.

This is the traveler's old difficulty once again. Allingham
scarcely realizes how empty his own "fulness" is, but
between dinners he can confess himself "Lonely. Walk,
field-path, Pennington Farm, standing corn. Ditch
crowded with wild-flowers. Would I had a companion!"
Until he makes his late marriage, the only thing he can do
is use the diary to pump up the meagerness of his enjoy-
ments into something resembling a bearable life. He uses
its pages to magnify his paltry hoard, but too often they
fail him, reflecting instead his nose pressed against the
glass. Lady Shelley tells him: " 'Come to us to-morrow
evening, if we're not gone' "; the next night, of course,
they are.

In his journal for April 26, 1841, Thoreau wrote that
"the civilized man has the habits of the house. His house
is a prison." Arthur Christopher Benson (1862–1925) was
more permanently and luxuriously at home, whether as
owner or guest, than William Allingham ever was, but in
most of the ways that count he was just as much a
prisoner of timidity and gloom as the Irish poet. Benson
could move confidently through Victorian and Edwardian England; he was, after all, the son of the Archbishop
of Canterbury, a master at Eton, Master of Magdalene

College, Cambridge, the chosen editor of Queen Victoria's letters, and a friend of writers like Edmund Gosse
and Henry James. But he wore his conventional security
like fat and, frightened of the dark energies he suspected
in his spirit, took care never to turn up the hard gemlike
flame with which Walter Pater had urged the men of his
time to burn.

Benson was scared, and he settled. He had strong literary ambitions, but he allowed himself to remain, as he
put it in 1906, a sensible don "stranded at 44 with a corner
in a tiny college, writing books that go straight to the
heart of a few hundred of the unctuous and sentimental
middle-class." Even when his fame grew, he knew he was
never to be more than an academic Arnold Bennett. And
part of him despised himself for it.

Sex was a large part of his problem, and in some ways
the inspiration for the more than four million words of
diaries he was to write. Benson loved young men, was
terrified of his urges, and chose, as schoolmaster, the
occupation most guaranteed to exalt and torment him on
a daily basis. According to his biographer, David Newsome, it was his reading of the diaries of William Johnson
Cory — an Eton schoolmaster who left " 'under a cloud' "
— that made Benson begin his own in earnest in 1897.
Those diaries would both check and compensate his
homosexual longings for the years he remained at Eton.
Even on December 8, 1903, as he is getting ready to leave
the school to edit Queen Victoria's letters and pursue his
literary career, his journal simultaneously rides to reverie
and keeps the reins tight:

In the evening I had my last Private. I examined the
boys in history. They did very well. As they filed out
I sate wondering — the lights bright, and a big fire
blazing, flickering over the benches and the maps, and
the inky forms, and the old books that I have known
so long . . . I feel a little tearful at the idea of the
work and the briskness and the young life all about —

and that all over; but I don't for one instant repent, and I would not alter my decision for one second, even if I could. The time has come naturally, and I must add very happily and sweetly to an end; the boys have been at their very best this half — sweet-tempered, considerate, good. And I have not slackened steam the least, but have bucketed on to the very end.

He never lets himself go. The diary "made my own weaknesses more and more clear to me" he writes. For safety's sake he has to observe, not participate in, storms of emotion. He sees himself standing "on the edge of Paradise," always aware of the frozen percipience of his stance: " 'I can see life as a series of beautiful pictures . . . I cannot live it.' "

So he looks about and makes an appallingly huge inventory of the eye, using the millions of words to describe all the great events of the day on whose edges he stands. When the Prime Minister lunches, he is there; when Gladstone is buried, he is watching; when Edward VII is crowned, he — like an unpissing, straitjacketed Pepys — is there for that, too. He hides his passions under mustaches and waistcoats and buries his need for love under the hideous Victorian appetite for work: Thursday, April 10, 1902: "I sate and wrote letters half the morning — 24 or so."

He suffers long and gruesome assaults of depression, especially between 1907 and 1910 and 1917 and 1923. At the start of the latter period he fears he will go mad; while frantically waiting to see a doctor, he writes down a prayer, puts the date and his signature to it, and secrets it in a drawer in his bedroom. His diary breaks off for a number of months after that. This is probably the greatest crisis in his life, and one of the rare occasions on which he is unable to confide in his journal. Normally he doesn't hide his sadness from it. He professes a dislike of those diaries kept by invalids, but is determined that his own — with all its hinted repressions and explicit sadness — will be more revealing than anyone's but Pepys's.

The latter's ciphered journals, kept by a man so thoroughly different from himself — a man who knew that the easiest thing to do about temptation is give in to it and *then* sit down to the day's correspondence — must have exerted a powerful grip on Benson's imagination in his later years, when he occupied the Master's Lodge at Magdalene College. All the time he was there, adding to his own five million words, he knew Pepys's million and a quarter were residing just across the garden and upstairs in the original bookcases of the Pepys Library. They had been there for two hundred years, keeping Pepys and his indulgences alive, day after day, night after night. Benson knew he could not exhibit himself as Pepys had done in life — it was not his destiny to *tocar* or *besar* a single *cosa* — but he was determined to exhibit his suppressions in death. He wanted the diaries read. However sad and unsatisfactory his own life might be, he set about preserving and shaping it with enough care and artifice ("I suppose if we could not gild our own lives a little we should hardly dare to live") that others would be able to keep looking at it. He once declared that the essence of beauty was continuity, the sense of longstandingness an old object can strike us with, and he continually planted what could someday be the evidence of his antiquity — not just the words in the diary, but "fetishes," little mementos of trips and visits, tiny egotistical time capsules — a piece of china, an old key, a tooth — that he buried under grounds he tramped over. Cheated of life, he would somehow cheat death.

His words now repose inside the same gates as those of Pepys, the man he strove so hard to imitate in so much but the art of living.

Arthur Crew Inman (1895–1963) beat Arthur Christopher Benson two to one: he wrote not a mere four, but ten million words of diaries before he shot himself to death. His journal was — for the forty years he expensively shut himself up in Boston, from the days of Coolidge to John Fitzgerald Kennedy — the instrument of immortality he fashioned. Early in life he, like Benson, had had a nervous breakdown; and, like Allingham, he was a failed poet. He lived something like a life, but it was a poor enough thing compared to the 155 typed volumes he put it into. Approaching the end of both enterprises, he offers a kind of summation of them on October 28, 1960:

I, Arthur Inman, am of years 65, a semi-invalid. This diary constitutes my major ambition, and keeping it my major work. Being fortunate enough to enjoy what is called an independent income, I am cared for physically by doctors who are also, in varying degrees, my friends, by my immediate family, by the friends who like me . . . I and my immediate family live in an old apartment building in a locality on the downslide in a city on the downslide, very comfortably for our purposes. My hobby and vindication is in endeavoring to make money trading in stocks. I own a lucrative apartment house. I suffer from weak nerves, weak ligaments, weak eyes, a tender digestive system, migraine attacks, too much energy for a fourth-class constitution . . . I lead, for me at any rate, an exciting life, though one I would as soon lose any night, which is spasmodic at best. I use Government talking-books, which are recordings of novels and serious works, to help pass the nights. Mornings I write in here, tend to business and hobbies; afternoons listen a bit to radio and correct what I have written mornings or study financial news; evenings talk to people or listen to Roderic or Evelyn [his wife] read aloud . . . I try to ride a very small way several mornings a week in my 1919 open Cadillac . . . I try to keep my hours both scheduled and full, but needs must rest in bed some 16 hours in 24. I have a curiosity about everything, perhaps an imagination, little or no intellect under command. I strive to keep my fears and annoyances under control. I make a good friend. I believe in nothing, actually, save perhaps time and pain. I have had more than my share of love and concern during my existence, and believe in returning it. I rule my actions and thoughts personally by the very clear adumbration of being good to those who are good to me, which, when followed, simplifies social behavior. I enjoy history. I enjoy people. My mind is always, like librating antennae, casting about. Being physically and nervously bankrupt gives me a feeling of some animal cornered in a cave, on guard from whatever portends danger. Though I am not happy, yet I am merry betimes. I know that my blessings are many, and count them daily. All about and in me is mystery, and past making reason. I enjoy helping people until they take advantage of my generosity, then kaput.

Instead of living, he collected: letters, news, whatever or whomever he could comfortably filter into his cave. He would advertise for "interesting people to talk to invalid," and those who answered his notice in the newspaper would get seventy-five cents an hour to tell him their stories while he stayed behind a black curtain.

He fanatically provided for his diary's future. Whoever edited it was to cut nothing (not even the compliments to Hitler). To make sure that it survived anything from fire to nuclear explosion, he had microfilms of it deposited in places unlikely to be bombed. The editor his diary has fallen to — make that "on" — is Daniel Aaron, a Harvard professor who has written a history of the American literary left and whose fascination with the diary's grotesque author and proportions conquered his squeamishness about spending the remaining years of his career with Arthur Crew Inman. Aaron told George Colt Howe: "He would kill, burn, or destroy for the diary's sake." Aaron, a nice, sane man who can usually be found bicycling around Harvard, is now committed to living with a hypochondriacal, phobic recluse for the rest of his scholarly life. There is even someone ready to succeed him "in case I die or lose my mind," he says; but he hopes to finish the job of Inman's immortality himself: "I'm going to make him famous."

Arthur Crew Inman is getting his wish.

If oddities of temperament kept him and Allingham and Benson from living fully in the world, it can at least be said that they were not wholly lacking in material means. Psychologically thwarted but not unduly deprived of money, none of them was truly desperate. But when a naturally troubled disposition is further beset by poverty the screws get genuinely tight. The real name of "Eve Wilson" is unknown to readers because she committed the shameful offense of falling out of the English middle class and into want shortly after the turn of the century. Her father had been a proud silk manufacturer in Manchester who married above himself and produced two sons and two daughters. By the time Eve was a young woman both her father and her mother had died, and she had the bad fortune to be caught female and unmarried. Everything in the father's business went to the two sons; the sister went to Scotland with her rich new husband — and the bulk of the furniture. Eve ended up at twenty-seven, after some years as a governess, as a stenographer at Miss de Burgh's Registry for "governesses, nursery nurses, and superior maids." She remained there for twenty-one years. When she started she earned thirty shillings a week; when she left her salary had yet to exceed three pounds. She left only because the chairman who took over the agency on Miss de Burgh's death fired everyone there. Eve Wilson died, alone and poor, nine months later.

A Miss Geraldine Waife, who worked with Eve, was later contacted and sent eight thick notebooks by her brother. She in turn gave them to an editor, in the hope that they could be fashioned into "a book for those, like

Eve, who have little time for reading, who read in a shaky bus, or hanging from a strap in the tube, or in a restaurant . . . I think there may be some who need its mental shelter." Miss Waife's image for *The Notebooks of a Woman Alone* (1935) is as apt as her intention was generous. The thick books were precisely that — a shelter — to Eve Wilson: a clean, well-lighted place festooned with observations and quotations that made her loneliness and fears more bearable.

Eve's work as a governess had not been as satisfying as that employment was to Ellen Weeton. Eve was a nervous and proud person who didn't like the idea of living where she worked. On the night she finds her job at Miss de Burgh's she exults in the chance she will have to live in a room of her own — years before Virginia Woolf celebrates that phrase as both symbol and substance of woman's freedom:

> I cannot think any woman is happier than I am tonight. I have at last got work which means making my own home away from the business place. What care I that it is only thirty shillings a week, that my room will only be a bed-sitting room, that baths will be a luxury, that my food will be bread, eggs, and cheese? It is all going to be my own. I can change when it is too uncomfortable, and yet not lose my work. And if the work is lost I have, anyway while my savings last, a place in which I have the right to stay, to be able to move about without the criticism of other people.
>
> I wish I knew if other women feel as I do. I don't think it is entirely the result of ten years earning my bread, sometimes with lots of butter, in other people's houses. I think I have always wanted alone-ness as a drunkard wants drink. How can I explain to these mothers, these employers of home-workers, that a room alone, a warmed one to which the employee can go, is a necessity?

If this passage shows Eve's independence, it also shows her fear that circumstances might once again deprive her of the chance to make a living and fulfill her compulsion toward solitude. But while she has her room she revels in it; and her notebooks are the wing she adds on in her imagination — a gay "shelter" decorated to her own taste.

Eve has the commonplace book habit. She quotes and copies with zest, and her selections give further proof of what seems to be an almost physical law: the more assiduously someone keeps his own diaries the more he will read others' as well. Eve Wilson reads the books of two figures we are soon to meet — Alice James and W. N. P. Barbellion — a woman and man whose circumstances made them obviously kindred to her. She also reads the diaries of Pepys, and is prompted to envy his endless and insouciant appetite for life:

> I think anxieties about ways and means have robbed me of thrills that I ought to have had. I wonder if it was my fault? Life is to me at times very frightening. I have always the feeling of living in a world that belongs to other people who must be placated or dodged. But surely living should be wonderful *sometimes* in spite of pain?

She is always aware of her predisposition toward fear and her imagination of disaster: "I think I naturally plant fears where others would think only in terms of a joke, or an adventure or an unusual event. I know I am likely to think, if I hear a child crying, that the child is in terror; and such is not *always* the case." What the diarists of the first chapter have in common with those in this last one is voluminousness. But the chroniclers needed so much space because their avidity and lack of suspicion toward life made them happy to rake and bag all of its details; the prisoners of one sort or another, like Eve Wilson, require room great enough in which to hide from the world, alternative planets onto which they can step when bad luck and odd moods evict them from this one.

Eve Wilson's greatest fear, from the very first day she finds work, is that she will lose it. When that calamity comes to pass, she is for a time too terrified to confide it even to her diary:

> I have lost my work. It is three weeks since I knew, but I did not dare to own to my book that the daily fear has become a certain fact. Am I now sorry I did not live the life of a miser on one pound a week — many would call that affluence — and save, first ten, and then forty, shillings a week? I had no dependents. I might have been able to do it. But my rises in salary were so uncertain. I do not think I should have ever made enough for safety even had I managed to live in dirt and cold all these years. Whenever I contemplated it I pushed the idea aside as impossible.

Her fears accelerate toward terror. She confides to her book the story of Rachel, a governess who lost work and had to stay in the workhouse until she could find new employment. Among the notebooks is an envelope Eve means to destroy after making guilt-ridden confessions on it in the middle of the night:

> Cheap lodgings, hard work, thin-natured, or mentally starved, people: I suppose it was all I deserved. And a psychologist once told me that we gravitate to what we want. Perhaps I was fitted for nothing else . . . Did I have other chances? Perhaps I did — dreadful thought — and never knew they were offered to me as a means of escape. To myself, though, just for once I will say that, when the chance seemed to be coming there was always someone crying for help, and I turned back. Very conceited and egoistic of me writing this. A psychologist would say it was my excuse for failing. I must leave it on paper, not in my book. I must destroy it to-morrow. — (Written one night about two a.m.).

Unlike Ellen Weeton, Eve Wilson never intends her books to be a bill of grievances. It was only her friend and accidental legatee, Miss Waife, who decided they would be such. So fully does Eve Wilson wish them to be the cheerful shelter where she can invent new life that she resists tarnishing them with her jobless panic. This is, after all, the book in which she once sketched her own version of utopia, a place where the hardest and least interesting jobs pay the most; so pleased is she with her fantasy that she writes a little paragraph of praise to the diary's assistance in her dream-making:

> I write for my own amusement. My bed-sitting room is not too warm; I cannot afford all the gas I want when a shilling-in-the-slot meter gives so little; my meal to-night was only a rather tired egg and a shrunken orange — I have heard this is the typical spinster's meal — for my landlady is angry that I did not go out this August Bank Holiday. But I have had a new book and been very contented thinking of a world as I would like it.

She came into the world with comfort and plenty; she left it with little more than the eight thick notebooks to her name.

In two essential respects Alice James (1848–1892) was Eve Wilson's opposite. Whereas the latter's London life ended on the rim of poverty, the former's concluded in genteel accommodations in Leamington Spa. And if Eve Wilson's work was the absolutely essential part of her existence, materially and emotionally, it was Alice James's invalidism that constituted her profession and identity. Her biographer Jean Strouse has described it as a sort of vocation, the only one socially and psycho-logically available to a highly strung woman in the peculiar family of overachievers that included her brothers Henry, the novelist, and William, the psycholo-gist. The victim of chronic and often undiagnosed ailments, Alice is for a time relegated to the position of her father's housekeeper. Recalling one of her earliest attacks of hysteria, she writes:

> As I used to sit immovable reading in the library with waves of violent inclination suddenly invading my muscles taking some one of their myriad forms such as throwing myself out of the window, or knocking off the head of the benignant pater as he sat with his silver locks, writing at his table, it used to seem to me that the only difference between me and the insane was that I had not only all the horrors and suffering of insanity but the duties of doctor, nurse, and strait-jacket imposed upon me, too.

She eventually settles in England with her companion Katharine Loring, increasingly roombound by indigestion, "nervousness," and, finally, breast cancer. But as her world contracts more and more, she makes a decision to turn the commonplace book she has been keeping into a full-blown diary. On May 31, 1889, she announces the deliberate metamorphosis of the perfunctory notebook she has used for the past three years:

> I think that if I get into the habit of writing a bit about what happens, or rather doesn't happen, I may lose a little of the sense of loneliness and desolation which abides with me. My circumstances allowing of nothing but the ejaculation of one-syllabled reflections, a written monologue by that most interesting being, *myself*, may have its yet to be discovered consolations. I shall at least have it all my own way and it may bring relief as an outlet to that geyser of emotions, sensations, speculations and reflections which ferments perpetually within my poor old carcass for its sins; so here goes, my first Journal!

She uses this ever more animate diary to chart the approach of what she calls in a letter to William "the most supremely interesting moment in life," namely, death. This was the one experience that Virginia Woolf (who would read Alice James's diary in 1934) once said she would never describe. But Alice James is determined not simply to chronicle its approach but to cheer it on as well. In September 1890 she laments that "the Monster Rebound" is cheating her of it, and worries that when she frees herself from his well-intentioned clutches she will be too insensible to participate fully: "A creature who has been denied all dramatic episodes might be allowed, I think, to assist at her extinction. I know I shall slump at the 11th hour, and it would complete it all so to watch the rags and tatters of one's Vanity in its insolent struggle with the Absolute, as the curtain rolls down on this jocose humbuggery called Life!" She unwaveringly holds to the dust-to-dust approach, poking fun at her own cage of flesh and ridiculing the consolations of religion. She is inclined to the definite, the aphoristic — and the accurate: "I suppose one has a greater sense of intellectual degradation after an interview with a doctor than from any human experience."

But for all its preoccupation with her illness, confinement, and resoluteness, Alice James's diary also manages to be hungrily and hilariously turned to the life outside herself. What an American patriot she was! Wonderfully devoid of her brother's Anglophilia, Alice manages to come up with her own acerbic view of English life, gleaning it through her observation of visitors and from her perusal of *Truth*, a scandal sheet often referred to in the diary, and shockingly disapproved of by one of her callers, the widow of the poet Arthur Clough (the same woman over whose invitation to the Tennysons' William Allingham shouted, "Hurrah!"). On January 21, 1891, Alice notes one of its items, which says that the Queen is going to have a special studio set aside for works of art being done with the Royal Family as subjects, because she is afraid her own subjects might come upon unfinished statues showing the Family's members undraped — in, in short, the marble raw. Alice comments:

"Isn't she the supreme grocer?" Herself an invalid and ex-patriate, she still marvels at the abundance of American energy and opportunity denied to the British types who come her way. A Leamington spinster: "She was a re-fined mortal, and although fifty years of age, embodied still, as K. said, the Wordsworthian maiden, having that wearying quality which always oozes from attenuated purity."

Alice may admire the tempestuousness of George Sand and the probity of George Eliot, but she knows her own field of vision has no need to be as fiery as the first's or as wide as the second's. Alice's room, like John Donne's body, is a little world made cunningly, and she recog-nizes that even on her "microscopic field, minute events are perpetually taking place illustrative of the broadest facts of human nature." Like all the tenants of this chap-ter, she knows that the jail and the bedsitter cannot cheat the world one can conjure inside oneself and project, like a shadow, onto the white screen of the diary's pages.

Having seen the winners and prizes of ordinary suc-cess, Alice swears she is happy never to have "had the ghost of a chance in the race." Still, her diary, once it gets going, is clearly intended as a work of art, a risk-free one that will not subject her to the critical strictures applied to novels. As Jean Strouse writes: "The anoma-lous literary realm occupied by the diary lay safely within the feminine province of the personal; Alice took no overt risk of appearing to compete either with men or with successful women like Eliot." Publication can be posthumous, but it is certainly something Alice wants. She dictates revisions to Katharine Loring (who became the diary's amanuensis on December 31, 1890) right up until the time of her death. This is not a diary written, like Virginia Woolf's, "faster than the fastest typewrit-ing." One doesn't hit upon phrases like "the fierce mus-tachios of the dashing defunct" — to describe the cavalry officer who was the first husband of an Englishwoman of her acquaintance — at the first click of the brain. The

casualness of most chroniclers is not for Alice James;
what she wants is more like the fastidiousness of those
pharaohs who laid out their tombs with everything they
would need after death. If Alice jokes about a story in
Truth, she makes sure to stick the relevant clipping into
the diary so that posterity will fully appreciate her wit.
If, in fact, she protests too much about anything, it is her
equanimity toward death.

Katharine Loring, who would live until 1943, performed the fealty of preserving and eventually publishing the book. Henry James remained unaware of its
existence for two years after Alice's death, but when he
finally read it he came to revere its unique spirit. He
also recognized that it was more than a diary, that, indeed,
it was his sister's alternative world, confirmation of "the
extraordinary intensity of her will and personality." His
assessment of Alice's diary was both loving and clear-
eyed, and it is good that he found it in him to make it,
for in reading his sister's book he had to deal with its
occasional function as apologia, the sort of thing Alice
indulged in on June 17, 1891: "H., by the way, has em-
bedded in his pages many pearls fallen from my lips,
which he steals in the most unblushing way, saying,
simply, that he knew they had been said by the family,
so it did not matter."

Alice James's invalidism was nearly lifelong. What surprises us most about her diary is that she began it so
late, so complete and instant was her success with it once
she took it up. For the Scottish poet William Soutar
(1898–1943), who came into the world not many years
after Alice left it, the habit of writing a diary came
earlier, when he was still a healthy naval officer and
aspiring writer during the First World War. In 1918
he became ill with something first thought to be rheuma-
tism but, as his vertebrae became crippled with rheuma-
toid arthritis over the next several years, was finally
realized to have come from streptococci that had been

in some long-ago meal. Semi-invalidism kept him from work as a journalist or teacher but freed him to continue, on his own, the university studies he had once pursued in a mediocre way. At the same time he made himself into a poet.

It was not until things became even darker, however, that he made himself into a great diarist. In 1929 he suffered from pneumonia; a year later he was operated on, without lasting success, to unlock the muscles in his right leg. During the next thirteen years he became almost entirely confined to his room. As his world shrank, his diaries bloomed from commonplace and appointment books into vivid accounts of his creative freedom amidst physical imprisonment. Alexander Scott, their editor, describes them: "From the date of the operation . . . the entries extend greatly, both in length and in range . . . The books in which his diary was kept belonged during this period to the *Collins Handy Diary* series, the page measuring 4″ × 3″, with twenty lines to the page — small dimensions, perhaps, to contain such richness; but Soutar's microscopic yet finely-legible script was able to make much of little." He kept separate notebooks for poetry and dreams. And when he knew he was dying, between July 5 and October 14, 1943, he wrote, separately, *The Diary of a Dying Man*.

Leaving the world was difficult for Soutar. He had been healthy long enough to develop a disposition that is said to have been athletic, spiritual, and sexy. Using his diaries to invent a surrogate world, or just magnify his shrunken one, could not have seemed inviting at first. But if he could no longer walk his way toward people he could still read himself in their direction, and be able to joke that his own confinement was only an exaggeration of ordinary Scottish insularity. Tuesday, February 17, 1931: "Finished reading *The Intimate Journals of Paul Gauguin*. Very fresh mind — he at once joins the company of those whom we wish we could have met. Such a distinctive French book makes a Scot feel that he is a rather dog-collared dog. We cannot recall Mary Stuart without seeing the shadow of Knox at her back."

Like Speer, he assigns himself immense journeys that can be taken without leaving his room. On July 29, 1931, he completes an "odyssey" he "began 8 years and 8 months ago" — through Chambers's *Twentieth Century Dictionary*. On October 1, 1930, he starts the *Encyclopaedia Britannica*, hoping to get through it in ten years. He learns to like his own company, and if his sentences are not really capable of the fast and malicious pirouettings of Alice James's, he remains free of any antiseptic saintliness. He can, it is true, incline toward blaming "some fatal flaw in [his] self's self for the humiliation of a fine body," but mostly he looks upon his failures to rise to the exigencies of his predicament with a self-dismissing humor: "How easy to become peevish in prison. Ella McQueen, should be in the garden, usually gives me a wave — today she didn't and I felt annoyed. Silly ass."

Seeking to capitalize on his difficulties without romanticizing them, Soutar wonders "if fit mortals realize that infirmity makes the most ordinary actions wonderful"; to a person like himself, "Everyday phrases can bring . . . a rounded image of loveliness mysteriously coloured by the consciousness that he himself can no longer enact them; phrases such as 'he lifted a stone,' 'he stood by the sea,' 'he walked into the wood.' " And he can keep himself aware of the bizarre privilege involved in being allowed to watch oneself die slowly: "Is it not a distinctive state of living to be under a doom and yet with time enough to contemplate the implications of such a state?"

Being conscious of his condition's compensations does not, however, blind him to the distortions it brings:

When one can no longer give free play to one's limbs the actions of others are followed with a more than normal intensity — so that one may enjoy movement vicariously, so to speak. Being a man, it is the move-

ments of women which have gained in attractiveness
— so that to watch either Bella or Gladys hanging out
clothes becomes an entertainment not without its so-
called sex-appeal. It is but natural that an unnatural
mode of life tends to proliferate through all one's
being — and there is the grave danger of becoming
sensually unbalanced. I know this danger only too well,
for I am blessed — or cursed — with a full-blooded
virility which is incompatible with my stagnant bodily
state.

Living amidst the stable parlor conditions of invalidism,
Soutar worries about misjudging the people one sees
only in one's room and not out behaving in the world:
"In short, the danger of the comfortable prisoner is to
expect the world to conform to the regulations of his
cell."

Like Allingham, he writes a poem to his diary, composing it on a day so dull that he must worry about what
"meaty morsel" he can find for his "hungry hound."
When he can find none he must reach inside himself
for the stuff of life that will give substance to his words:

> I bleed myself to be your drink:
> Is not the blood of poets — ink?

What he customarily comes up with are sketches of
character types — a loud salesman, the "easeful divine"
— reflections on art, philosophy, religion, and his condition. Despite being chair-ridden Soutar remains an
admirer of D. H. Lawrence's theories about the integra-
tion of body and mind.

He does not want posterity's pity. On Friday November 3, 1933, considering the anniversary of his condition's being recognized as irreversible, he writes, "*Three
years.*" But he is careful that any future reader not mistake what is meant as an aid to reflection for a cry of
anger. The next day he adds the following note: "Lest
any who may, at some future date, turn over these

pages, be tempted to sentimentalize upon the laconic note at the top of the previous page, let me confess that as I lifted my pen after writing it I found myself whistling: but without comfort, or calling, then might bitterness abide." He is aware of his own flaws and limits and, even with his invalidism, the comforts he enjoys relative to those forced to do heavy labor or bear the even harder burden of being unemployed. And he is suspicious of his own addiction to the diary, sometimes sensing that he fills it with a spurious awareness:

> A diary is like drink; we tend to indulge in it over often: it becomes a habit which would ever seduce us to say more than we ought to say and more than we have the experiential qualifications to state . . . A diary is an assassin's cloak which we wear when we stab a comrade in the back with a pen. And here is this diary proving its culpability even to its own harm — for how much on this page is true to the others?

Soutar writes that he continues to fill his diary's pages not only because there is little else he can do, but also because he is possessed of the ordinary human egocentricity that tells him that "not a single other creature in all the history of the world has been just as ourself — not another will be like us." His vitality is such that he cannot let any certainty remain unexamined. He forces himself to wonder whether he isn't becoming "a shrunken spirit which prefers a garden to a world"; perhaps he never loved the outside world with enough fervor to regret its movement away from him.

He kept the diary until the day before he died in October 1943. He harbored the expressed or secret wish of every diarist to live beyond his time. For Soutar, that wish was stated two months before pneumonia finally killed him, in sentences of calm frankness and great beauty:

Why do we wish to be remembered, even when none remain who looked upon our face? Surely, though it must retain an element of self-consideration, it is a last acknowledgment that we need to be loved; and, having gone from all touch, we trust that memory may, as it were, keep our unseen presence within the borders of day.

It is a wish whose granting he deserved more than most of us. Scott's collection of Soutar's journals, *The Diaries of a Dying Man*, is a neglected classic, and Soutar's name is kept too close to the dusky fringes of day's border to satisfy literary and personal justice. How disappointing, how in need of amendment it is, that one can open the endlessly obliging *Oxford Companion to English Literature* to check on his dates — and find he isn't there.

The *Oxford Companion* also omits Bruce Frederick Cummings (a.k.a. W. N. P. Barbellion), and that would keenly disappoint him were he still here to get the news. But he would be exceptionally pleased to know that he did manage to crash the *Dictionary of National Biography*. Here is his citation in the concise version:

CUMMINGS, BRUCE FREDERICK (1889–1919), diarist and biologist; generally known by pseudonym W. N. P. BARBELLION; in Natural History Museum, South Kensington, 1911–17; published extracts from his diaries, *The Journal of a Disappointed Man*, 1919.

What disappointed him? The frustration of his literary ambitions by editors; the thwarting of his amatory ones by beautiful women; the years of waiting on the certain death that finally overtook him at thirty; mostly the knowledge that life would never love him as much as he loved himself. Even the wife who took him on could not hope to compete with his regard for his own vitality, imprisoned as it was in a frame being eaten by disseminated sclerosis: "The truth is I think I am in love with her: but I am also mightily in love with myself. One or the other has to give." With his lot in life so little, with death giving such chase, and with such huge ambitions shouting to get out, there is nothing else for Barbellion to do but turn the diary he had begun when he was thirteen from a book into a universe over which he is ruler and in which there is only one subject: himself. The last years of his life are to be a race between ego and death: "Even as I sit and write, millions of bacteria are gnawing away my precious spinal cord, and if you put your ear to my back the sound of the gnawing I dare say could be heard."

Oh, occasional bits of Barbellion's small "real" world creep into the diary — such as the arrival of large mailings of houseflies to his museum in 1916 from people excited by a letter to the *Times* concerning their winter habits. But what are his daytime work as a naturalist and his nighttime recumbancy as an invalid compared to the huge energies forever being stanched inside him? "During a walk or in a book or in the middle of an embrace, suddenly I awake to a stark amazement at everything. The bare fact of existence paralyses me — holds my mind in mortmain. To be alive is so incredible that all I do is to lie still and merely breathe — like an infant on its back in a cot." Here he is with so much ego, self-consciousness, percipience, and pent-up animation that he feels like Gulliver among the Lilliputians when he walks down High Street on market day, and nobody pays him the slightest attention. Here he is with so much appetite for every sensation life can give that he intends to pull the communication cord of an express train as soon as he can spare the five-pound penalty ("My hands tingle as often as I look at it")—and life traps him in the corner of a museum in a body that's a farce. Yes, he can certainly read all the books the library porter can bring him, especially journals — the Goncourts, Maurice de Guérin —

but even so, it's only *he* who can really understand the life in them: "The Porter spends his days in the Library keeping strict vigil over this catacomb of books, passing along between the shelves and yet never paying heed to the almost audible susurrus of desire — the desire every book has to be taken down and read, to live, to come into being in somebody's mind. He even hands the volumes over the counter, seeks them out in their proper places or returns them there without once realising that a Book is a Person and not a Thing. It makes me shudder to think of Lamb's *Essays* being carted about as if they were fardels."

All the while his body is giving out, he knows the books are breathing. So there is only one thing to do: get himself into a book. Others did it — look at Marie Bashkirtseff, the Russian girl whose journal made such a success with English readers when it was translated in 1890: "I am simply astounded," Barbellion writes when he reads it. "It would be difficult in all the world's history to discover any two persons with temperaments so alike . . . We are identical! Oh, Marie Bashkirtseff! how we should have hated one another!"

There is no room in Barbellion's world for anyone but himself, and fortunately, the kind of book he chooses to make his respirator — the diary — needn't have anybody else hooked up to it. He hates the healthy and impercipient, the ones with bodies capable of appreciating the sensations they so complacently squander:

From the drawing-room window I see pass almost daily an old gentleman with white hair, a firm step, broad shoulders, healthy pink skin, a sunny smile — always singing to himself as he goes — a happy, rosy-cheeked old fellow, with a rosy-cheeked mind . . . I should like to throw mud at him. By Jove, how I hate him. He makes me wince with my own pain. It is heartless, indecently so, for an *old* man to be so blithe.

The man is like an incarnation of the "trickling, comfortable Essays" of Mr. A. C. Benson that Barbellion so loathes, blocked by his own pressing egotism from imagining that Benson might secretly be filling his own desk drawers with millions of words.

As early as July 14, 1912, Barbellion knows a drastic metamorphosis has to occur: "I cannot for the life of me rake up any excitement over my own immediate decease — an unobtrusive passing away of a rancorous, disappointed, morbid, and self-assertive entomologist in a West Kensington Boarding House — what a mean little tragedy! It is hard not to be somebody even in death." With his egotism "driven underground" the only thing left to do is become his diary, a transmutation eventually so successful that by 1915 he knows that if the journals perish it will mean the end of his "real self" — "and as I should take no pleasure in the perpetuation of my flabby, flaccid, anaemic, amiable puppet-self, I should probably commit suicide." Every quiver of his crippled body, every fantasy of his profligate mind, goes down onto the page.

Unable to stop watching himself, he compares his journal to a lover, to an alcoholic's drink, to an addiction so strong he hates it, sometimes wants to destroy it and cheat posterity of the chance to criticize his obsession:

Yet thro' all my nausea, here I remain happy to discuss myself and my little mishaps. I'm damned sick of myself and all my neurotic whimperings, and so I hereby and now intend to lead a new life and throw this Journal to the Devil. I want to mangle it, tear it to shreds. You smug, hypocritical readers! you'll get no more of me. All you say I know is true before you say it and I know *now* all the criticism you are going to launch. So please spare yourself the trouble. You cannot enlighten me upon myself. I *know*. I disgust myself — and you, and as for you, you can go to the Devil with this Journal.

Of course, like Stendhal, he is addressing posterity on the same page he swears it will never see. He can't stop. He is too far gone; the identification of self and page is too complete. He will never throw away the diary. He hasn't walked through the looking-glass; he's become it. He knows that each action and every thought exists only for how it will appear on the paper. He admits to lying out of vanity; and he admits to making such a confession out of vanity, too: "So that one way or another I am determined to make kudos out of myself. Even this last reflection is written down with an excessive appreciation of its wit and the intention that it shall raise a smile."

In order to be so obsessed with his survival, and the attention the future will pay him, Barbellion must first be obsessed with his death. As far back as 1907 he is imagining "cinema pictures" of it. Will he make it through the night? Should he try suicide? No, even that would be insufficient orchestration of his own demise. What he decides on, after he at last finds a publisher for the diary, is this: he will put "Barbellion died on December 31" in brackets at the bottom of the last page. So what if it's not true? If he can invent himself on paper, surely he can kill himself there, too. Let the public guess at it.

But first the journals have to be kept safe for that publication. He has a special brass-handled cabinet made for them, which he calls his "coffin." When a friend comes to dinner he will "with some show of deliberation select a volume to read to him, drawing it from its division with lavish punctiliousness, and inquiring with an oily voice, 'A little of 1912?' as if we were trying wines." He is terrified by the possibility that they will perish in a World War I zeppelin bombing, or because of a fire in his rooms, or because someone will carelessly toss them into the fireplace. Or, with so much life inside them, they might just spontaneously combust: "All day they make a perfect uproar in their solitary confinement — although no one hears it. And at night they become phosphorescent, though nobody sees it."

After Barbellion finds a publisher for *The Journal of a Disappointed Man* he cannot resist keeping one *Last Diary*. It runs from March 21, 1918, to June 3, 1919, covering the period during which he awaits the book's printing and his imminent death. He is living in the care of a nurse for part of this period, spending months on end in bed without being able to go outside. The race is going to end in a photo finish: the bacilli eating his spine seem to be moving just as fast as the presses at Chatto and Windus. But he has faith the book will win. It will be his revenge ("The world has always gagged and suppressed me — now I turn and hit it in the belly"), and its publication a last burst of "oxygen." His book will soon be breathing along with those he overheard on the library shelves more than ten years before.

He hopes for a big sale (just like the one Marie Bashkirtseff got), and he reflects on what he spent all those years doing. He is for the most part pleased at having been "the scientific investigator of myself," but as he waits he also goes crazy with boredom, counting the patterns on the wallpaper, the panes of glass in the window, the spools in the back of his chair.

Finally, the race ends on March 27, 1919, and the victory is his:

> I've won! This morning at 9 a.m. the book arrived. C. and W. [Chatto and Windus] thoughtfully left the pages to be cut, so I've been enjoying the exquisite pleasure of cutting the pages of my own book. And nothing's happened. No earthquake, no thunder and lightning, no omen in a black sky. In fact, the sun is shining. Publication next week.

The book sells very well. But in the weeks after publication the literal-minded reviews make him uneasy, make him doubt the years of transmutation. On May 18 he writes: "In the Journal I can see now that I made myself out worse than I am, or was. I even took a morbid pleasure in intimating my depravity — self-mortification. If I had spoken out more plainly I should have escaped all this censure. The reviewers are only too ready to take me at my word, which is but natural. I don't think on the whole my portrait of myself does myself justice." How could it have? And how could the Fleet Street Lilliputians be expected to understand the overflowing, sclerotic Gulliver? Barbellion is not so much conscious of failure here as he is disappointed that there is nothing left for him to do. There is no more inventing of himself possible — no time for any more retouchings and additions to his "self-erected monument."

He died on October 22.

Barbellion never quite reached adulthood, a state attained when one comes to accept, or at least intuit, that God, biology, and our so-called fellow men have no intention of accommodating our dreams. He chose to answer back life's mean jokes, and when it countered by letting loose the bacilli in his spine he dug in his heels and began his imaginative tantrum. Barbellion was no Progoffian attempting with painful sincerity to get in touch with the streams of his emotion. He was determined to flood the land with his lunatic vitality. He didn't want the world his way; he wanted the world to have him his. So he wrote his ludicrously moving journals, never unaware of their crazy bravura. Few people read them anymore, but that cannot undo his improbable accomplishment. In a genre to which it is impossible to ascribe formulas and standards, he forces one to render a judgment — namely, that his is the greatest diary a man has written.

Epilogue

June 13, 1983, 3:15 P.M.
The Fellows Garden, Magdalene College, Cambridge

I'll be going home a week from today, carrying the whole manuscript with me. I wanted to come here this afternoon — just down the hill from where I've lived these last few months — to sit on the bench and think about it. The Master's Lodge here is now a sort of modernist chalet, not what Benson lived in, but pretty much all else is the same, I think: the gardens, the quadrangles, and Pepys's diary upstairs. "MENS CUIUSQUE IS EST QUISQUE" — that's his motto on the bookplates. It should have been "DID PONER MI MANO SUB HER JUPE"!

I'm thinking about him now, and I'm thinking about Benson thinking about him. I'm thinking about so many of the ones who came between, too: Boswell up in Scotland, provoking Johnson; Laurel Lee being casually saintly in her hospital bed; Weston setting up his peppers in the sunlight; Ellen Weeton tramping about and hoping for work; Joshua Naples going out to the graveyard with his shovels. It seemed right to come here today and wonder about all of them. The book will soon be edited and printed and set out in the stores. Hard to believe!

I suppose this one on my lap won't be finished until I am.

This is quite a day. This morning's *Herald Tribune* reports that Pioneer 10, a little gold-and-silver spaceship launched eleven years ago, will pass beyond the solar system this afternoon, the only manmade object to do so. In fact, it's already gone (it was supposed to get past the last planetary orbit at 1:00 P.M. GMT). It's expected to keep traveling for a minimum of two billion years.

The first star it passes will be Barnard's Star — but that won't be for 10,507 years. If people live on Barnard's Star, and they decide to snatch Pioneer 10 out of the sky, they're going to find on board the sketch of an atom of hydrogen; a diagram showing the earth's position in the solar system — and a drawing of a man and a woman.

Some scientists thought to put those things on it before the launch in 1972.

O gold-and-silver ship, Godspeed into the darkness — for what are you but a last, fragile diary? Are you not the planet's very own, forever whispering into the cosmos what all those other diaries shall forever whisper from their cupboards?

I was, I was — I am.

A Reader's Bibliography

Allingham, William. *The Diary of William Allingham*. Introduction by Geoffrey Grigson. Fontwell, Sussex: Centaur Press Ltd., 1967.

Amato, Antony, and Katherine Edwards [pseudonyms]. *Affair*. New York: Putnam, 1978.

Auden, W. H. *A Certain World*. New York: Viking, 1970.

———. and Christopher Isherwood. *Journey to a War*. New York: Random House, 1939.

Barbellion, W. N. P. [pseudonym]. *The Journal of a Disappointed Man*. Introduction by H. G. Wells. London: Chatto and Windus, 1919.

———. *A Last Diary*. Preface by Arthur J. Cummings. New York: George H. Doran, 1920.

Beauvoir, Simone de. *America Day by Day*. Translated by Patrick Dudley. London: Duckworth, 1952.

Benson, A. C. *The Diary of Arthur C. Benson*. Edited by Percy Lubbock. 4th ed. London: Hutchinson, 1926.

———. *Edwardian Excursions: From the Diaries of A. C. Benson 1898–1904*. Edited by David Newsome. London: John Murray, 1981.

Bentley, Toni. *Winter Season: A Dancer's Journal*. New York: Random House, 1982.

Bevington, Helen. *Along Came the Witch: A Journal in the 1960's*. New York: Harcourt Brace Jovanovich, 1976.

Bliss, Joseph. "Sensory Experiences of Gilles de la Tourette Syndrome," *Archives of General Psychiatry* 37, no. 12 (December 1980): 1343–47.

Boswell, James. *Journal of a Tour to the Hebrides*. Edited by Frederick A. Pottle and Charles H. Bennett. New York: McGraw-Hill, 1961.

Bremer, Arthur. *An Assassin's Diary*. Introduction by Harding Lemay. New York: Harper's Magazine Press, 1973.

Byron, George Gordon Noel. *Byron's Letters and Journals*. 12 vols. Edited by Leslie A. Marchand. Cambridge, Mass.: Belknap Press of Harvard University Press, 1973–1982.

Camus, Albert. *Notebooks 1935–1942*. Translated by Philip Thody. New York: Harcourt Brace Jovanovich, 1978.

Capote, Truman. *In Cold Blood.* New York: Random House, 1965.

Carrington, Dora. *Letters and Extracts from Her Diaries.* Introduction by David Garnett. New York: Holt, Rinehart and Winston, 1970.

Carroll, Jim. *The Basketball Diaries.* Timbouctou, Calif.: Timbouctou Books, 1978. (Paperback available from Bantam Books.)

Carroll, Lewis. *The Russian Journal and Other Selections from the Works of Lewis Carroll.* Edited and with an introduction by John Francis McDermott. New York: Dover, 1977.

Crossman, Richard. *The Diaries of a Cabinet Minister.* New York: Holt, Rinehart and Winston, 1975.

Darwin, Charles. *The Voyage of the Beagle.* Introduction by H. Graham Cannon. London: J. M. Dent, 1959.

Degas, Edgar. *The Notebooks of Edgar Degas.* 2 vols. Edited by Theodore Reff. Oxford: Clarendon Press, 1976. (Translations by the author.)

Dillard, Annie. *Holy the Firm.* New York: Harper and Row, 1977.

Dodington, George Bubb. *The Political Journal of George Bubb Dodington.* Edited by John Carswell and Lewis Arnold Dralle. Oxford: Clarendon Press, 1965.

Dostoevski, Fyodor. *The Notebooks for "Crime and Punishment."* Edited and translated by Edward Wasiolek. Chicago and London: University of Chicago Press, 1967.

Dreyfus, Alfred. *Five Years of My Life: The Diary of Captain Alfred Dreyfus.* Introduction by Nicholas Halasz. New York and London: Peebles Press, 1977.

Dwight, S. E. *The Life of President Edwards.* New York: G. & C. & H. Carvill, 1830. (For the diary of Jonathan Edwards.)

Fitzgerald, F. Scott. *The Notebooks of F. Scott Fitzgerald.* Edited by Matthew J. Bruccoli. New York and London: Harcourt Brace Jovanovich/Bruccoli Clark, 1978.

Fothergill, Robert. *Private Chronicles: A Study of English Diaries.* London: Oxford University Press, 1974.

Frank, Anne. *The Diary of a Young Girl.* New York: Doubleday, 1967.

Fremantle, Anne, ed. *The Wynne Diaries.* 3 vols. London: Oxford University Press, Humphrey Milfold, 1935–1940.

Fussell, Paul. *Abroad: British Literary Traveling Between the Wars.* New York: Oxford University Press, 1980.

Gascoyne, David. *Paris Journal 1937–1939.* Preface by Lawrence Durrell. London: The Enitharmon Press, 1978.

Gauguin, Paul. *Noa Noa: Voyage to Tahiti.* New York: Reynal, 1962.

Ginsberg, Allen. *Journals: Early Fifties, Early Sixties.* Edited by Gordon Ball. New York: Grove Press, 1977.

Goebbels, Joseph. *Final Entries 1945: The Diaries of Joseph Goebbels.* Edited by Hugh Trevor-Roper. New York: Putnam, 1978.

Gold, Gerald, ed. *The Watergate Hearings: Break-In and Cover-Up. Proceedings of the Senate Select Committee on Presidential Campaign Activities as edited by the staff of The New York Times.* New York: Viking, 1973.

Goncourt, Edmond, and Jules de Goncourt. *Pages from the Goncourt Journal.* Edited, translated and introduction by Robert Baldick. Oxford: Oxford University Press, 1978.

Gosse, Edmund. *Father and Son: A Study of Two Temperaments.* New York: Norton, 1963.

Graham, Martha. *The Notebooks of Martha Graham.* Introduction by Nancy Wilson Ross. New York: Harcourt Brace Jovanovich, 1973.

Greene, Douglas C., ed. *Diaries of the Popish Plot.* Delmar, N.Y.: Scholars' Facsimiles and Reprints, 1977.

Greene, Graham. *The End of the Affair.* New York: Viking, 1951.
———. *In Search of a Character: Two African Journals.* New York: Viking, 1962.

Gregory, Augusta. *Journals.* Edited by Daniel J. Murphy. New York: Oxford University Press, 1978.

Hakluyt, Richard. *Hakluyt's Voyages.* Edited by Richard David. Boston: Houghton Mifflin, 1981.

Hammarskjöld, Dag. *Markings.* Translated by Leif Sjöberg and W. H. Auden. Foreword by W. H. Auden. New York: Knopf, 1964.

Haydon, Benjamin. *The Diary of Benjamin Robert Haydon.* 5 vols. Edited by Willard Bissell Pope. Cambridge, Mass.: Harvard University Press, 1960–1963.

Hinz, Evelyn J., ed. *A Woman Speaks: The Lectures, Seminars and Interviews of Anaïs Nin.* London: W. H. Allen, 1978.

Holliday, Laurel. *Heart Songs: The Intimate Diaries of Young Girls.* New York: Methuen, 1980.

Hopkins, Gerard Manley. *The Note-Books and Papers of Gerard Manley Hopkins.* Edited by Humphrey House. London and New York: Oxford University Press, 1937.

Horney, Karen. *The Adolescent Diaries of Karen Horney.* New York: Basic Books, 1980.

Howe, George Colt. "Historian of the Present," *Harvard Magazine* 83, no. 5 (May–June 1981): 47–52. (Contains extract from Arthur Crew Inman's diary and a profile of Daniel Aaron.)

Huyghe, Patrick. "Diary Writing Turns a New Leaf," *The New York Times Magazine*, November 8, 1981, 98–108.

Isherwood, Christopher. *The Berlin Stories*. New York: New Directions, 1963.

———. *Christopher and His Kind, 1929–1939*. New York: Farrar, Straus & Giroux, 1976.

James, Alice. *The Diary of Alice James*. Edited by Leon Edel. New York: Dodd, Mead, 1964.

Jerome, Jerome K. *Diary of a Pilgrimage*. Gloucester, England: Alan Sutton Publishing Ltd., 1982.

Joyce, James. *A Portrait of the Artist as a Young Man*. New York: Viking, 1964.

Kafka, Franz. *The Diaries of Franz Kafka, 1914–1923*. Translated by Martin Greenberg. Edited by Max Brod. New York: Schocken, 1965.

Kaplan, Chaim A. *The Warsaw Diary of Chaim A. Kaplan*. Edited and translated by Abraham I. Katsh. New York: Collier, 1973.

Kemble, Fanny. *The Terrific Kemble: A Victorian Self-Portrait from the Writings of Fanny Kemble*. Edited and with an introduction by Eleanor Ransome. London: Hamish Hamilton, 1978.

Kierkegaard, Søren. *The Last Years: Selections from the Journals, 1853–1855*. Edited and translated by Ronald Gregor Smith. New York: Harper and Row, 1965.

Kunen, James Simon. *The Strawberry Statement: Notes of a College Revolutionary*. New York: Random House, 1969.

Lahr, John. *Prick Up Your Ears: The Biography of Joe Orton*. New York: Knopf, 1978.

Larrea, Jean-Jacques. *The Diary of a Paper Boy*. New York: Putnam, 1972.

Le Corbusier [Charles Edouard Jeanneret-Gris]. *Sketchbooks*. Vol. 1, *1914–1948*. Introduction by Maurice Besset. New York: The Architectural History Foundation, and Cambridge, Mass.: The M.I.T. Press, 1981.

Lee, Laurel. *Walking Through the Fire: A Hospital Journal*. New York: E. P. Dutton, 1977.

Leonardo da Vinci. *The Notebooks of Leonardo da Vinci*. 2 vols. Compiled and edited by Jean-Paul Richter. New York: Dover, 1970.

Lewis, C. S. *A Grief Observed*. New York: The Seabury Press, 1963.

Lewis, Meriwether, and William Clark. *The Journals of Lewis and Clark*. Edited by Bernard DeVoto. Boston: Houghton Mifflin, 1953.

Liddon, Henry Parry. *The Russian Journal—II*. Edited and with an introduction and notes by Morton N. Cohen. Carroll Studies No. 3. New York: The Lewis Carroll Society of North America, 1979.

Lindbergh, Anne Morrow. *Hour of God, Hour of Lead: Diaries and Letters of Anne Morrow Lindbergh, 1929–1932*. New York: Harcourt Brace Jovanovich, 1973.

Lindbergh, Charles. *The Wartime Journals of Charles Lindbergh*. New York: Harcourt Brace Jovanovich, 1970.

Louis Philippe, King of the French. *Diary of My Travels in America*. Translated by Stephen Becker. New York: Delacorte Press, 1977.

MacNeice, Louis. *Autumn Journal*. New York: Random House, 1940.

McNeill, Elizabeth [pseudonym]. *Nine and a Half Weeks: A Memoir of a Love Affair*. New York: E. P. Dutton, 1978.

Manningham, John. *The Diary of John Manningham of The Middle Temple, 1602–1603*. Edited by Robert Parker Sorlien. Hanover, N.H.: University Press of New England, 1976.

Mansfield, Katherine. *Journal of Katherine Mansfield*. Edited by J. Middleton Murry. New York: Howard Fertig, 1974.

Marcus, Stephen. *The Other Victorians: A Study of Sexuality and Pornography in Mid-Nineteenth Century England*. New York: Basic Books, 1974.

Mather, Richard. *Journal of Richard Mather*. Boston: David Clapp, 1850.

Matthews, William. *American Diaries*. Boston: J. S. Canner, 1959.
———. *British Diaries: An Annotated Bibliography of British Diaries Written Between 1442 and 1942*. Berkeley and Los Angeles: University of California Press, 1950.

Maurois, André. *From My Journal*. Translated by Joan Charles. New York & London: Harper & Bros., 1948.

Merton, Thomas. *The Secular Journal of Thomas Merton*. New York: Farrar, Straus and Cudahy, 1959.

Mićunović, Veljko. *Moscow Diary*. Translated by David Floyd. Garden City, N.Y.: Doubleday, 1980.

Milburn, Clara. *Mrs. Milburn's Diaries*. Edited by Peter Donnelly. London: George Harrap, 1979.

Moffatt, Mary Jane, and Charlotte Painter, eds. *Revelations: Diaries of Women*. New York: Random House, 1974.

My Secret Life. Introduction by G. Legman. New York: Grove Press, 1966.

Naples, Joshua. *The Diary of a Resurrectionist*. Edited by James Blake Bailey. London: Swan Sonnenschein, 1896.

Narayan, Jayaprakash. *Prison Diary*. Edited by A. B. Shah. Seattle: University of Washington Press, 1978.

Newberry, Julia. *Julia Newberry's Diary*. Introduction by Margaret Ayer Barnes and Janet Ayer Fairbank. New York: Norton, 1933.

Newsome, David. *On the Edge of Paradise: A. C. Benson the Diarist*. Chicago and London: University of Chicago Press, 1980.

Nicolson, Harold. *Diaries and Letters, 1930–1939. Edited by Nigel Nicolson*. New York: Atheneum, 1966.

Nijinsky, Vaslav. *The Diary of Vaslav Nijinsky*. Edited by Romola Nijinsky. Berkeley and Los Angeles: University of California Press, 1971.

Nin, Anaïs. *The Diary of Anaïs Nin*. Volume 4, *1944–1947*. Edited by Gunther Stuhlmann. New York: Harcourt Brace Jovanovich, 1971.

O'Brien, Kate. *English Diaries and Journals*. London: Collins, 1943.

Olmstead, Alan H. *Threshold: The First Days of Retirement*. New York: Harper and Row, 1975.

Orwell, George. *1984*. New York: Harcourt Brace Jovanovich, 1977.

Oswald, Lee Harvey. "Historic Diary," in *Report of the Warren Commission on the Assassination of President Kennedy*. New York: McGraw-Hill, 1964.

Pepys, Samuel. *The Diary of Samuel Pepys*. Edited by Robert Latham and William Matthews. Berkeley: University of California Press, 1970–1983.

Plath, Sylvia. *The Journals of Sylvia Plath*. Edited by Frances McCullough. New York: The Dial Press, 1982.

Ponsonby, Arthur. *English Diaries: A Review of English Diaries from the Sixteenth to the Twentieth Century with an Introduction on Diary Writing*. New York: George H. Doran, 1922.

———. *More English Diaries: Further Reviews of Diaries from the Sixteenth to the Nineteenth Century with an Introduction on Diary Reading*. New York: George H. Doran, 1927.

———. *Scottish and Irish Diaries from the Sixteenth to the Nineteenth Century*. New York: George H. Doran, 1927.

Progoff, Ira. *At a Journal Workshop*. New York: Dialogue House Library, 1975.

Reck-Malleczewen, Friedrich Percyval. *Diary of a Man in Despair*. Translated by Paul Rubens. New York: Collier, 1972.

Reid, B. L. *The Lives of Roger Casement*. New Haven and London: Yale University Press, 1976.

Rhys, Jean. *Smile Please: An Unfinished Autobiography.* Foreword by Diana Athill. New York: Harper and Row, 1979.

Roncalli, Angelo [Pope John XXIII]. *Journal of a Soul.* Translated by Dorothy White. New York: McGraw-Hill, 1965.

Rorem, Ned. *An Absolute Gift: A New Diary.* New York: Simon and Schuster, 1978.

Rowse, A. L. *Sex and Society in Shakespeare's Age: Simon Forman the Astrologer.* New York: Scribner's, 1974.

Sackville-West, Vita. *Knole and the Sackvilles.* London: Heinemann, 1931.

Sand, George. *The Intimate Journal of George Sand.* Edited and translated by Marie Jenney Howe. Chicago: Academy Press, 1977.

Saroyan, Aram. *Last Rites: The Death of William Saroyan.* New York: Morrow, 1982.

Sarton, May. *Journal of a Solitude.* New York: Norton, 1977.

Sassoon, Siegfried. *Diaries 1915–1918.* Edited by Rupert Hart-Davis. London: Faber and Faber, 1983.

Schlissel, Lillian, ed. *Women's Diaries of the Westward Journey.* New York: Schocken, 1982.

Scott-Maxwell, Florida. *The Measure of My Days.* New York: Knopf, 1968.

Sewall, Samuel. *The Diary of Samuel Sewall.* 2 vols. Edited by M. Halsey Thomas. New York: Farrar, Straus & Giroux, 1973.

Shelley, Mary. *Mary Shelley's Journal.* Edited by Frederick L. Jones. Norman: University of Oklahoma Press, 1947.

Shelley, Percy Bysshe. *Note Books from the Originals in the Library of W. K. Bixby.* 3 vols. Edited by H. Buxton Forman. New York: Phaeton Press, 1968.

Shields, David. *A History of Personal Diary Writing in New England, 1620–1745.* Ann Arbor, Michigan: University Microfilms, 1982.

Smith, Lucy Toulmin, ed. *A Commonplace Book of the Fifteenth Century.* Norwich, England: Agas H. Goose, 1886.

Soutar, William. *The Diaries of a Dying Man.* Edited by Alexander Scott. London: W. & R. Chambers, 1954.

Sparks, Beatrice, ed. *Go Ask Alice.* Englewood Cliffs, N.J.: Prentice-Hall, 1971.

———. *Jay's Journal.* New York: Times Books, 1979.

Speer, Albert. *Spandau: The Secret Diaries.* New York: Macmillan, 1976.

Stendhal [Marie Henri Beyle]. *The Private Diaries of Stendhal.* Edited and translated by Robert Sage. Garden City, N.Y.: Doubleday, 1954.

Sterne, Laurence. *A Sentimental Journey through France and*

Italy by Mr. Yorick to which are added The Journal to Eliza and A Political Romance. Edited by Ian Jack. London: Oxford University Press, 1968.

Strong, George Templeton. *The Diary of George Templeton Strong.* 4 vols. Edited by Allan Nevins and Milton Halsey Thomas. New York: Macmillan, 1952.

Strouse, Jean. *Alice James: A Biography.* Boston: Houghton Mifflin, 1980.

Tayler, William. *Diary of William Tayler, Footman: 1837.* Edited by Dorothy Wise. London: St. Marylebone Society Publications Group, 1962.

Thoreau, Henry David. *The Heart of Thoreau's Journals.* Edited by Odell Shepard. New York: Dover, 1961.

Trilling, Diana. *Mrs. Harris: The Death of the Scarsdale Diet Doctor.* New York: Harcourt Brace Jovanovich, 1981.

Trotsky, Leon. *Trotsky's Diary in Exile 1935.* Translated by Elena Zarudnava. Cambridge, Mass.: Harvard University Press, 1958.

Victoria, Queen of Great Britain. *Victoria in the Highlands: The Personal Journal of Her Majesty Queen Victoria.* London: Frederick Muller, 1968.

Voltaire, François Marie Arouet de. *The Complete Works of Voltaire.* Edited by Theodore Besterman and others. Geneva: Institut et Musée Voltaire; Toronto: University of Toronto Press, 1968–   . (Translations by the author.)

———. *Voltaire's Household Accounts 1760–1778.* Edited in facsimile by Theodore Besterman. New York: Pierpont Morgan Library, 1968.

Warren, Robert Penn. *All the King's Men.* New York: Harcourt Brace, 1946.

Waugh, Evelyn. *The Diaries of Evelyn Waugh.* Edited by Michael Davie. Boston: Little, Brown, 1976.

Weeton, Ellen. *Journal of a Governess.* 2 vols. Edited by Edward Hall. London: Oxford University Press, 1936–1939.

Weston, Edward. *The Daybooks of Edward Weston.* 2 vols. Edited by Nancy Newhall. Millerton, N.Y.: Aperture, 1973.

Willy, Margaret. *Three Women Diarists.* London: Longmans, Green, 1964.

Wilson, Edmund. *The Thirties.* Edited by Leon Edel. New York: Farrar, Straus & Giroux, 1980.

Wilson, Eve [pseudonym]. *The Note Books of a Woman Alone.* Edited by M. J. Ostle. London: J. M. Dent, 1935.

Woodforde, James. *The Diary of a Country Parson 1758–1802.* Edited by John Beresford. Oxford: Oxford University Press, 1979.

Woolf, Virginia. *The Diary of Virginia Woolf.* 5 vols. Edited by Anne Olivier Bell. New York: Harcourt Brace Jovanovich, 1977– .

———. "The Legacy," in *A Haunted House and Other Short Stories.* New York: Harcourt Brace Jovanovich, 1944.

Wordsworth, Dorothy. *Journals of Dorothy Wordsworth.* Edited by E. de Selincourt. New York: Macmillan, 1941.

Wordsworth, Dorothy, and William Wordsworth. *Home at Grasmere: Extracts from the Journal of Dorothy Wordsworth and from the Poems of William Wordsworth.* Edited by Colette Clark. New York: Penguin, 1978.

Wynne, Elizabeth. [*See* Fremantle, Anne.]

Acknowledgments

Grateful acknowledgment is made for permission to quote from materials listed below:

My Sister and Myself, by J. R. Ackerley. Reprinted by permission of David Higham Associates Ltd.

The Diary of William Allingham. Reprinted by permission of Centaur Press Ltd., Fontwell, Sussex, England.

Go Ask Alice (anonymous). Copyright © 1971 by Prentice-Hall, Inc. Reprinted by permission of Prentice-Hall, Inc., Englewood Cliffs, N.J.

A Certain World: A Commonplace Book, by W. H. Auden. Copyright © 1970 by W. H. Auden. A William Cole Book. Reprinted by permission of Viking Penguin, Inc.

"The Horatians," from *Collected Poets*, by W. H. Auden. Copyright © 1976 by Edward Mendelson, William Meredith, and Monroe K. Spears, executors of the Estate of W. H. Auden. Reprinted by permission of Random House, Inc.

A Diary Without Dates, by Enid Bagnold. Reprinted by permission of William Heinemann Ltd.

The Journal of a Disappointed Man and *A Last Diary*, by W. N. P. Barbellion. Chatto and Windus Ltd.

America Day by Day, by Simone de Beauvoir, trans. Patrick Dudley. Reprinted by permission of Duckworth and Co. Ltd.

Extracts from the diaries of Arthur Christopher Benson. Reprinted by permission of The Master and Fellows of Magdalene College, Cambridge University.

Winter Season: A Dancer's Journal, by Toni Bentley. Copyright © 1982 by Toni Bentley. Reprinted by permission of Random House, Inc.

Along Came the Witch, by Helen Bevington. Copyright © 1976 by Helen Bevington. Reprinted by permission of Harcourt Brace Jovanovich, Inc.

An Assassin's Diary, by Arthur H. Bremer. Copyright © 1972 by *Harper's Magazine*. All rights reserved. Reprinted from the January 1973 issue by special permission.

Volumes 4 and 8 of *Byron's Letters and Journals*, ed. Leslie A. Marchand. Copyright © 1974, 1978 by John Murray. Reprinted by permission of Harvard University Press.

Notebooks 1935–1942, by Albert Camus, trans. Philip Thody. Copyright © 1963 by Hamish Hamilton Ltd. and Alfred A. Knopf, Inc. Reprinted by permission of Alfred A. Knopf, Inc.

In Cold Blood, by Truman Capote. Copyright © 1965 by Truman Capote. Reprinted by permission of Random House, Inc.

The Basketball Diaries, by Jim Carroll. Copyright © 1978 by Jim Carroll. Reprinted by permission of Jim Carroll. Published by Timbouctou Books and Bantam Books.

The Russian Journal—II: A Record Kept by Henry Parry Liddon of a Tour Taken with C. L. Dodgson in the Summer of 1867. Reprinted by permission of the Lewis Carroll Society of North America.

The Lives of Roger Casement, by B. L. Reid. Reprinted by permission of Yale University Press.

Diaries of the Popish Plot, ed. Douglas C. Greene. Reprinted by permission of Scholars' Facsimiles and Reprints, Inc.

The Notebooks of Edgar Degas, ed. Theodore Reff. Reprinted by permission of Oxford University Press.

The Concise Dictionary of National Biography, Part II, 1901–1950. Reprinted by permission of Oxford University Press.

Holy the Firm, by Annie Dillard. Copyright © 1977 by Annie Dillard. Reprinted by permission of Harper & Row Publishers, Inc.

The Political Journal of George Bubb Dodington, ed. John Carswell and Lewis Arnold Dralle. Reprinted by permission of Oxford University Press.

The Notebooks for "Crime and Punishment," trans. and ed. Edward Wasiolek. Copyright © 1967 by The University of Chicago. Reprinted by permission of The University of Chicago Press.

Five Years of My Life: The Diary of Captain Alfred Dreyfus, ed. Nicholas Halasz. Reprinted courtesy of Peebles Press International, Inc.

Collected Poems, by Alan Dugan. Reprinted by permission of Alan Dugan.

The Great Gatsby, by F. Scott Fitzgerald. Copyright © 1925, 1953 by Charles Scribner's Sons. Reprinted with the permission of Charles Scribner's Sons.

Excerpt from Simon Forman as quoted in *Sex and Society in Shakespeare's Age: Simon Forman the Astrologer* is reprinted with the permission of Charles Scribner's Sons. Copyright © 1974 by A. L. Rowse.

The Diary of a Young Girl, by Anne Frank. Copyright © 1952 by Otto H. Frank. Reprinted by permission of Doubleday & Co., Inc.

Paris Journal 1937–1939, by David Gascoyne. Reprinted by permission of The Enitharmon Press.

Journals: Early Fifties, Early Sixties, by Allen Ginsberg. Reprinted by permission of Grove Press, Inc. Copyright © 1977 by Allen Ginsberg.

Reality Sandwiches, by Allen Ginsberg. Copyright © 1963 by Allen Ginsberg. Reprinted by permission of City Lights Books.

Final Entries 1945: The Diaries of Joseph Goebbels. Reprinted courtesy of G. P. Putnam's Sons.

Pages from the Goncourt Journal, ed. Robert Baldick. Reprinted by permission of Oxford University Press.

Father and Son, by Edmund Gosse. New York: Charles Scribner's Sons, 1907. Reprinted with the permission of Charles Scribner's Sons.

The Notebooks of Martha Graham. Copyright © 1973 by Martha Graham. Reprinted by permission of Harcourt Brace Jovanovich, Inc.

Gregory, Augusta. *Journals*, ed. Daniel J. Murphy. Published in the United States by Oxford University Press. Reprinted by courtesy of Colin Smythe Ltd., publishers of the Coole Edition of Lady Gregory's works.

Markings, by Dag Hammarskjöld. Trans. by Leif Sjöberg and W. H. Auden. With a foreword by W. H. Auden. Copyright © 1964 by Alfred A. Knopf, Inc., and Faber and Faber Ltd. Foreword copyright © 1964 by W. H. Auden. Reprinted by permission of Random House, Inc.

Hakluyt's Voyages, ed. Richard David. Reprinted courtesy of Richard David and Houghton Mifflin Co.

The Diary of Benjamin Robert Haydon, ed. Willard Bissell Pope. Copyright © 1963 by the President and Fellows of Harvard College. Reprinted by permission of Harvard University Press.

The Adolescent Diaries of Karen Horney. Copyright © 1980 by Basic Books, Inc. Reprinted courtesy of Basic Books, Inc.

The Note-Books and Papers of Gerard Manley Hopkins, ed. Humphrey House. Reprinted by permission of Oxford University Press.

Arthur Crew Inman's diary. Reprinted with permission of Daniel Aaron.

Christopher and His Kind, by Christopher Isherwood. Copyright © 1976 by Christopher Isherwood. Reprinted courtesy of Farrar, Straus & Giroux, Inc.

The Diary of Alice James. Reprinted by permission of Dodd, Mead & Co., Inc.

Alice James, by Jean Strouse. Copyright © 1980 by Jean Strouse. Reprinted by permission of Houghton Mifflin Company.

Diary of a Pilgrimage, by Jerome K. Jerome. Reprinted by permission of Alan Sutton Publishing Ltd.

The Diaries of Franz Kafka, 1914–1923, by Franz Kafka. Copyright © 1949 by Schocken Books, Inc.

The Warsaw Diary of Chaim A. Kaplan, trans. and ed. by Abraham I. Katsh. Copyright © Abraham I. Katsh 1965, 1973. Reprinted by permission of Macmillan Publishing Co., Inc.

The Terrific Kemble, ed. and intro. by Eleanor Ransome. Reprinted by permission of Hamish Hamilton Ltd.

The Last Years: Journals 1853–1855, by Søren Kierkegaard, ed. and trans. Ronald Gregor Smith. Copyright © 1965 by Ronald Gregor Smith. Reprinted by permission of Harper & Row Publishers, Inc.

The Strawberry Statement, by James Simon Kunen. Copyright © 1968, 1969 by James S. Kunen. Reprinted by permission of the Sterling Lord Agency, Inc.

A Young Girl's Diary ("Gretchen Lainer"), ed. E. & C. Paul. Reprinted by permission of George Allen & Unwin (Publishers) Ltd.

The Diary of a Paper Boy, by Jean-Jacques Larrea. Copyright © 1972 by Jean-Jacques Larrea. Published by G. P. Putnam's Sons. Reprinted by permission of The Putnam Publishing Group.

Le Corbusier/Sketchbooks, Volume 1, 1914–1948, intro. by Maurice Besset; notes by Françoise de Franclieu. Copyright © 1981 by the Fondation Le Corbusier and the Architectural History Foundation. Reprinted by permission of The M.I.T. Press.

Walking through the Fire, by Laurel Lee. Copyright © 1977 by Laurel Lee. Reprinted by permission of E. P. Dutton, Inc.

A Grief Observed, by C. S. Lewis. Copyright © 1961 by N. W. Clerk. Used by permission of The Winston/Seabury Press, Minneapolis, Minnesota 55404.

The Journals of Lewis and Clark, ed. Bernard DeVoto. Copyright © 1953 by Bernard DeVoto. Copyright © renewed 1981 by Avis DeVoto. Reprinted by permission of Houghton Mifflin Co.

The Wartime Journals of Charles Lindbergh. Copyright © 1970 by Charles A. Lindbergh. Reprinted by permission of Harcourt Brace Jovanovich, Inc.

Diary of My Travels in America, by Louis Philippe, King of France, 1830–1848. Translated from the French by Stephen Becker. Preface by Henry Steele Commager. Translation copyright © 1977 by Dell Publishing Co., Inc. Reprinted by permission of Dell Publishing Co., Inc.

Nine and a Half Weeks, by Elizabeth McNeill (pseud.). Copyright © 1978 by E. P. Dutton. Reprinted by permission of E. P. Dutton, Inc.

The Diary of John Manningham of the Middle Temple, 1602–1603, ed. Robert Parker Sorlien. Reprinted by permission of University Press of New England. Copyright 1976 by Trustees of the University of Rhode Island.

The Journal of Katherine Mansfield, by Katherine Mansfield. Copyright © 1927 by Alfred A. Knopf, Inc. Renewal copyright © 1955 by J. Middleton Murry.

From My Journal, by André Maurois. Copyright © 1947, 1948 by André Maurois. Reprinted by permission of Georges Borchardt, Inc.

The Secular Journal of Thomas Merton, by Thomas Merton. Copyright © 1959 by Madonna House. Reprinted courtesy of Farrar, Straus & Giroux, Inc.

Moscow Diary, by Veljko Mićunović. Translation and introduction copyright © 1980 by Doubleday & Co., Inc. Reprinted by permission of Doubleday & Co., Inc.

Mrs. Milburn's Diaries, by Clara Milburn, ed. Peter Donnelly. Copyright © 1979 by Judy Milburn and Peter Donnelly. Reprinted by permission of Schocken Books, Inc.

Prison Diary, by Jayaprakash Narayan, ed. A. B. Shah. Reprinted by permission of University of Washington Press.

Julia Newberry's Diary, by Julia Newberry. Reprinted by permission of W. W. Norton & Co., Inc. Copyright © 1933 by W. W. Norton & Co., Inc. Copyright renewed 1961 by Margaret Ayer Barnes.

Harold Nicolson: Diaries and Letters, 1930–1939. Edited by Nigel Nicolson and reprinted with the permission of Atheneum Publishers. Copyright © 1966 by William Collins & Sons & Co. Ltd.

The Diary of Vaslav Nijinsky. Reprinted by permission of University of California Press.

The Diary of Anaïs Nin, Volume Four, 1944–1947. © 1971 by Anaïs Nin. Preface © 1971 by Gunther Stuhlmann. Reprinted by permission of Harcourt Brace Jovanovich, Inc.

Threshold, by Alan H. Olmstead. Copyright © 1975 by Alan H. Olmstead. Reprinted by permission of Harper & Row Publishers, Inc.

Extracts from the diaries of Joe Orton quoted in *Prick Up Your Ears* by John Lahr are reprinted by permission of the Estate of Joe Orton.

1984, by George Orwell. Copyright © 1949, by Harcourt Brace

Jovanovich, Inc.; renewed 1977, by Sonia Brownell Orwell. Reprinted by permission of the publisher.

The Diary of Samuel Pepys, ed. by Robert Latham and William Matthews. Reprinted by permission of A. D. Peters & Co. Ltd.

The Journals of Sylvia Plath, ed. Ted Hughes and Frances McCullough. Copyright © 1982 by Ted Hughes as executor of the Estate of Sylvia Plath. A Dial Press Book. Reprinted by permission of Doubleday & Co., Inc.

At a Journal Workshop, by Dr. Ira Progoff. Reprinted by permission of Dialogue House Library.

Diary of a Man in Despair, by Friedrich P. Reck-Malleczewen, trans. Paul Rubens. Translation copyright © 1970 by Paul Rubens. Reprinted by permission of Macmillan Publishing Co., Inc.

Smile Please: An Unfinished Autobiography, by Jean Rhys. Copyright © 1979 by the Estate of Jean Rhys. Reprinted by permission of Harper & Row Publishers, Inc.

Lydia Rudd's diary of overland journey from St. Joseph, Missouri, to Burlington, Oregon, reproduced by permission of The Huntington Library, San Marino, California.

Journal of a Soul, by Pope John XXIII (Angelo Roncalli). Trans. Dorothy White. Reprinted by permission of Geoffrey Chapman, a division of Cassell Ltd.

Knole and the Sackvilles, by Vita Sackville-West. Reprinted by permission of Nigel Nicolson.

The Intimate Journal of George Sand, ed. Marie Jenney Howe. Reprinted by permission of Cassandra Editions, Academy Press Ltd.

Journal of a Solitude, by May Sarton. Copyright © 1973 by May Sarton. Reprinted by permission of W. W. Norton & Co., Inc.

The Measure of My Days, by Florida Scott-Maxwell. Copyright © 1968 by Florida Scott-Maxwell. Reprinted by permission of Random House, Inc.

Women's Diaries of the Westward Journey, ed. Lillian Schlissel. Copyright © 1982 by Schocken Books, Inc.

Last Rites, by Aram Saroyan. Copyright © 1982 by Aram Saroyan. Reprinted by permission of William Morrow & Co., Inc.

Diaries 1915–1918, by Siegfried Sassoon. Reprinted by permission of Faber and Faber Ltd.

The Diary of Samuel Sewall, Volumes 1 & 2, ed. M. Halsey Thomas. Copyright © 1973 by Farrar, Straus & Giroux, Inc. Reprinted by permission of Farrar, Straus & Giroux, Inc.

Mary Shelley's Journal, ed. Frederick L. Jones. Copyright 1947 by the University of Oklahoma Press. Reprinted by permission.

Jay's Journal, ed. Beatrice Sparks. Copyright © 1979 by Beatrice Sparks. Reprinted by permission of Times Books / The New York Times Book Co., Inc.

Spandau: The Secret Diaries, by Albert Speer, trans. Richard Winston and Clara Winston. Translation copyright © 1976 by Macmillan Publishing Co., Inc. Reprinted by permission of Macmillan Publishing Co., Inc.

Stendhal (Marie Henri Beyle). The Private Diaries of Stendhal. Trans. and ed. Robert Sage. Copyright © 1958 by Robert Sage. Reprinted by permission of Doubleday & Co., Inc.

A Sentimental Journey through France and Italy by Mr. Yorick to which are added The Journal to Eliza and A Political Romance, by Laurence Sterne, ed. Ian Jack. Reprinted by permission of Oxford University Press.

The Diary of George Templeton Strong, 4 vols. Ed. Allan Nevins and Milton H. Thomas. Copyright © 1952 by Macmillan Publishing Co., Inc., renewed 1980 by Milton Halsey Thomas. Reprinted by permission of Macmillan Publishing Co., Inc.

Trotsky's Diary in Exile: 1935, by Leon Trotsky, trans. Elena Zarudnaya. Reprinted by permission of Harvard University Press.

All the King's Men, by Robert Penn Warren. Reprinted by permission of Harcourt Brace Jovanovich, Inc.

The Diaries of Evelyn Waugh, by Evelyn Waugh, ed. Michael Davie. Reprinted courtesy of Little, Brown and Co.

Journal of a Governess, 1807–1811, by Ellen Weeton, ed. Edward Hall. Reprinted by permission of Oxford University Press.

Daybooks, by Edward Weston. Copyright © 1981 Arizona Board of Regents, Center for Creative Photography. Reprinted by permission.

The Note Books of a Woman Alone, ed. M. G. Ostle. Reprinted by permission of J. M. Dent & Sons Ltd.

The Thirties, by Edmund Wilson. Copyright © 1980 by Helen Miranda Wilson. Reprinted courtesy of Farrar, Straus & Giroux, Inc.

Drury Lane Journal: Selections from James Winston's Diaries, 1819–1827, by James Winston, ed. Alfred L. Nelson and Gilbert B. Cross. Reprinted by permission of the Society for Theatre Research.

The Diary of a Country Parson, 1758–1802, by James Woodforde. Reprinted by permission of Oxford University Press.

The Diary of Virginia Woolf. Volume One, Volume Two, Volume Three, copyright © 1977, 1978, 1980 by Quentin Bell and Angelica Garnett. Reprinted by permission of Harcourt Brace Jovanovich, Inc.

Journals of Dorothy Wordsworth, ed. Mary Moorman. Reprinted by permission of Oxford University Press.

The Wynne Diaries, 3 vols. Ed. Anne Fremantle. Reprinted by permission of Oxford University Press.

Index